CITY MOVES

CITY MOVES

A User's Guide to the Way Cities Work

Stephen Friedman

McGRAW-HILL PUBLISHING COMPANY

New York   St. Louis   San Francisco   Bogotá
Hamburg   Madrid   Mexico   Milan   Montreal
Paris   São Paulo   Tokyo   Toronto

1 2 3 4 5 6 7 8 9 DOC DOC 8 9 2 1 0 9

ISBN 0-07-022431-5

Library of Congress Cataloging-in-Publication Data
Friedman, Stephen.
City moves : a user's guide to the way cities work / Stephen Friedman.
p. cm.
Includes index.
ISBN 0-07-022431-5
1. Sociology, Urban—United States. 2. City and town life—United
States. 3. Cities and towns—United States. I. Title.
HT123.F78 1989
307.7'6'0973—dc19   88-29036
                                                                      CIP

Book design by Sheree L. Goodman

For Jesse and Johanna

About the Author

STEPHEN FRIEDMAN has a Ph.D. in environmental and social psychology from the University of California at Berkeley. He has taught, done research, and consulted in a wide range of settings in both this country and abroad. Among his publications are *Environments* (Pacific Grove, Calif.: Brooks/Cole, 1974) and a selection in *Color for Architecture* (London: Studio Vista, 1976; New York: Van Nostrand Reinhold, 1977), a choice of the Library of Urban Affairs. He has taught for the European Division of the University of Maryland, the School of Architecture of Oxford Polytech, Boston College, the Nathan Mayhew Seminars of Martha's Vineyard, and the San Francisco Art Institute. He is presently an associate professor in the psychology department of Montclair State College in New Jersey and a member of the visiting faculty of the School of Architecture of Pratt Institute.

Among those cities the author has regularly "moved" in, sometimes staggering and sometimes locomoting with a little more elegance and grace, are New York, Boston, San Francisco, Oakland, Newark, Washington D.C., Paris, Jerusalem, Florence, Athens, London, and Oxford. He delights in the many forms and events encountered in the city, and this book is an outgrowth of those urban enthusiasms.

About the Book

CITY MOVES is a resource book for people who use American cities. Although the large majority of this country's population live in or near cities, there are very few books that can help them make sense of the totality of their urban experience, that is, *both* the people *and* the places of the city. Those books that are available are generally specialist in orientation, with a very narrow range of focus, and are also usually written in a technical language which makes it impossible for the layperson to apply what is being read to everyday experience. There *are* books on the workings of the mind, and books on the workings of the solar system, and books on all kinds of natural environments from deserts to deciduous forests, but there exist no books that can serve as general guides to the American urban experience. *City Moves* addresses itself to a wide audience on a broad range of subjects relating to everyday city life.

Acknowledgments

First, there are the many artists, writers, and scholars whose work has both informed my own experience of the city and inspired this book. Many of those people have been cited, and as is always the case in an endeavor of this sort, many others whose influence was undoubtedly as strong, but perhaps not quite as direct, have not. To have done so, even if I had been capable of it, would have resulted in a manuscript as long, but now containing just a list of names of people responsible for books, buildings, ideas, social movements, and every other manner of urban activity and artifact. Perhaps not a bad idea, but not exactly the move I had in mind for this effort.

And then there are the friends and colleagues who were gracious enough to share their perceptions of various aspects of this project with me. A heartfelt thanks to Eileen Bradley, Dan Bucsescu, Michael Feldberg, Ruth Feldberg, Tom Ford, Ruth Pasquine Lacey, Johanna Lion Friedman, Kenneth Friedman, Danny Klein, Katinka Matson, Kathleen Mock, Ronald Mock, Harry Rosenzweig, Amy Gilman Srebnick, Dan Weaver, Phil Winter, and all the folks of the Ecologistics Research Group.

Contents

Introduction

MOVES

THIS IS A BOOK ABOUT CITIES AND THE MOVES PEOPLE MAKE IN them. If you look up the word *move* in the *Oxford English Dictionary*, among the definitions you will find are the following: "a proposal or motion, a change of house or place of sojourn, the changing of position of a piece in the regular course of a game, a device or trick or action calculated to secure some end, to shake or disturb."

In *City Moves* there will be "devices and tricks," attempts to "shake and disturb," "utterances and proposals," and a myriad of things calculated to help you "change your position" and think about cities in new and different ways. One of the more ironic aspects of life in today's United States is that it's often easier to get information about the distant and the exotic—a television special about a Stone Age tribe in New Guinea or newspaper photographs of the far side of the moon—than it is to learn about the everyday events and objects that surround our immediate lives.

I myself knew quite a bit about the geology of the far side of the moon long before I had any specific information about the grid system of streets I navigated on a daily basis—somewhat alienating from immediate experience to say the least and not

1

very helpful if you're trying to think coherently about a redevelopment or zoning problem facing a municipality you're involved with.

Are the people who live in cities colder and less friendly than those who live other places (Move #19)? What exactly is going on at that construction site, and why am I so intrigued by it (Move #13)? What has been the impact of the automobile on the American city (Move #9)? How do people use and not use their eyes in urban situations (Move #18)? What is the nature of community in contemporary American cities (Move #22)? *City Moves* will answer these and other similar questions by providing strategies and information for understanding the people and places of urban America. At the center of these strategies is the idea of action and movement.

This book takes the position that to really understand a phenomenon one has to become completely immersed in it. Learning isn't a spectator sport, and not much of it can be accomplished by merely reading or sitting back and listening to other people talk. It's something like trying to get in shape by looking at videos of other people working out—one of my favorite strategies but, alas, not very effective. Of course, since the city is the place where most of us lead a good part of our lives already, much of the advice about "doing" particular things—going to the top of a building or making a list or reflecting on the nature of "home" —can be taken with a grain of salt. Many of these experiences are at the heart of urban life, so when the instructions in *City Moves* get very specific, you can either take them literally or use the Move as a vehicle for reflecting on cities and city life as you've already experienced it.

This disclaimer aside, I think it's important to point out that certain activities usually associated with much earlier parts of our lives—the third grade, for example, where teachers were always telling us to sit up straight in our seats, or to write a paragraph on a particular theme, or to list the major products of Peru—can be very useful when trying to comprehend something as complex as urban life. While it's a mistake to equate possession of these discrete bits of isolated information with understanding, and this is a mistake committed everywhere in contemporary society from game shows such as "Wheel of Fortune" to the Scholastic Aptitude Tests that every applicant for college takes, concentrating on specifics can be helpful at times.

For example, even a seemingly juvenile task such as making a list of fifteen adjectives to describe the scene witnessed from the top of a tall building (Move #1) can be useful in forcing you to abstract out from the multitude that you see below. It demands that you make choices and look critically in a way that probably wouldn't happen without this kind of instruction. My temptation to engage in a brief digression on the nature of lists becomes impossible if I stay within the form of the subject itself, a vertical column of words or simple expressions that somehow relate to each other, and this is the strength of this strategy. The absolute elimination of everything not on the list can provide us with a place to begin our reflections.

Although *City Moves* will provide you with many ways for integrating these discrete bits of information, and these ways will include images, metaphors, and conceptual frameworks borrowed from social science and the design disciplines, there is some sympathy for the words of Mies van der Rohe, "God is in the details."

City Moves is divided into five general sections—"Overview," "Patterns in Time and Space," "Building Buildings," "The Urbanite," and "The Community"—and each section is made up of "Moves." A Move will first present an urban experience, ranging from a tour of a specific part of the city to a structured fantasy, to a collection of readings and information on a particular topic, and will then provide notes to help the reader more fully understand the Move just made.

If a particular Move is composed mainly of readings and information (Moves #4, #5, #7, #25), then the notes section will be eliminated. When notes *are* present, they will also contain additional references on themes dealt with in the Move so that the reader can further pursue any topics of interest. Additional resources will also be given at the end of each Move for the same purpose. Throughout the text, Moves will be cross-referenced so that readers may easily refer to other relevant parts of the book.

Whenever the # sign appears, followed by a number, the theme or topic under discussion recieves additional treatment in the Move cited. You may want to turn to that Move; refer to the list of Moves in the Table of Contents.

As is often the case with things urban, a bit of hopping around can be both enlightening and enjoyable, but opportunities presented need not always be taken, *cannot* always be taken. You'd be in for a fairly dizzying non-ending ride if you immediately turned to the cross-referenced Move every time you encountered the # sign. Treat them the way you would any other alternative path on a move through the city: Follow the ones that seem most interesting, ignore the rest, and maybe even double back on those that intrigued you but didn't seem worth exploring at the time.

Given the incredible diversity of urban America, *City Moves* can hope to provide the reader with only an introduction to a wide variety of topics and themes, but it can also provide the resources for obtaining more information. In this sense, *City Moves* can be thought of as a resource book for the user of American cities. In *Language, Counter-Memory, Practice* (Ithaca: Cornell University Press, 1977), the French philosopher Michel Foucault wrote that for him a book was a toolbox that could help the reader understand the rules of other books and texts. The image of the toolbox is congenial to the spirit with which this book was created.

While some Moves use specific examples from particular American cities, all these strategies have been chosen to help the reader deal with a large number of urban scenes. Cities are by no means all the same, and it's emphatically not the case that "if you've seen one, then you've seen them all," but there *are* many ways in which cities are similar. The Moves in this book will focus on the themes, continuities, and regularities that run throughout American cities and can be seen repeatedly in the urban landscape. These Moves are a sort of generic guide to the American city and city life, or perhaps even a set of annotated urban experiences.

In one sense this book is very different from the guidebooks that attempt to familiarize the reader with places and events of significance in new and unknown urban situations. Where are the best parks in St. Louis? What are the most interesting neighborhood festivals in Newark and New Orleans? Which museums are worth visiting in Dallas? What is the location of the tallest building in Los Angeles?

While *City Moves* does contain new information, on everything from the history of the skyscraper (Move #12) to the origins of the many ethnic and racial groups that make up today's American population (Move #25), in a deeper and more interesting sense it's an introduction to the familiar, the ordinary, the everyday, the mundane, an introduction which, on occasion, will ask more questions than it answers, in the firm belief that it's often more important to be aware of the significant questions than it is to be concerned exclusively with the answers. This book is a tool that supports participation in activities and helps you to make *City Moves*.

AMERICAN ATTITUDES TOWARD URBANIZATION

The United States is clearly a nation of cities. History reaffirms what our eyes tell us every day. In 1790, the year of the first U.S. census, only 1 in 20 Americans lived in towns with populations greater than 2,500. New York and Philadelphia were the only two such cities. New York had a population of 49,401; Philadelphia was second largest with 28,522. One hundred and ninety years later, in 1980, seven out of ten Americans were classified as urbanites by the U.S. Bureau of the Census.

Globally, the trend has been the same. In 1800, seven cities in the world were populated by half a million inhabitants or more. By 1900, 42 had achieved that size, and today there are more than 200 cities with half a million inhabitants. Projections are that by the year 2000, 40 percent of the world's population will live in cities.

Americans have generally had negative attitudes toward the city. Thomas Jefferson captured the feelings of many when he wrote, "I view great cities as pestilential to the morals, the health and the liberties of men." In their classic study *The Intellectual Versus the City: From Thomas Jefferson to Frank Lloyd Wright* (Cambridge: Harvard University Press, 1962), Morton and Lucia White traced the development of this anti-urban bias. True, the scholar Leo Marx, in an essay entitled "The Puzzle of Anti-Urbanism" (*Literature and the Urban Experience*; New Brunswick, NJ: Rutgers University Press, 1980), criticized their conclusion for being overly simplistic, claiming that what the writers whom the Whites studied were objecting to were larger transformations in society of which the city was only a part. Nevertheless, there's no denying the fact that a lot of anti-urban sentiment *does* run throughout American writing.

This sentiment reached a zenith in the early part of this century when some of the members of the Chicago school of urban sociology postulated that living in cities would literally drive people mad. Louis Wirth, following the lead of the German urban scholar Georg Simmel (Move #16), argued that the fragmentary nature of urban social relationships and the continuous barrage of stimuli would result in symptoms of mental illness. In his classic essay "Urbanism as a Way of Life," he wrote about the "schizoid" character of urban personality. Fortunately, city people don't seem to be crazier than anyone else, but as we'll see later (Moves #16, #17, #21, #22), the ways in which people cope with the potential psychological difficulties of the city *do*, to a great degree, influence how they behave.

Have Americans had any *positive* things to say about the city? Ralph Waldo Emerson spoke of the "City of God whose gates stand always open free to all comers," and Walt Whitman wrote, "This is the city and I am one of its citizens." But then there were Hawthorne, Thoreau, and Poe, who attacked the city for being too civilized, while John Dewey and Henry James didn't find it civilized enough. The city has always received, at best, mixed reviews, and any look at the American city must begin from this paradox: The United States is a nation of urbanites, most of whom don't particularly like the city. We see this dislike reflected in everything from attitude polls to the collective fantasies of the nation as expressed in television advertising and political choices. When was the last time a candidate for a major national office turned his or her back on rural America and came out for a national image with the city at its center? What typical response would you expect if you asked people to free-associate to the word *city*? What things first come to your mind when *you* hear the word *city*?

A Gallup poll in 1978 asked people where they would prefer to live if given the choice among city, suburb, small town, and farm. Only 13 percent chose the city, and, even more significant, of those who at the time lived in cities, only 21 percent cited the city as their preferred place of residence. This is quite remarkable when you realize that in the most recent census two out of three Americans were classified as urbanites, and it's often been argued that the third person might just as well have been. Today, even in rural America, people lead lives dominated by urban institutions: the mass media, the financial community, and educational institutions. They also think and behave in ways that are more traditionally associated with urban societies than they are with pre-urban hunter-gatherer or agrarian societies (Move #4).

"Specialization," that inevitable consequence of the rise of cities, is everywhere in America. We constantly divide up space (Moves #2, #6, #7, #17, #19, #24) and time (Moves #2, #4, #5, #21) and even our relationships with other people (Move #14) into precise, specialized components. We then spend enormous amounts of time and energy maintaining the boundaries between these elements. There are "business districts" and "shopping centers" and "cultural centers" and "living rooms" and "dining rooms" and "recreation rooms" and "lunch time" and "overtime" and "friends" and "family" and "business associates," and these categories are all generally kept distinct and separate from one another.

Think for a moment about all those zoning regulations designed to maintain the integrity of residential areas (Move #7) and the radical transformations in attitude and behavior that most people go through when going from "work" to "home" (Move #14). This is as true for someone living in a small town in rural Kansas as it is for the inhabitants of places such as New York and Chicago and Los Angeles.

City Moves has not been written from an anti-urban perspective; on the contrary, the objects and events it deals with are often viewed as worthy of celebration. It's here in the city that anything and everything can be found, and it's here that certain special conditions—particularly those of density and heterogeneity—create the possibility for much that is innovative and noble in the human spirit to emerge.

Unfortunately there is also the city of poverty, violence, crime, racism, hatred, and individual and corporate greed, which the media, and at times our own experience, acquaint us with on a daily basis. Although the economic and political conditions that generate these urban catastrophes are reflected in *City Moves*— ranging from the racist motivation of much early zoning legislation (Move #7) and suburbanization (Move #9) to reading tall buildings as symbols of corporate power (Move #1)—they're not the major focus of this book. There *are* works cited in *City Moves* that more directly treat these themes. Two important volumes that should be added to any such list are William Ryan's *Blaming the Victim* (New York: Vintage Books, 1971) and Robert Goodman's

After the Planners (New York: Simon & Schuster, 1971). While horror stories can be found in American cities of today—and in all cities of all times, for that matter, although this by no means removes the obligation and immediate need to remedy the situation—what's amazing is that so many objects and events can still inform and delight. Contrary to the images on the eleven o'clock news, which to a large extent are a function of a definition of "news" that has at its center elements of the dramatic and the atypical, it's still possible to walk neighborhood streets (Move #24) many places and not be mugged or caught up in a "Miami Vice" drug war. You'll never hear on the news that for 99 percent of the population in any metropolitan region on any given day everything was every bit as ordinary as it always is or that the large, large majority of the buildings did *not* fall down. That's not really what's demanded of the news, but the danger is that somehow the atypical and unusual comes to be treated as if it were the everyday and ordinary, and as a result, people cut themselves off from a good deal of possibly rewarding experience.

AMERICAN CITIES

Listed in Table 1 are the twenty largest American cities, along with their population figures going back to the first census of 1790. The twenty largest Standard Metropolitan Statistical Areas (SMSAs) are given in Table 2. This is a term coined by the U.S. Bureau of the Census to refer to concentrations of people that extend beyond the geographical boundary of a city into the broader surrounding region. It's a necessary idea in a time when the border between the city and the surrounding area has been changed from a concrete thing such as a wall or a gate (Move #2) to little more than a line, often seemingly drawn somewhat arbitrarily, on a map. It's possible in modern America to turn your head at the wrong moment and miss that usually hidden, always innocuous, sign that typically marks the edge (Move #1) of the city. This puts us in a position of regularly asking a question that during the first 5,500 years of urban history could have been asked only by a lunatic: "Is this the city?" The old rules, under which if you saw groups of big buildings (Move #12) you were in the city and if you saw groups of trees (Move #8) you were in the country, no longer seem to apply.

Table 1 The Twenty Largest Cities in the United States

Rank	City	1980	1970	1960	1950	1900	1850	1790
1	New York, NY	7,071,030	7,895,563	7,781,984	7,891,957	3,437,202	696,115	49,401
2	Chicago, IL	3,005,072	3,369,357	3,550,404	3,620,962	1,698,575	29,963	...
3	Los Angeles, CA	2,966,763	2,811,801	2,479,015	1,970,358	102,479	1,610	...
4	Philadelphia, PA	1,668,210	1,949,996	2,002,512	2,071,605	1,293,697	121,376	28,522
5	Houston, TX	1,594,066	1,233,535	938,219	596,163	44,633	2,396	...
6	Detroit, MI	1,203,339	1,514,063	1,670,144	1,849,566	285,704	21,019	...
7	Dallas, TX	904,078	844,401	679,684	434,462	42,638	...	...
8	San Diego, CA	875,504	697,471	573,224	334,387	17,700	...	...
9	Baltimore, MD	786,775	905,787	939,024	949,706	508,957	169,054	13,503
10	San Antonio, TX	785,410	654,153	587,718	408,442	53,321	3,488	...
11	Phoenix, AZ	764,911	584,303	439,170	106,818	5,544	...	...
12	Honolulu Co., HI	762,874	630,528	294,194	248,034	39,308	...	...
13	Indianapolis, IN	700,807	736,856	476,258	427,173	169,164	8,091	...
14	San Francisco, CA	678,974	715,674	740,316	775,357	342,782	34,776	...
15	Memphis, TN	646,356	623,988	497,524	396,000	102,320	8,841	...
16	Washington, D.C.	637,651	756,668	763,956	802,178	278,718	40,001	...
17	San Jose, CA	636,550	459,913	204,196	95,280	21,500	...	...
18	Milwaukee, WI	636,212	717,372	741,324	637,392	285,315	20,061	...
19	Cleveland, OH	573,822	750,879	876,050	914,806	381,768	17,034	...
20	Columbus, OH	564,871	540,025	471,316	375,901	125,560	17,882	...

Table 2 **The Twenty Largest SMSAs in the United States**

SMSA	1980		1970	
	Rank	Pop.	Rank	Pop.
New York, NY–NJ	1	9,119,737	1	9,973,716
Los Angeles–Long Beach, CA .	2	7,477,657	2	7,041,980
Chicago, IL	3	7,102,328	3	6,974,755
Philadelphia, PA–NJ	4	4,716,818	4	4,624,110
Detroit, MI	5	4,352,762	5	4,435,051
San Francisco–Oakland, CA . .	6	3,252,721	6	3,109,249
Washington, DC–MD–VA . .	7	3,060,240	7	2,910,111
Dallas–Fort Worth, TX . . .	8	2,974,878	12	2,377,623
Houston, TX	9	2,905,350	16	1,999,316
Boston, MA	10	2,763,357	8	2,899,101
Nassau–Suffolk, NY	11	2,605,813	9	2,555,868
St. Louis, MO–IL	12	2,355,270	10	2,410,884
Pittsburgh, PA	13	2,263,694	11	2,401,362
Baltimore, MD	14	2,174,023	13	2,071,016
Minneapolis–St. Paul, MN–WI .	15	2,114,256	17	1,965,391
Atlanta, GA	16	2,029,618	18	1,595,517
Newark, NJ	17	1,965,304	15	2,057,468
Anaheim–Santa Ana–Garden Grove, CA	18	1,931,570	20	1,421,233
Cleveland, OH	19	1,898,720	14	2,063,729
San Diego, CA	20	1,861,846	23	1,357,854

We live in a society dominated by cities, where it's often impossible to tell at any given moment if we're even *in* a city. It's as if Gertrude Stein's quip about Oakland, "There's no *there* when you get there," has been turned on its ear. Now the "there" is everywhere. Is it any wonder that most people have negative attitudes toward the city?

City Moves is about these places and the many others in the United States like them. In a short story called "City Life" by Donald Barthelme, a character says:

> "Ramona thought about the city. I have to admit we are locked in the most mysterious exquisite muck. This muck heaves and palpitates. It is multidirectional and has a mayor. To describe it takes many hundreds and thousands of words. Our muck is only part of a much greater muck—the nation state—which is itself the creation of that muck of mucks, human consciousness. Of course all these things also have a touch of sublimity."

The task is to help make sense of that "muck" and reach through with human consciousness for a "touch of sublimity."

A FINAL WORD ABOUT USING THIS BOOK

While it's probably a good idea to start with the three Moves in Part I, "Overview," this book is nonlinear in the same sense that the city itself is. Colin Rowe and Fred Koetter compare the city to a collage in *Collage City* (Cambridge: MIT Press, 1978). The idea of a beginning, a middle, and an end shouldn't be taken too literally in either this book or the city. *City Moves* can be gone through from front to back, or it can be used like any other resource book—the dictionary, *Guide Michelin*, the *Whole Earth Catalog*, or Dr. Spock's baby book. Pick the topics that interest, amuse, concern, or confuse you, look them up, and then begin to make your Moves.

I

OVERVIEW

The goal of the three Moves in this section is to gather some impressions of the city in its entirety. Take a step back and gain some perspective. As a follower of Marshall McLuhan commented, "I'm not sure who it was who discovered water, but I *am* pretty sure it wasn't a fish."

In this section, you'll take a step back by rising above the city to take a look, by closing your eyes and imagining a scene, and by reading some definitions, metaphors, and nicknames that poets, scholars, chambers of commerce, and others have used to describe the city.

MOVE #1

Bird's-Eye View

THE ANCIENT EGYPTIAN HIEROGLYPH FOR THE CITY WAS THE "CROSS-roads within the wall": ⊗. And while it's been suggested that in the United States today this could more accurately be stated as the "crossroads within the sprawl," the beauty of this symbol is that it provides clues about *what* to look at—"roads" and "walls" or, more generally, "paths" and "edges"—and also *how* to look. Get above it all and look down. Architects and city planners call this angle of vision a "plan" and find it quite useful when dealing with complex objects and spaces. It often reveals things that can't be seen at ground level.

Listed in Table 3 are some of the major tall buildings in leading American cities.

A trip to the top of one of these buildings can be useful and informative. This is the vantage point of the writer of the Egyptian hieroglyph, and from this height it is now possible to see all of the city at once. If the whole is greater than the sum of its parts, which seems a reasonable proposition when examining something as complex as a piece of music, or a person's face, or a city, then this is a good place to start. The great nineteenth-century planner Camillo Sitte was said to have always asked first for the best tower from which to view the city when arriving at a new place. He would also request a good map of the place (Move #17)

Table 3 **Tall Buildings in Leading American Cities**

	Height in feet	Number of stories
New York, N.Y.		
World Trade Center (2 towers)	1,350	110
Empire State, 34th St. & 5th Ave.	1,250	102
TV tower, 164 ft., makes total	1,414	...
Chrysler, Lexington Ave. & 43d St.	1,046	77
American International Bldg., 70 Pine St.	950	67
40 Wall Tower	927	71
Citicorp Center	914	46
RCA Bldg., Rockefeller Center	850	70
1 Chase Manhattan Plaza	813	60
Pan Am Bldg., 200 Park Ave.	808	59
Eichner Bldg.	799	70
Woolworth, 233 Broadway	792	60
1 Penn Plaza	764	57
Exxon, 1251 Ave. of Americas	750	54
Equitable Center Tower West	750	58
1 Liberty Plaza	743	50
Citibank	741	57
World Financial Center, Tower C	739	54
One Astor Plaza	730	54
Metropolitan Tower, 146 W. 57th St.	716	56
Chicago, Ill.		
Sears Tower (world's tallest)	1,454	110
Amoco	1,136	80
John Hancock Center	1,127	100
Water Tower Place (a)	859	74
First Natl. Bank	852	60
Three First National Plaza	775	57
Olympia Centre	727	63

Table 3 **Tall Buildings in Leading American Cities** *(continued)*

	Height in feet	Number of stories
IBM Plaza	695	52
One Magnificent Mile	673	58
Daley Center	662	31

Los Angeles, Cal.

	Height in feet	Number of stories
First Interstate Bank	858	62
Crocker Center, North	750	53
Security Pacific Natl. Bank	735	55
Atlantic Richfield Plaza (2 bldgs.)	699	52
Wells Fargo Bank	625	48
Crocker-Citizen Plaza	620	42
California Plaza	578	42
Century Plaza Towers (2 bldgs.)	571	44
Citycorp Plaza	534	42
Union Bank Square	516	41

Philadelphia, Pa.

	Height in feet	Number of stories
City Hall Tower, incl. 37-ft. statue of Wm. Penn	548	7
Commerce Sq., #1	530	41
1818 Market St.	500	40
Provident Mutual Life	491	40
Fidelity Mutual Life Ins. Bldg.	490	38
Phila. Saving Fund Society	490	39
Central Penn Natl. Bank	490	36
Centre Square (2 towers)	490/416	38/32
Philadelphia National Bank	475	25
Two Mellon Plaza	450	30
One Reading Center	417	32
Fidelty Bank Bldg.	405	30
Industrial Valley Bank	400	32

Table 3 Tall Buildings in Leading American Cities *(continued)*

	Height in feet	Number of stories
One Logan Square	400	32
Lewis Tower, 15th & Locust	400	33

Baltimore, Md.

U.S. Fidelity & Guaranty Co.	529	40
Maryland National Bank Bldg.	509	34
6 St. Paul Place	493	37
World Trade Center Bldg.	395	32
Tremont Plaza Hotel	395	37
250 W. Pratt St.	360	26
Harbor Court.	356	28
Blaustein Bldg.	342	30
Union Trust Tower	335	24
Central Savings Bank Bldg.	330	28
Charles Center South	330	26

San Antonio, Tex.

Tower of the Americas	622	...
Tower Life	404	30
Interfirst Plaza	387	28
Nix Professional Bldg.	375	23
Natl. Bank of Commerce	310	24
Interfirst NW Financial Center	302	20

Phoenix, Ariz.

Valley National Bank	483	40
Arizona Bank Downtown	407	31
First Interstate Bank Plaza	372	27
United Bank Plaza	356	28
First Federal Savings Bldg.	341	26
Hyatt Regency	317	20

Table 3   Tall Buildings in Leading American Cities (continued)

	Height in feet	Number of stories
Honolulu, Hi.		
Ala Moana Americana Hotel	395	38
Pacific Tower	350	30
Franklin Towers	350	41
Honolulu Tower	350	40
Discovery Bay	350	42
Hyatt Regency Waikiki	350	39
Mailo Court Hotel	350	43
Regency Tower, 2525 Dale St.	350	42
Pearlridge Square	350	43
Yacht Harbor Towers	350	40
Canterbury Place	350	40
Royal Iolani	350	38
Island Colony	350	44
Century Center	350	41
Pacific Beach Hotel	350	43
Hawaiian Monarch Hotel	350	43
Waikiki Hobron	350	43
San Francisco, Cal.		
Transamerica Pyramid	853	48
Bank of America	778	52
101 California St.	600	48
5 Fremont Center	600	43
Embarcadero Center, No. 4	570	45
Security Pacific Bank	569	45
One Market Plaza, Spear St.	565	43
Wells Fargo Bldg.	561	43
Standard Oil, 575 Market St.	551	39
One Sansome-Citicorp	550	39

Table 3 Tall Buildings in Leading American Cities (continued)

	Height in feet	Number of stories
Shaklee Bldg., 444 Market	537	38
Aetna Life	529	38
First & Market Bldg..	529	38
Metropolitan Life	524	38
Crocker National Bank	500	38
Hilton Hotel	493	46
Pacific Gas & Electric	492	34
Union Bank	487	37

Oakland, Cal.

	Height in feet	Number of stories
Ordway Bldg., 2150 Valdez St..	404	28
Kaiser Bldg..	390	28
Lake Merritt Plaza	371	27
Raymond Kaiser Engineer Bldg.	336	25
Clorox Bldg..	330	24

Memphis, Tenn.

	Height in feet	Number of stories
100 N. Main Bldg.	430	37
Commerce Square	396	31
Sterick Bldg..	365	31
Clark, 5100 Poplar	365	32
Morgan Keegan Tower, 50 Front St.	341	23
First Natl. Bank Bldg.	332	25
Hyatt Regency	329	28

Seattle, Wash.

	Height in feet	Number of stories
Columbia Center	954	76
Seattle–1st Natl. Bank Bldg.	609	50
Space Needle	605	...
First Interstate Center	574	48
Seafirst 5th Ave. Plaza	543	42

Table 3 Tall Buildings in Leading American Cities *(continued)*

	Height in feet	Number of stories
Bank of Cal., 900 4th Ave.	536	42
Rainier Bank Tower, 4th & Univ.	514	42
Smith Tower	500	42

Miami, Fla.

	Height in feet	Number of stories
Southeast Financial Center	764	55
Centrust Tower	562	35
Metro-Dade Administration Bldg.	510	30
Edward Ball Bldg.	484	35
One Biscayne Corp.	456	40
Amerifirst Bldg.	375	32
Hotel Inter-Continental Miami	366	35
Venitia, 1635 Bayshore Dr.	365	42

Boston, Mass.

	Height in feet	Number of stories
John Hancock Tower	790	60
Prudential Tower	750	52
Boston Co. Bldg., Court St.	605	41
Federal Reserve Bldg.	604	32
International Place, 100 Oliver St.	600	46
First National Bank of Boston	591	37
One Financial Center	590	46
Shawmut Bank Bldg.	520	38
Exchange Place, 53 State St.	510	39
Sixty State St.	509	38
One Post Office Sq.	507	40
One Beacon St.	507	40
New England Merch. Bank Bldg.	500	40
U.S. Custom House	496	32
John Hancock Bldg.	495	26

Table 3 **Tall Buildings in Leading American Cities** *(continued)*

	Height in feet	Number of stories
Pittsburgh, Pa.		
U.S. Steel Bldg.	841	64
One Mellon Bank Center	725	54
One PPG Place	635	40
One Oxford Centre	615	46
Gulf, 7th Ave. and Grant St.	582	44
University of Pittsburgh	535	42
Mellon Bank Bldg.	520	41
1 Oliver Plaza	511	39
Grant, Grant St. at 3rd Ave.	485	40
Koppers, 7th Ave. and Grant	475	34
Equibank Bldg.	445	34
Dallas, Tex.		
Interfirst Plaza, 901 Main St.	939	73
First International Bldg.	710	56
LTV Center	686	50
Arco Tower, 1601 Bryan St.	660	49
Thanksgiving Tower, 1600 Pacific Ave.	645	50
Two Dallas Centre	635	50
First National Bank	625	52
Republic Bank Tower	598	50
First City Center, 1700 Pacific Ave.	595	49
SW Bell Admin. Tower	580	37
One Lincoln Plaza	579	45
Olympia York, 1999 Bryan St.	562	37
Reunion Tower	560	50
Southland Life Tower	550	42
Diamond Shamrock, 717 N. Harwood St.	550	34
2001 Bryan St.	512	40

Table 3 **Tall Buildings in Leading American Cities** *(continued)*

	Height in feet	Number of stories
San Diego, Cal.		
First Interstate Bank	398	24
California First Bank	388	27
First National Bank	379	27
The Meridan	371	27
Imperial Bank	355	24
Wells Fargo Bldg.	348	20
1010 Second	340	25
Great American	339	24
Central Federal	320	22
Union Bank	320	22
Indianapolis, Ind.		
American United Life Ins. Co.	533	38
Indiana Natl. Bank Tower	504	37
City-County Bldg.	377	26
Merchants Plaza/Hyatt Regency Hotel	328	26
Indiana Bell Telephone	320	20
Atlanta, Ga.		
IBM Tower, 1179 W. Peachtree	813	50
Westin Peachtree Plaza	723	71
Georgia Pacific Tower	697	51
Southern Bell Telephone	677	47
First National Bank, 2 Peachtree	556	44
Marriott Marquis	554	52
Concourse Tower, 1001 Hammond Dr.	534	34
Equitable Building, 100 Peachtree	453	34
101 Marietta Tower, 101 Marietta St.	446	36
Atlanta Center	443	35
Park Place, 2660 Peachtree	420	34

Table 3 **Tall Buildings in Leading American Cities** *(continued)*

	Height in feet	Number of stories
National Bank of Georgia	409	32
Peachtree Summit No. 1	406	31
North Avenue Tower, 310 North Ave.	403	26
Tower Place, 3361 Piedmont Road	401	29

Denver, Col.

	Height in feet	Number of stories
Republic Plaza	714	56
Mountain Bell Center	706	54
United Bank of Denver	697	52
1999 Broadway	544	43
Arco Tower	527	41
Anaconda Tower	507	40
Tabor Center, #2	493	39
One Denver Place	467	35
Amoco Bldg., 17th Ave. & Broadway	450	36
17th Street Plaza	438	34
Brooks Towers, 1020 15th St.	420	42
Mellon Financial Center	415	32
Stellar Plaza	410	32
Tabor Center, #1	405	32
Energy Center 1	404	29

Cleveland, Oh.

	Height in feet	Number of stories
Terminal Tower	708	52
Sohio Tower	650	46
Erieview Plaza Tower	529	40
One Cleveland Center	450	31
Justice Center, 1250 Ontario	420	26
Federal Bldg.	419	32
National City Complex	410	35
Cleveland Trust Tower No. 1	383	29

Table 3 **Tall Buildings in Leading American Cities *(continued)***

	Height in feet	Number of stories
Eaton Center	360	28
Ohio-Bell Hqs.	360	22

St. Louis, Mo.

	Height in feet	Number of stories
Gateway Arch	630	...
Metropolitan Square Tower	591	40
S.W. Bell Telephone Bldg.	587	44
Mercantile Trust Bldg.	550	37
Centerre Bldg.	433	31
Laclede Gas Bldg., 8th & Olive	400	30
S.W. Bell Telephone Bldg.	398	31
Civil Courts	387	13
Queeny Tower	321	24
Counsel Tower	320	30

Fort Worth, Tex.

	Height in feet	Number of stories
City Center Tower II	546	36
1st United Tower	536	40
Mobil Bldg.	430	31
Mart Hotel	400	29
Fidelity Union Tower	400	33
One Dallas Centre	386	30
Southwestern Bell Toll Bldg.	372	22

Detroit, Mich.

	Height in feet	Number of stories
Westin Hotel	720	71
Penobscot Bldg.	557	47
15000 Town Center Dr.	554	40
Guardian	485	40
Renaissance Center (4 bldgs.)	479	39
Book Tower	472	35

Table 3 **Tall Buildings in Leading American Cities** *(continued)*

	Height in feet	Number of stories
Prudential Town Center.	448	32
13000 Town Center Dr..	443	32
Cadillac Tower	437	40
David Stott	436	38
Mich. Cons. Gas Co. Bldg.	430	32

Houston, Tex.

	Height in feet	Number of stories
Texas Commerce Tower	1,002	75
Allied Bank Plaza, 1000 Louisiana	985	71
Transco Tower	899	64
RepublicBank Center	780	56
Heritage Plaza, 1111 Bagby	762	53
InterFirst Plaza	744	55
1600 Smith St.	729	54
Gulf Tower, 1301 McKinney	725	52
One Shell Plaza (not incl. 285 ft. TV tower)	714	50
Four Allen Center	692	50
Capital Natl. Bank Plaza	685	50

New Orleans, La.

	Height in feet	Number of stories
One Shell Square	697	51
Place St. Charles	645	53
Plaza Tower	531	45
Energy Centre	530	39
LL&E Tower, 901 Poydras	481	36
Sheraton Hotel	478	47
Marriott Hotel	450	42
Texaco Bldg.	442	33
Canal Place One	439	32
1010 Common	438	31
Int'l Trade Mart Bldg.	407	33

and the hotel where the best food could be had—not a bad strategy at all.

In a brilliant essay, the French philosopher Roland Barthes said of the Eiffel Tower, "the bird's-eye view, which each visitor to the Tower can assume in an instant for his own, gives us the world to read and not only to perceive . . . permits us to transcend sensation and to see things in their structure . . . every visitor to the Tower makes structuralism without knowing it . . . he separates and groups."

The same thing can be said of this Move. To look down on an American city from a high place is somehow to take a step back so that you can observe the essence of the place. You can get to the heart of the matter without having to deal with any of the distractions that are always there at ground level (Move #18). This is the traditional Western strategy of being objective by establishing some distance from the thing to be known or understood, and it underlies everything from experimentation and the scientific method to the cool, detached, professional look of that anchorperson on the eleven o'clock news. To know it is to take a step back and then have a look. But then the questions become: How exactly do you look, and at what do you look?

One good strategy is to scan the city to form some general impression. Sometimes it's easier to take things in and look at everything before you look at any one thing. The discipline of putting things down on paper can also be helpful. If you were to write a short descriptive paragraph about the view, what would it be like? If complete sentences and paragraphs aren't your style, then lists may be more appropriate. What five, ten, or fifteen adjectives could be used to describe what it is you're seeing? Do any metaphors come to mind when describing the scene below (Move #3)? Of course, to use any of these strategies you're going to have to make some decisions about how to take the thing below apart and break it down into manageable units so that it can be thought about in a systematic fashion.

From the height of these structures, you can easily imagine the history of the place. What was the city like thirty years ago? Fifty years ago? A century ago? How did the place look when it was first settled (Move #5)? Long before there were cities at all (Move #4)? And what will things be like in the future? In fifty years? A hundred years?

Sometimes it can be helpful to pick a specific feature, such as a downtown building site or a main boulevard, and imagine what it was like at different moments in time. Knowledge of some local history and a familiarity with novelistic and cinematic portrayals of the future can also help with this leap of the imagination.

Another set of questions worth thinking about involves the buildings themselves. Why would anyone want to build a structure this tall? And what's the appeal of climbing to the top and looking down? You undoubtedly engaged in this activity long before *City Moves* came along and advised you to start climbing and looking. Why? Some reflections on your motivation might reveal something about the nature of cities. As a matter of fact, it probably makes sense to make this Move more often, to pull it out of the category of "things to be done with tourists" and make it a more frequent occurrence. Literally "keep the city in view" and see whether any of the material in *City Moves* changes what it is you see below.

NOTES

Numbers, Holism, and Density

One of the first impressions when you look down on the city from above is of numbers and density. These seem to be defining characteristics of the place, and every observer of the city has commented on them. Everywhere you look there's stuff, and it's all packed together pretty tightly. The United States has more than thirty urban centers with more than a million people in them and more than one hundred cities with populations of more than three hundred thousand. More people need more buildings, streets, cars, plazas, and all those other things that serve as props and sets for city life (Move #14). The numbers of the city are overwhelming.

Here's a day in the life of New York City through the numbers reported in *New York* magazine: On March 1, 1983, 320,000 street lights were burning on 6,000 miles of streets; 3,409 bars were doing business; there were 460 miles of waterfronts; 9,531 patients occupied beds in the city's public hospitals; 94 million kilowatt hours of energy were supplied by Con Edison; New Yorkers used 1.29 billion gallons of water in their tubs, showers, sinks, fountains, water glasses, and sewers; 116,778 cars drove across the George

Washington Bridge; J.F.K. International Airport had 768 arriving and departing flights carrying 62,862 passengers, along with 511 tons of mail and 2,937 tons of cargo; included in the last figure were 411,859 flowers.

The thing about these numbers is their immensity, their incredible precision—*exactly* 116,778 cars on the George Washington Bridge and not a single one more or less—and the delight people seem to take in encountering them even though the numbers themselves are often impossible to comprehend. What exactly is 1.29 billion gallons of water? Or 320,000 street lamps? And why would *New York* magazine want to inform its readers that on March 1, 1983, J.F.K. International Airport received 411,859 flowers?

Social critics such as Friedrich Engels and, more recently, Roland Barthes (*Mythologies*; New York: Hill & Wang, 1972) claim that one of the mythologies of modern society, born of this love of numbers that are themselves urban creations (Move #4), is the mistaken assumption that most differences in the world are quantitative rather than qualitative. Barthes called this a "cheapening of experience." Can the experience of 6 million pounds of food be captured by envisioning 24 million quarter-pounders just like the one you had for lunch? It's clearly an impossible task, and this is one of the reasons the city so often eludes us. The numbers overwhelm the imagination, and in a desperate bid at understanding, we try to reduce the incomprehensible magnitudes to multiples of smaller units that we *can* understand.

It would be a mistake to assume that the city you're looking down at is *just* a small town multiplied many, many times. Although differences among cities are often described in quantitative terms, and in some senses a city of seven and a half million people *is* ten times bigger than a city of three-quarters of a million, the kinds of vast increases in magnitude regularly seen in the city result in qualitative differences. The whole *is* greater than the sum of its parts, and just as is the case in music, the things happening in between the notes are often more important than the notes themselves.

If the American city is the place of numbers, then it's also the place of density—extreme density. This density is a relatively recent historical development. Anthropologists postulate that hunter-gatherers of the Paleolithic era, the Stone Age, which lasted from about 500,000 B.C. to 9,000 B.C., needed anywhere from a half to a full square mile of land to support themselves. This vast amount of space was needed to gather enough food to insure survival. About 6,000 years later, after the domestication of dogs and cattle and the development of more sophisticated farming techniques (Move #4), early agriculture could support densities of thirty or more people per square mile.

Table 4 **Population Density in American Cities**

Rank	City	Density per square mile	Rank	City	Density per square mile
1	New York	23,282.94	23	Los Angeles	6,395.26
2	San Francisco	14,955.37	24	Oakland	6,353.71
3	Jersey City	14,803.44	25	Minneapolis	6,319.44
4	Newark	13,639.10	26	Huntington Beach	6,245.60
5	Chicago	13,173.44	27	Anaheim	5,807.51
6	Philadelphia	12,986.23	28	Seattle	5,391.33
7	Boston	12,239.00	29	Norfolk	5,075.65
8	Washington, D.C.	10,385.19	30	Cincinnati	4,935.43
9	Miami	10,114.61	31	St. Paul	4,873.40
10	Yonkers	9,086.09	32	Flint	4,866.19
11	Baltimore	8,645.88	33	Warren	4,711.52
12	Detroit	8,619.91	34	Louisville	4,577.47
13	Providence	8,292.12	35	Honolulu	4,359.99
14	Pittsburgh	7,638.52	36	Akron	4,235.30
15	Cleveland	7,560.24	37	Worcester	4,231.51
16	Santa Ana	7,489.45	38	Denver	4,221.62
17	St. Louis	7,403.35	39	San Jose	4,215.56
18	Buffalo	7,215.12	40	Dayton	4,179.59
19	Long Beach	7,212.25	41	St. Petersburg	4,165.52
20	Milwaukee	6,641.04	42	Toledo	4,157.50
21	Syracuse	6,588.11	43	Grand Rapids	4,049.95
22	Rochester	6,586.95	44	Omaha	3,814.94

Table 4 Population Density in American Cities *(continued)*

Rank	City	Density per square mile	Rank	City	Density per square mile
45	Albuquerque	3,809.04	73	Phoenix	2,428.36
46	Portland, Ore.	3,663.83	74	Dallas	2,417.32
47	Richmond	3,507.42	75	Riverside	2,369.99
48	Tacoma	3,341.79	76	Knoxville	2,360.04
49	Lincoln	3,338.48	77	Memphis	2,228.81
50	Fort Wayne	3,314.01	78	Shreveport	2,121.80
51	Baton Rouge	3,310.50	79	Lubbock	2,116.53
52	Spokane	3,294.23	80	Chattanooga	2,045.42
53	Tucson	3,253.32	81	Tulsa	2,027.63
54	Tampa	3,217.09	82	Arlington, Texas	2,026.87
55	Madison	3,165.42	83	Colorado Springs	1,957.69
56	Atlanta	3,125.16	84	Jackson	1,925.00
57	Columbus, Ohio	3,086.72	85	Indianapolis	1,867.82
58	Aurora	3,067.47	86	El Paso	1,771.91
59	Fresno	3,030.58	87	Little Rock	1,747.09
60	Las Vegas	2,994.07	88	Fort Worth	1,540.56
61	San Antonio	2,979.55	89	Corpus Christi	1,489.08
62	Sacramento	2,936.54	90	Kansas City, Kan.	1,464.43
63	Charlotte	2,900.80	91	Kansas City, Mo.	1,418.22
64	Des Moines	2,893.98	92	Mobile	1,411.63
65	Birmingham	2,890.38	93	Montgomery	1,381.28
66	Houston	2,867.06	94	Virginia Beach	1,013.52
67	Austin	2,790.08	95	Nashville	854.88
68	New Orleans	2,752.99	96	Columbus, Ga.	769.49
69	Salt Lake City	2,744.66	97	Lexington	721.43
70	San Diego	2,711.38	98	Jacksonville	654.05
71	Wichita	2,653.42	99	Oklahoma City	620.33
72	Greensboro	2,568.35	100	Anchorage	88.50

Major modern American cities range in density from a high in New York of more than 23,000 people per square mile to a low of 88.5 people per square mile in Anchorage, Alaska (see Table 4)—a geometric increase from Paleolithic times. Even these figures are modest compared with those of cities such as Hong Kong and Tokyo, which can run ten times as high. Nevertheless, things are dense in the American city. One-fifth of the American population now lives on 1.8 percent of the land of the continental United States, and it's within these areas that the term "population explosion" has any meaning. Within a ten-minute walk of the desk of a worker in midtown Manhattan on a typical weekday are close to a quarter of a million people.

Of course, any measure of density must somehow take into account the fact that many cities have incorporated within their boundaries large areas that sometimes contain few, if any, people in them. For example, one reason for Anchorage's low density is that at 1,955 square miles it's more than twice the area of its nearest rival, Jacksonville, Florida. The following list, showing the twenty largest cities in terms of absolute (geographic) size, clearly reveals this and provides another definition of city size.

1. Anchorage: 1,995 square miles
2. Jacksonville: 827 square miles
3. Oklahoma City: 650 square miles
4. Honolulu: 604 square miles
5. Houston: 556 square miles
6. Nashville: 533 square miles
7. Los Angeles: 463.9 square miles
8. Dallas: 378 square miles
9. Indianapolis: 375.2 square miles
10. Phoenix: 325.2 square miles
11. San Diego: 322.9 square miles
12. Kansas City: 316.3 square miles
13. New York: 303.7 square miles
14. Memphis: 290 square miles
15. Lexington: 283 square miles
16. San Antonio: 263.6 square miles
17. Virginia Beach: 258.7 square miles
18. Fort Worth: 250 square miles
19. El Paso: 240 square miles
20. Chicago: 228.1 square miles

As this list shows, Anchorage, Alaska, is larger than Los Angeles, New York, Chicago, San Antonio, Kansas City, and Phoenix combined. Will there ever come a time when population figures also reflect this?

The pros and cons of high density have been strongly debated (Move #16), but there's no denying that a lot of life in the city, and a good deal of what you see when you look down in Move #1, is the result of high density. While some experts claim that high density is the cause of many urban woes—including crime, pollution, and psychological stress—others argue that it's one of the things that generate all the excitement that has been attracting people from the surrounding countryside for thousands of years. Lewis Mumford, in *The City in History* (New York: Harcourt Brace Jovanovich, 1961), offered a graphic analogy: "As with gas, the very presence of the molecules within that limited space produced more social collisions and interactions within a generation than would have occurred in many centuries if still isolated in their native habitats, without boundaries."

Parts of the City

Seeing the whole city at once (from above) allows you to observe how different parts of the city relate to one another. Why this pattern of roads and that arrangement of tall buildings (Moves #12, #13)? How was it decided to put that park there (Move #8)? From this height, you can see that the city is a collection of physical objects, and any questions on the arrangement of these objects must be preceded by some thoughts on the elements of physical form. How can we divide up the things below so that they can be thought about in a systematic fashion? More simply put, what are the parts of the city?

In a pioneering work (Move #17) titled *The Image of the City* (Cambridge: MIT Press, 1960), Kevin Lynch described five different urban elements. He asked residents to draw maps of Boston, Los Angeles, and Jersey City and then asked them how to get from one place to another in each of these cities. Examining the information they provided, he derived several categories. Not surprisingly, three of those categories—"paths," "edges," and "nodes"—were the same as those in the Egyptian hieroglyph.

"Paths" are channels along which people move. Streets, sidewalks, transit lines, canals, and railroad lines are all examples of this type of element. For most people, paths are major elements in their image of the city (Move #17), and almost all commentators see them as extremely important parts of the city. Between 40 and 70 percent of the land of the modern American city is devoted to the automobile. While not all these spaces are paths—parking lots and storage facilities being the notable exceptions—the large majority of them are.

"Edges" are linear elements not used as paths. People often experience them as borders and boundaries. The edge of the modern city has been almost entirely broken down by the dispersion of population that was made possible with the development of high-speed transportation and communication systems (Move #19). Particularly significant in this regard has been the automobile (Move #9). Today, the wall around the crossroads would be more accurately depicted by a less regular, more diffuse line: maybe $\langle x \rangle$ instead of $\otimes$. According to Lewis Mumford, we've moved away from the image of the city as a container to the image of the city as an electronic net (Part V).

In a book titled *Close Up: How to Read the American City* (Columbia: University of Missouri Press, 1981), Grady Clay proposed the term "front" as a replacement for "edge." "Front" is being used here the way weather forecasters and military strategists use it, and Clay believed that this word takes into account the dynamic, shifting conditions that exist at modern city boundaries. A city boundary is not just a wall fixed in place the way it was in earlier times, but rather two sets of forces—development interests versus preservationist interests or people who want more housing, factories, and shopping centers lined up against those who want to maintain farms and greenbelts—in active conflict with each other. Clay is clearly right when referring to the outer boundaries of most cities in the United States, but the idea of edge still has a lot of utility in describing many of the internal boundaries that exist within the city itself. The boulevard that marks the border of a large urban park (Move #8) and the elevated train tracks that indicate the boundary of an ethnic neighborhood (Move #24) are both better described by the term "edge," with its image of precision and crispness. Of course, edges often evolve into fronts and vice versa.

"Districts" are those areas of the city that have common identifying features. Water, open land in parks (Move #8), single-family homes in residential areas, the downtown high rises (Move

#12), neighborhoods (Move #24) made up of three- and four-story row houses are all examples of districts. Districts can also be characterized by either the kind of people who inhabit them—in ethnic, racial, or socioeconomic terms (Move #25)—or the kinds of activities that take place there. The garment district, the waterfront, and the railroad yards are often visible even from this height.

"Nodes" and "landmarks" are the final two categories. Nodes are usually parts of transportation systems and are often located at the crossing of paths. Large train and bus stations, traffic circles, and complex intersections where a number of different roads come together are all examples of nodes. They can also be simple concentrations such as a street corner hangout or one of the small parks and plazas (Move #15) that are becoming popular in many downtown areas. Unless they're quite prominent, they're often not visible from this height, but when they can be seen, they're quite dramatic with all that traffic moving through them.

Like nodes, landmarks are points of reference. They're often used as navigational aids when locomoting through the city (Move #17). They're usually rather simply defined physical objects, buildings, or features of the natural landscape which have been given great symbolic significance. In all likelihood, the building from which you're making this observation is, in Lynch's terms, a landmark.

Power

Height and ascension have always been associated with power. This is something language communicates with such phrases as "moving up in the world," "getting to the top," and "overcoming obstacles." There's a wonderful scene in the Charlie Chaplin movie *The Great Dictator* in which Chaplin, playing the Hitler-like Hinkel, has a meeting with a Mussolini clone played by Jack Oakie. This is literally a summit meeting; the two men are in barber chairs that they keep cranking higher and higher, realizing that whoever can get the uppermost position and force the other to look up when he talks will have an advantage, perhaps an "insurmountable" advantage. The scene ends with the two wildly waving men moving up and out of sight off the top of the screen. This is really being kicked upstairs—would that all troublesome heads of state could be so easily disposed of.

The city has traditionally been the place of power and has

usually housed the secular and religious rulers of society. Often this competition has taken the form of capturing the high ground with tall buildings. The passion and eroticism of much of this modern competition has been humorously depicted by Rem Koolhaas in a book called *Delirious New York* (New York: Oxford University Press, 1978). Imagine the Chrysler Building caught in the act of making love to the Empire State Building, while a spent Goodyear Blimp lies limply between them.

"Higher and higher" has almost always been interpreted as meaning more and more powerful. This is as true of architecture as it is of interpersonal relationships and theological images. In Boston, for example, the John Hancock Building and the Prudential Center, both homes of insurance companies, seem to be trying to stare each other down in some modern version of *High Noon*. This has been true throughout urban history. Think about those early power brokers, the builders of the Tower of Babel, who wanted to deal directly with God and not be talked *down* to. NASA astronauts have talked about the thrill of looking down at meteors flashing through the sky below.

The list of tall buildings provided at the beginning of this Move can be read as statements on the competition for power among different groups in the city and among different cities themselves. Do two World Trade towers of 1,350 feet each top one Sears Tower of 1,454 feet? What do we make of the fact that the Sears Tower, built in an age of incredible technological sophistication, is only three times as high as the 5,000-year-old pyramid of Cheops?

Elevators

Without elevators, there'd be no high-rise buildings. This is a good example of how technology has made a particular urban form possible. It's a theme that runs throughout this book and that can be seen everywhere from the relationship between the automobile and the mall (Move #9) to the impact television has had on our sense of place (Move #19). In fact, without certain technological advances in food production that allowed for increased population density (Move #4), the city itself would not have emerged. Technology runs throughout urban history and is not, as is often stated, a recent addition to city life (Move #19).

In 1850 Henry Waterman invented the first platform freight

elevator, and in 1854 Elisha Grave Otis completed his first hy-draulic elevator with a safety device so that passengers would feel secure. By 1871 passenger elevators were used in office build-ings, by 1887 the first electric elevator was in use, and by 1904 the first gearless traction elevator was installed. The development of the elevator, along with certain innovations in the technology of structure—particularly the steel skeleton, which was first used by Chicago engineer William LeBaron Jenney in the Home In-surance Building of 1883 (which, unfortunately, was demolished in 1931 to make room for a larger structure)—made it possible to build up rather than out in the city.

Although there *are* examples of multistoried buildings from much earlier times, these innovations made them much easier and more practical to build. Since high rises allowed more inten-sive land use and greater profit, they became very popular. Build-ing up resulted in dramatic increases in density, and the skyscraper soon became one of the most dominant building forms of urban America (Move #12).

FIGURE 1: The ultimate bird's-eye view: a satellite picture of the United States at night. *(Argonaut Press, Madison, WI)*

ADDITIONAL READING

Barthes, Roland. *Eiffel Tower and Other Mythologies*. New York: Farrar, Straus & Giroux, 1979. Roland Barthes's essay "Eiffel Tower" in this book is an important celebration of the joys of ascension and should be looked at by every climber of tall buildings. For Barthes, Paris is the "text" that can be "read" from the vantage point of the Tower.

Clay, Grady. *Close Up: How to Read the American City*. Columbia: University of Missouri Press, 1981. This is an interesting work on recent changes in American city form and seems to take into account the spatial dispersion—spreading out across the landscape—that the automobile (Move #9) and electronic media (Move #19) permit and, perhaps, even demand.

Lynch, Kevin. *The Image of the City*. Cambridge: MIT Press, 1960. This is a pioneering work in urban environmental perception and the elements of city form.

MOVE #2

Empty Room/Full Room

or,
"It's Starting to Get Crowded in Here, Shall We Dance?"

THIS MOVE IS A GOOD EXERCISE FOR BEGINNING TO UNDERSTAND the dynamics of urban behavior. If the city is that fantastic collection of designed objects you see when you look down in Move #1, then it's also groups of people behaving toward one another in particular ways. It's not that people in cities are so different from others; rather, the situations they regularly confront have unique characteristics that often demand a different kind of behavior than that which would be appropriate in other kinds of settings. While Parts IV and V go into greater detail about the individual urbanite and city communities, this exercise will provide you with a central image that should be of great help whenever you think about the dynamics of urban behavior, people in the city, and why they do what they do.

Relax, close your eyes, and imagine yourself standing in the middle of a large room—a very large room, the biggest you've ever seen. The place is so big that you can't even see the walls that mark the edges, but somehow you sense that they're out there somewhere. A few people are standing off in the distance, but most of what you see is open empty space.

As time passes, the room slowly fills. At first a few friends and family and then, for no apparent reason, more and more people seem to be showing up. Gradually, there's less and less room. You begin to feel the presence of other people, and slowly

39

you're forced to move closer and closer to them. You see them all the time and, because of their proximity, sometimes even touch them. Some are talking and gesturing in your direction, and some aren't. Some you know, and many you don't. Some are doing things that make sense, while others are behaving in ways you don't quite understand.

Now keep that image in your head and think about how different your behavior would be in the full room compared with the empty one. Clearly, with the restriction of space and the exposure to a whole host of new people, you'd have to think, feel, and act differently, and as a result of this, your attitudes toward space, time, and other people would undoubtedly change. Reflecting on the nature of these changes can be helpful in understanding urban behavior. Return to the two images. What exactly would be the difference in your behavior in the crowded room compared with your behavior in the empty one?

NOTES

With its high numbers and density, the full room can be compared to the urban situation. As the room gets more and more crowded, those in it have to develop techniques for staying out of other people's way—both physically and psychologically. *Coordination* becomes a major issue, and cities are places where people have a sophisticated battery of techniques for coordinating their behavior with that of others. These techniques range from the tools and machines of technology—traffic lights and telephones, for example (Move #19)—to particular attitudes about space and time.

Attitudes Toward Time

If the crowded room is something like a dance with lots of other people, then the whole issue of time and timing becomes important. To choreograph your moves with theirs, you must pay close attention to the passage of time. Meeting someone for lunch at 1:30 or figuring out whether the 5:20 is running on schedule requires a particular orientation toward time. Instruments have to be developed to measure it precisely, and it must be valued as a resource. Time is a nonrenewable resource whose movement, seen as expenditure, is difficult, if not impossible, to control.

Certainly we can freeze it and capture a particular moment with a photograph, and film and video even afford the luxury of seemingly reversing it, but all in all, time has resisted our more assertive attempts at manipulation, and dreams of time travel and immortality remain just that, dreams.

There would also have to be a certain standardization of measurement to eliminate the situation that existed before 1883 when the traveler between New York and San Francisco encountered more than 200 local times.

Precision in measurement has increased dramatically over the last 125 years. According to David S. Landes in *Revolution in Time* (Cambridge: Belknap Press of Harvard University Press, 1983), when Cambridge and Oxford met in March 1864 for the world's first dual track meet, officials used watches that beat 14,400 times an hour, and the races were timed in quarter seconds. At Stockholm in 1912, the Olympic Games used photographic-electric timers clocking tenths of a second. In Paris in 1924, instruments were used that could measure hundredths of a second. Today, atomic clocks at national observatories use quartz crystal oscillators with frequencies of 2.5 megacycles per second checked by cesium-beam resonators vibrating at 9,192,631,770 plus or minus 20 cycles per second. When these people say, "eight o'clock sharp," they're not fooling.

Scholars have often written about the significance of the development of accurate clocks for the emergence of the city. Think for a moment about what city life would be like without clocks, watches, and radio time checks. Suddenly coordination on the crowded stage becomes more difficult because it's impossible to plan with any precision. If airport scenes are chaotic now with frequent delays and changes of schedule, imagine the situation where precision on this scale would be impossible even to think about because of the lack of adequate tools. I wouldn't want to be the one to orchestrate all the flights arriving at a major metropolitan airport at "dawn," rather than at 5:48, 5:51, 6:02, and so on. Even makers of music have difficulty without a rhythm section.

And the advertising world reminds us daily of the almost totemic significance that watches have in modern urban society —totems whose meaning and significance goes far beyond any simple utilitarian function that they may serve. What possible use is there for a watch that can tell time 300 feet under the water or that loses only a tenth of a second a year? What that watch really does is communicate to the world that its owner takes time very seriously, even 300 feet under the water (where you really wouldn't want to miss an important meeting), and therefore is a person who should in turn be taken seriously. Just exactly what is the solid steel shell of the Rolex protecting? The inner workings of the machine or our own fragile psyches from the inevitable movement of time?

In a society dominated by cities, if you don't take time seriously, you won't be liked or respected. Conversely, if you're not liked or respected, the accusation will be made that you don't take time seriously. It's amazing how much the descriptions of all those "outcast" groups in urban societies seem to resemble one another, the classic description of the "other." Henry Mayhew talks about the urban poor of London in the middle of the last century in *London Labor and London Poor* (London: G. Newbold/New York: Harper, 1851), "[He] is distinguished from the civilized man by his repugnance to regular and continuous labor—by his want of providence in laying up a store for the future—by his inability to perceive consequences ever so slightly removed from his immediate apprehension by his passion for stupefying herbs and roots, and, when possible, for intoxicating fermented liquors."

This portrait could just as easily have been given by the sexist of a woman, by the racist of a black or Hispanic, by the European colonial of the "native," by the northern European of the southern European (Move #25), by the nonpoor of the poor, and by almost all those other groups who stand in antagonistic relationships to each other.

The specific language changes, from everyday words such as *childlike* and *impulsive* to the social science jargon, *present-time oriented* and *inability to delay gratification*, but the general picture is the same. The consistency of these descriptions over such a wide range of people and situations indicates that more is being revealed about the people providing the descriptions than about the people being described. And one of the things that is being said is that the people in the crowded room must be continually conscious of the passage of time, and the accusation of being unaware of this movement is almost always included in negative stereotypes.

The crowded room and its counterpart, the city, also demand a strong appreciation of the time to come, the future. Spontaneity and impulsivity are characteristics not traditionally valued in urban societies. You don't want the driver of that downtown bus to "do his own thing" when you're going to a business appointment. This is even more true if you're alongside his vehicle in heavy morning traffic. "His own thing" has to mesh somehow with the plans you've made for the rest of the day—including staying alive, which is in some ways dependent on his *not* deciding that the lane markers are trivial and not to be honored because they dampen his individuality and constrain his freedom—and the plans his employers have made with the public—that is, the bus schedule. Any last-minute changes would disrupt the choreography of all these relationships. I'm always a bit leery of automobile bumper stickers that proclaim the driver to be a blithe spirit—the same way pilots carrying tomes on epistomology or ontology make me nervous. It's not the personality type or the intelligence that is worrisome, but rather the nagging doubt that the person might suddenly come to the conclusion that things aren't really the way they seem and as a consequence totally innovative behavior is appropriate. I don't need to think about this while speeding along the highway or flying at 30,000 feet. Impulsive behavior is possible in the empty room where interdependency isn't as much a fact of life, but in the crowded room of the city, it would result in chaos. That's why it's absolutely necessary to plan.

The number of plans and schedules projecting into the future we carry around in our heads is amazing: plans for the next thirty seconds when this page is concluded, a schedule for the next hour, the rest of the day, the week, month, the year, vacation plans, life plans, retirement plans, and even perpetual care for that cemetery plot that has been purchased in advance because when the need arises, there literally won't be any time left. It will have all run out.

A number of therapies have emerged in the past thirty years, often encountered under the names Gestalt therapy and T groups, where the emphasis is strictly on the "here and now," and any attempt to introduce other material is seen as an evasion. In part, this is an attempt to remedy the often-reported situation where people spend so much time focusing on the future that somehow they feel the present is lost. The experience of thinking only about vacation while at work and thinking only about work while on vacation is a fairly common one.

Close Stranger and Distant Friend

Another difference between the full room and the empty room is that in the empty room there's a greater correspondence between physical space and psychological space. That is, in the empty room, it's usually the case that people who are emotionally and psychologically close are also physically close. This happens so often in encounters between people that the language of space is often used to describe emotional relationships: "I feel *close* to you." "You're *distancing* yourself from me." "Something you said *touched* me." These are all examples of this metaphoric use of language, which works because in most situations people *do* try to get physically close to other people they like and stay away from those they don't like.

The city is the place where physical and psychological space often *don't* correspond, and a central element of the crowded room is the *paradox of the close stranger and distant friend*. In the city you regularly rub elbows with strangers while your friends are often miles away.

Attempts to deal with this paradox help to explain a lot of urban behavior. Many of the things people do in the crowded room can best be understood as attempts to keep the close stranger at a distance. These techniques include the way we manage the small spaces around us (Move #15), the way perceptions and thoughts are screened and filtered (Move #16), the way eyes are used in the city (Move #18), technological devices such as Walkman-type personal stereos and telephone-answering machines (Move #19), the status of speed in modern urban society (Move #21), and restrictive immigration legislation (Move #25).

Attitudes toward Space

The transition from the empty room to the crowded room also results in a different set of attitudes toward space. Suddenly there's a need for making order out of what at times can seem to be chaos, in a way that wasn't quite necessary when the room was empty. Space, like time, must be thought of as objective, homogeneous, measurable, and universal in its qualities. The unique, the idiosyncratic, the particular, can't be attended to as closely if we are all to coordinate our activities with each other. This is reflected in ways of dividing up space, such as the grid (Move

#6), and the establishment of rules such as zoning ordinances, which further regulate how space can be used (Move #7). In the empty room, it doesn't make much sense to worry about what gets built where, but in the crowded city, this becomes an important issue.

Issues of "turf," or protection from the many people who are suddenly all over the place, emerge in the city. This theme is enacted on the scale of "home as castle" (Move #11), the "neighborhood" as a group of people in a particular part of the crowded room who lend each other support (Move #24), and the emergence of the image of "gate" as a useful tool for thinking about the crowded room.

Image of Gate

The image of the gate is an ancient one in the history of the city. It was these openings through the "edge" of the old city wall that contained and constricted the flow of traffic and strongly influenced what people and activities would encounter one another. To close the city gates at night meant locking out people whom one didn't want to encounter in the dark and keeping certain other people in. Even today, the nicknames of many American cities (Move #3) indicate that it's still a popular image, but now the vision is the entire city serving as the entrance to a broader region. Here the image is always one of "entering" through the gate.

The city can be thought of as an environment with a series of gates or potential barriers to movement and perception. These gates give access to some groups and activities and deny access to others. They can be "opened" and "closed" in the fashion of doors, windows, walls, screens, filters (Move #16), fences, broad boulevards and highways, plantings of trees and hedges (Move #8), the ghetto and "the other side of the tracks." To "open" them is to make any changes that increase the possibility of access between the elements on either side of the gate, while to close them is to diminish this access.

The "ghetto" is a classic example of the gate. The word itself is Italian and may be derived from the Hebrew word *get*, meaning "letter of divorce," or "divorce," and hence implying separation. Other theories of its origin trace it back to an abbreviation of *borghetto*, the diminutive of *borgo* or *borough*, or to *gietto*, one of the foundaries of Venice located near the Jewish quarter. The term was first used in 1516 in Venice to designate the Jewish quarter, but in contemporary American cities it generally refers to poor, black, and Hispanic areas.

Gates are everywhere on the crowded stage, and the ghetto, like other examples of this form, *both* reflects the underlying values that have resulted in its being built and also helps maintain those values. The loony circle of reasoning goes, "Let's put them behind gates because we don't want to hang out with them because they're dirty, dangerous, visually distasteful, and there's always a danger we'll catch it from them," but once the group is put behind the gate, it becomes much easier to sustain the negative stereotypes because reality testing becomes almost an impossibility. Now there's no way of telling if the group has any of those characteristics because we keep our distance from it.

Not that it doesn't make sense to put certain things behind gates—no one wants to live next door to a steel plant or a treatment center for contagious diseases—but it should be realized that once a group or activity is placed behind a series of gates, the chances for interaction with it become highly diminished. As a consequence, it's much easier to entertain rather unrealistic, even fantastic, notions of what the thing behind the gate is.

Children raised in purely residential areas, for example, talk very differently about the nature of work than do those who encounter it on a daily basis because of zoning and site placement. It's the difference between the child of three who sees most of the adults in the immediate environment go off daily to this mysterious place called "work" and then return home hours later with cryptic messages—"How was work, honey?" "Fine"—and the child who daily encounters adults of both sexes engaged in a wide variety of activities.

How many "town-gown" conflicts (ongoing wars in a locality between educational communities such as universities and others) are maintained long beyond the life of the initial cause of the dispute because the gates between the two combatants were essentially closed, and as a result, both the townies and the gownies could entertain highly unrealistic negative images of each other.

The social psychologist Kurt Lewin talked about the importance of the "gatekeeper" in a study designed to change American eating habits during World War II. Meat was being rationed, but there was an abundance of organ meat—sweetbreads, hearts, lungs, and brains—available, and Lewin's task was to develop strategies for increasing the consumption of these cuts. He decided to concentrate on the gatekeeper, the family member who purchased, prepared, and served food in the home, and he found that through a discussion of the issue with groups of these people, their food selection could be changed in the desired direction.

In his book *Managing the Flow of Technology* (Cambridge: MIT Press, 1977), Thomas J. Allen also discussed the significance of the gatekeeper, in this case the person who helps provide access to technological information outside the immediate organization. Research has shown that product and process development projects are more successful when a gatekeeper is on the team. There's also evidence that, in general, gatekeepers tend to be promoted into management.

Zoning regulations (Move #7), the use of "filters" to deal with "cognitive overload" in the city (Move #16), and the elimination of the distinction between front stage and back stage (Move #14) which some media scholars claim has been caused by television (Move #19) are all examples where "access" is the major theme. This theme can be further explored through the use of the image of the gate. This image suggests a number of questions. What specific forms do the gates take? What groups of people and/or activities are being separated? Who are the gatekeepers, and how do they decide when to open and close the gate?

ADDITIONAL SUGGESTIONS

Fantasy behavior can be enhanced by placing yourself in what you consider to be a "safe" situation and then using some of the qualities of the place itself as points of departure for structuring the images. Gaston Bachelard even identifies this function as the major purpose of the home, "protection for the daydreamer" (Move #11).

Two other strategies can be helpful: Return repeatedly to the imaginary scene—in the case of this Move, the empty room slowly transforming itself to a place crowded with people—and make the Move a collective one where groups of people elaborate on the scene together.

And, although this Move has been structured around a fantasy experience, you can deal with similar themes using observational techniques. In the settings you've observed that resemble the "empty room" and the "full room"—actual rooms like those in apartments, dormitories, and barracks or the outdoor rooms of the city such as Olmsted's parks (Move #8) and those vest pocket parks and plazas that are in front of a lot of downtown skyscrapers (Move #15)—how do people go about dealing with the "close stranger and distant friend"? And what about the kind of gates used in these situations?

MOVE #3

The Name of the Place
Definitions, Nicknames, and Metaphors

DEFINITIONS

WHAT OTHER FACTORS HAVE TO BE INCLUDED IN ANY OVERVIEW OF the city? One of the shortest definitions of the city was that given by the urban sociologist Louis Wirth in what has probably been one the most cited and influential articles in American sociology, "Urbanism as a Way of Life" (*American Journal of Sociology*, July 1938), when he wrote that the city is a "relatively large, dense and permanent settlement of socially heterogeneous individuals." While this can be a useful starting point, it does have a number of shortcomings. First, some of the elements of the definition need modification or, at the very least, elaboration.

The term "dense," for example, needs clarification. Many observers of the modern American city have pointed out that scientific advances have given us the option of spreading out in space while still maintaining the interpersonal contacts necessary for city life. Why be crowded together when it's now possible to stay in touch via the automobile (Move #9) and the television and telephone (Move #19)? Of course, this can all come to a quick screeching halt if the machines break down, but why not enjoy it while it lasts? And besides, it gives more Americans a chance to aspire to that part of the "American Dream," which includes a single-family detached house on a piece of land (Move #11). "Don't go to Los Angeles, wait until Los Angeles comes to you" is the way it's sometimes put. Instead of people going to the city, now it's the city going to the people.

The image of "permanency" has been challenged by some twentieth-century thinkers, too. The Archigram group of London has proposed building mobile cities capable of locomoting around the landscape (see Figure 2). If the two poles of human existence are movement and settlement, with the city traditionally seen as one of the great exemplars of the latter, then things seem to be changing. Bedouins have few good words to say for those whose dwellings stayed fixed in one place, and with film sequels and American and Soviet space programs going "where no one has gone before," residential movement on the local, national, and global scales may be one of the dominant themes of the twenty-first century. In an era when it's not unusual to see someone driving his or her motor *home* down the highway, with bicycles and motorcycles tied to the wall of the dwelling, the process seems to have already begun.

Another problem with the Wirth definition is that it neglects the physical aspects of the city—the streets, buildings, parks, and plazas seen when you look down in Move #1—instead emphasizing people and social relationships. A complete definition has to include *both* these components if it is going to be of any help in making Moves through the city. The city is collections of people who behave in certain ways *and* collections of designed objects that surround these behaviors, a theater with performers using the stage, sets, and props to support their performances (Move #14).

FIGURE 2: "Walking City Visits New York" by Ron Herron of Archigram.

Throughout the history of the modern city, all those disciplines and professions that have attempted to describe, analyze, and, on occasion, provide remedies for its ills have almost invariably emphasized one or the other of these two components. Urban sociology, urban anthropology, urban psychology, and city planning have traditionally concentrated on what it is people *do* in the city and, in the case of city planning, what it is they *should* be doing, while engineering, architecture, and urban design have typically concentrated on the physicality of the place—its streets, plazas, and buildings. This fragmentation of the definition of the city, ironically an example itself of the specialization that always accompanies urbanization, has unfortunate consequences. It leads to a situation similar to one where those designing or trying to understand the front of the car don't have much to say to those designing the back of the car. Or, if your preferences run to scholarly pursuits and organic metaphors, the people examining the front of the elephant aren't able to communicate with the people studying the rear of the elephant. And we know what happened in the Sufi tale of the blind men and the elephant.

For urban sociologists, the major defining characteristic of the city is a particular kind of social organization—a way people have of behaving toward one another that has been called "civilization." For Robert Redfield in *The Primitive World and its Transformations* (Ithaca: Cornell University Press, 1965), civilization was a set of social bonds that

> result from mutual usefulness, from deliberate coercion or from the mere utilization of the same means. In [this] . . . order, men are bound by things, or are themselves things. They are organized by necessity or expediency. Think, if you will, of the orderly way which automobiles move in response to the traffic light or the policeman's whistle, or think of the flow of goods, services and money among the people who together produce, distribute and consume some commodity such as rubber.

These social connections rest on impersonal, specialized relations that are in strong contrast to the way primitive, pre-urban societies operate. This is something like the relationship the reader of this book has with those who produced it.

> The major contrast between civilized and primitive societies lies in the bonds unifying the society. Although their technologies

differed, hunting-gathering groups and Neolithic farm-villages were alike in being small . . . both were self contained, for virtually all the group needed to know was obtained within its own confines. They were homogeneous, for even though the Neolithic allowed permanent settlement, both of these technological levels required every individual to devote full attention to obtaining food; thus the major distinctions were those of age and sex, since all the individuals had the same occupation and attendant property and wealth. In all Stone Age societies, kinship was very important, and the family, performing economic, educational, leadership and other functions, was the major social unit.

The distinction being made here (in N. Gist and S. Fava, *Urban Society*; New York: Thomas Y. Crowell, 1964) is between a collection of people all of whom pretty much did the same thing and a collection of people who do a wide range of things. As specialists, people in the latter group often find it impossible to communicate to those outside the specialization exactly what it is they do, how they do it, or the problems they face in both action and thought as they go about their specialization.

For example, the Move from the cave painters of Lascaux in Neolithic France 15,000 years ago, who were clearly engaged in a communal activity revolving around the hunt, to today's minimalist and neorealist painters can be understood only within the context of their history. Looking at artwork such as the beer cans, flags, and targets of the American painter Jasper Johns is a different experience for those who are familiar with the period of abstract expressionism that preceded him and that, to some extent, he was reacting against than it is for those who don't have this information. Much of contemporary painting, like many other human activities in American urban society, makes sense only if you're a member of that small part of the tribe that is familiar with the rules and history of this specialization. If those outside this comparatively small group don't know what the paintings mean, it's because they weren't painted for them in the same way that the Lascaux paintings *were* made for the whole tribe. This doesn't mean that the work can't be viewed and even enjoyed— it's not totally inaccessible—but it does mean that the two seemingly similar experiences, looking at paintings on a wall, are in fact very different. Perhaps the closest we civilized folk can come to the pre-urban experience is when we look at family photographs where the visual object is always experienced in a wide range of communal and individual contexts. Little Freddie's graduation picture may have for me as much personal and tribal significance as did the animal figures on the wall for the Neolithic hunter.

The distinction between "primitive" and "civilized" suggests that one way of arriving at an overview or definition of the city is to examine pre-urban situations. To know about city look at noncity. Although travel is always recommended, the difficulty with this strategy is twofold. First, in a rapidly urbanizing world, it's possible to find places that are not cities in the physical sense but difficult to find people who haven't been influenced by urban values and behaviors. This is particularly true in the United States. But even if you could find that nonurban tribe, in your very observation of it you'd be bringing the city that's within you along to the experience. Obviously, all the ways of thinking and behaving that are intimately associated with urban life (see Part IV) have been internalized by the time we're adults and color everything we see.

PARADOX

Inevitably, any scientific treatment of the city denies something of its complexity and paradoxical nature. The goal of science, whether social or otherwise, is to simplify and introduce order and regularity where there at first may seem to be none. This is as true for urban scholarship and city life as it is for botany and plant life. This always results in a rather lean, stark portrayal of the thing being studied. Hence the appeal of numbers to scientists as the most extreme exemplars of the belief that "less is more" (Move #12). Traditionally, poets, novelists, and visual artists have taken it upon themselves to flesh out these lean pictures. In a catalog of visionary cities being described by Marco Polo to Kublai Khan (in *Invisible Cities*; New York: Harcourt Brace Jovanovich, 1974), the Italian writer Italo Calvino spoke directly to this issue:

> With cities, it is as with dreams: everything imaginable can be dreamed, but even the most unexpected dream is a rebus that conceals a desire or, its reverse, a fear. Cities, like dreams, are made of desires and fears, even if the thread of their discourse is secret, their rules are absurd, their perspectives deceitful, and everything conceals something else.

In *The Lawless Roads* (London: Penguin Books, 1971), the English novelist Graham Greene despaired of ever describing it:

> How to describe the city? Even for an old inhabitant it is impossible: one can present only a simplified plan, taking a house here, a park there, as symbols of the whole.

In an important comment on the physicality of the city, Lewis Mumford, in *The Culture of Cities* (New York: Harcourt Brace Jovanovich, 1938), took issue with all those who saw the city as somehow a less worthy setting for human life because, being a product of human minds and hands, it wasn't "natural":

> The city is a fact of nature, like a cave, a run of mackerel or an ant-heap. But it is also a conscious work of art, and it holds within its communal framework many simpler and more personal forms of art . . . With language itself, it [the city] remains man's greatest work of art.

Claude Levi-Strauss repeated the theme in his classic work *Tristes Tropiques* (New York: Atheneum, 1974):

> Cities have often been likened to symphonies and poems, and the comparison seems to me a perfectly natural one. They are in fact objects of the same kind. The city may even be rated higher since it stands at the point where nature and artifice meet. A city is a congestion of animals whose biological history is enclosed within its boundaries, and yet every conscious and rational act on the part of these creatures helps to shape the city's eventual character. By its form as by the manner of its birth, the city has elements of biological procreation, organic evolution and aesthetic creation. It is both a natural object and a thing to be cultivated; individual and group; something lived and something dreamed. It is the human invention par excellence.

METAPHOR

Because of its complex and paradoxical nature, metaphor has always been a useful approach to the city. The two metaphors that appear again and again are those of the "city as a living organism" and the "city as a machine."

The French sociologist Emile Durkheim made extensive use of

organic and machine metaphors when describing societies as they evolved from small-scale communities to nation-states. He likened the former situation to that of a machine where everyone did pretty much the same thing and people were held together by their similarity to one another. *Organic solidarity* was the term Durkheim used to describe the situation in urban society where people play complementary roles (Move #14) and, like the organs of the body, are interdependent. A division of labor exists: One person grows grain, another harvests it, a third produces a popular breakfast cereal, a fourth sells it, and a fifth appears on the package to convince the first four, and the rest of us, to buy it.

Machine metaphors were particularly popular early in the twentieth century. When Frank Lloyd Wright said, "my god is machinery," and I. A. Richards stated, "a sentence is a machine for understanding," they were only reaffirming a traditional American faith in technology (Move #19). Admittedly, in the several-hundred-year history of this country's existence, machines have produced some of our more notable successes. Under the onslaught of exploding space shuttles and environmental pollution, much of this enthusiasm for machines is diminishing in the second half of the twentieth century, but the "city as machine" still remains a powerful image in both popular and professional settings.

In a provocative work entitled *The Uses of Disorder* (New York: Knopf, 1970), the sociologist Richard Sennett argued that one negative consequence of the machine metaphor has been the equating of any kind of conflict with malfunction, which in the case of the machine is obviously to be avoided. No one wants a car that doesn't run or a food processor that doesn't process. According to Sennett, this has resulted in people's wanting a certain kind of homogeneity and blandness that curtails their development and freezes them in a perpetual state of adolescence. And this is a developmental stage where conflict, risk, and variety are often avoided. "Purity" is the goal, and everything has that incredible lack of ambiguity, the true mark of innocence. The city, whose very elements of numbers, variety, and density are usually portrayed as something negative to be coped with (Move #16), can be used to overcome this state of perpetual adolescence, but if it is to do so, the image cannot be that of the smoothly running machine.

Sennett proposed dense, decentralized cities where people

would be routinely in contact with a wide range of other people and events and the choices inherent in such a complex situation could be fully experienced. For example, actual conflict on the streets where neighbors are forced to resolve disputes because the police won't respond every time there's a noise complaint forces people to learn something about compromise and cooperation. This is the "real" world, not the world as a media creation where everyone can afford to remain pure and be concerned with abstract notions of honor and privacy. This is a world where the endings aren't neat, precise, and clean, and you don't automatically move on to another show every thirty minutes, sixty minutes, or maybe even a couple of hours (if it's a special on World War II, for instance). Cities organized too rigidly around order, with "a place for everything and everything in its place" (Move #7), don't allow for this type of growth and personal development.

A number of these ideas are reminiscent of those of Stephen Carr in an essay titled the "City of the Mind" (in W. R. Ewald [ed.], *Environment for Man*; Bloomington: Indiana University Press, 1967). He proposed that urban designers stimulate people to explore new settings and experiences by designing some degree of novelty and complexity in urban forms. A similar impulse also seems to be behind much of the work of the postmodernists (Moves #9, #12).

The language of the organic metaphor is so pervasive that it has even crept into everyday speech. Expressions such as "urban revitalization," "heart of the city," and "dying neighborhoods" are all examples of the organic metaphor. The Chicago School made extensive use of images of plant and animal communities in their studies of such urban institutions as neighborhoods (Move #24). While these two metaphors *can* be quite useful, it's important to remember that the language used to describe a thing strongly influences the way the thing being described will be perceived and dealt with. The differences among "fat," "full figured," and "Rubenesque" are less in poundage and more in attitude toward that poundage.

Whenever metaphors are used—and later in the book the metaphor of drama or theater will be presented as being particularly useful (Move #14)—the important words to remember are *as if*. Think of the city *as if* it were a living organism. Therefore, while plants and animals must die, this may not be the case for neighborhoods (Move #24). Consider the city *as if* it were a machine; while an important aspect of machines is the interchangeability of their parts—the alternator for one 1966 Plymouth Valiant will work equally well for any other 1966 Plymouth Valiant—this isn't often the case for cities. To think of a downtown cultural center as a machine part is to deny all regional and local qualities of the culture to be displayed. "Context" is an important idea in postmodernist design, and the machine metaphor denies this significance. An engine is an engine is an engine, and it always works the same way no matter where it is.

Just as metaphors have been used to attempt to gain an understanding of the city, the city itself has been appropriated as a metaphor to explain other complex events. Ludwig Wittgenstein observed in *Philosophical Investigations* (3d. ed.; New York: Macmillan, 1958): "Our language can be seen as an ancient city: a maze of little streets and squares, of old and new houses, and of houses with additions from various periods; and this surrounded by a multitude of new boroughs with straight regular streets and uniform houses."

NICKNAMES

Another approach to the question of urban definition is to take a look at how people in different American cities have chosen to portray themselves through the use of nicknames. While the motivation for these nicknames ranges from attempting to encourage tourism to passing negative judgments on the places being named, generally these labels capture a particular quality that is often quite prominent. In the following list are the nicknames for some of America's leading cities.*

NEW YORK

The Big Apple
The Empire City
The Metropolis
Gotham
The Melting Pot

Fun City
Capital of Finance
City that Never Sleeps
Father Knickerbocker

---

*From Joseph N. Kane and Gerald L. Alexander, *Nicknames and Sobriquets of U.S. Cities, States and Counties*, 3d. ed. (Metuchen, NJ: Scarecrow Press, 1979).

CHICAGO

Chi
Hogopolis
City of Big Shoulders
Second City
Windy City

Convention City
City by the Lake
Country's Greatest Rail
  Center
The Queen of the Lakes

LOS ANGELES

L.A.
The Movie City
Glamour Capital of the
  World
The City of Angels
Smog City

One Hundred Suburbs in
  Search of a City
The City Built in a Day
The City of Make-Believe
The City of Liquid
  Sunshine

PHILADELPHIA

Philly
The City of Brotherly Love
The Birthplace of the Nation

America's Convention City
The Cradle of Liberty
The Quaker City

HOUSTON

Space City, U.S.A.
Babylon on the Bayou
The Oil Center of the World

The Land of the Big Inch
America's Growingest City
The First City of Texas

DETROIT

The Motor City
Renaissance by the River
The City of Progress

The Dynamic City
The City of Straits
Fordtown

DALLAS

Big "D"
The Southwest Metroplex
  (with Fort Worth)
Athens of the Southwest

The All-American Town
The City of Opportunity
The Fastest Growing City

SAN FRANCISCO

Frisco
Baghdad by the Bay
Gateway to the Orient
City of the Golden Gate

City of One Hundred Hills
The Suicide Capital of the
U.S.

BOSTON

Beantown
The Hub
The Cradle of Liberty

The Athens of America
The Puritan City
City of Paul Revere

ST. LOUIS

The Gateway Arch City
The Shoe Capital of
America
The Great River City

The Memphis of the
American Nile
The Mound City
The Gateway to Space

ATLANTA

The Big Peach
The Capital of the New
South

The Dogwood City
The Gate City
The New York of the South

MINNEAPOLIS

The Twin Cities
(with St. Paul)
The City to Watch
Milltown

Gateway to the Northwest
The Sawdust City
The City of Lakes

SEATTLE

The American Gateway to
Alaska and the Orient
The City of Seven Hills
The World's Greatest
Halibut Port

The Little Portage
The Cannery City
The Evergreen Playground

MIAMI

The Action City
The Gateway to Latin
 America
The Sunshine Capital of the
 World

The Tropic Metropolis
The Magic City
The Town that Climate
 Built

NEW ORLEANS

The Creole City
The Gulf City
The Alexandria of America

The City of the Mardi Gras
The Heart of Dixie
The Convention City

ALBUQUERQUE

The Duke City
The Miracle of the
 Southwest
The Hot Air Balloon Capital
 of the World

The Metropolis of New
 Mexico
The Marketing and Trading
 Center
The Growing City

ADDITIONAL READING

Calvino, Italo. *Invisible Cities*. New York: Harcourt Brace Jovanovich, 1974. In this wonderful series of tales the explorer Marco Polo tells the Kublai Khan about the cities in his kingdom that Polo has visited. Calvino writes about the city of imagination and possibility and, in a way, the ultimate utopian visions (Move #10).

Mumford, Lewis. *The Culture of Cities*. New York: Harcourt Brace Jovanovich, 1938.

Tonnies, F. *Community and Society*. Edited by Charles Loomis. New York: Harper & Row, 1963. Tonnies, who published this book in 1887, was the first to articulate differences in types of human relationships—what he termed *gemeinschaft* and *gesellschaft*. The former were relationships found in extended families and rural villages and were based on sentiment, tradition, and common bonds. These rested on natural will, which in turn was based on the family and "soil." The latter were found in modern capitalistic states and were characterized by rationalism, individualism, and emotional disengagement. These two orientations were seen as opposites.

Weber, Max. *The City*. New York: The Free Press, 1958. This work first appeared in 1905 and is usually thought of as the first modern effort in urban studies.

Weber considered cities to be places that encouraged social individuality and innovation, places of historical change. But along with this, he believed that the cities of his day were primitive, undeveloped institutions, and he chose to study cities of the late Middle Ages in the low countries and the slightly later early Renaissance cities of Italy as examples of cities that exhibited the full possibilities of urban culture—places that bred many different urban styles of life.

Wirth, Louis. "Urbanism as a Way of Life." *American Journal of Sociology* 44:8–20, July 1938. This classic article cites three population characteristics, size, density, and heterogeneity, as important in influencing urban styles of life. Although strongly criticized in its particulars, the work has had enormous influence on a whole host of writers on the city (Move #16) and is often seen as following the grand European tradition of Tonnies, Weber, Durkheim, and Simmel.

II

PATTERNS IN TIME & SPACE

THE SEVEN MOVES IN THIS SECTION FOCUS ON FAC-
tors that have been major influences on the overall
shape of the city, factors that give the place its
special look and feel and help to determine what
goes where and how the different parts should relate to one another.

In an essay called "The Nature of Cities" (*Annals
of the American Academy of Political and Social Science,*
November 1945) the urban sociologists Chauncy
Harris and Edward Ullman offered some ideas on
why cities were located where they were. They presented three different relationships the city could
have with the surrounding countryside. It could be
a "central place" performing comprehensive services for the surrounding area or a "transport" city
"performing break-of-bulk and allied services along
transport routes, supported by areas which may be
remote in distance but close in connection because
of the city's strategic location on transport channels." The third type, the "specialized function"

city, performed a single service such as mining, manufacturing, or recreation for a large area.

Another urban sociologist, also of the Chicago School, which had been responsible for some of the classic studies of cities and city life, has provided what has probably been the most enduring image of the internal structure of the city. Ernest Burgess, in his "Growth of the City" (in R. E. Park and E. W. Burgess, *The City*; Chicago: University of Chicago Press, 1925), pictured a series of concentric circular zones, starting at the center with a central business district and moving out to a "commuters' zone" (see Figure 3). Critics of this image have argued that additional factors, such as geography and history (Move #5), have resulted in cities' being more complex and less regular than concentric zone theory would have one believe.

"Sector theory" and "multiple nuclei" have been the major alternatives offered to Burgess's picture of concentric zones. Homer Hoyt developed the sector theory by studying the housing market of Chicago from 1840 to 1940. He also argued that the development of the city begins in the center but then moves outward in wedge-shaped sectors— something like the slices of a pie—and not in concentric circles.

Each of the wedges has a specific function. For example, industry and luxury housing may both start in the center of the city, but as time goes on, they spread out in different directions. Luxury housing is likely to spread toward high ground and prestigious sites such as Central Park (New York), Nob Hill (San Francisco), and Beacon Hill (Boston), while industry will use other criteria for making locational choices. Availability of adequate transportation systems and zoning considerations (Move #7) are always important for heavy industry. In their multiple nuclei theory, Harris and Ullman disputed the idea that the city begins with a single center. They pictured a situation where different

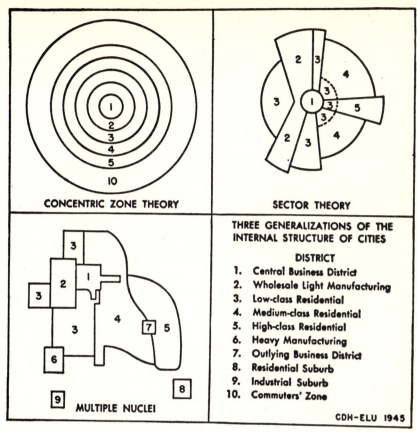

FIGURE 3: Three theories of city growth from Chauncy Harris and Edward Ullman, "The Nature of Cities," *Annals of the American Academy of Political and Social Science*, November 1945.

activities and groups of people start from different places in the city.

Moves #4 and #5 deal with the history and prehistory of the city. Attitudes such as those of modern architecture, where history was viewed as a burden to be overcome and not something of significance to be analyzed and reflected on, clearly don't make much sense when dealing with a phenomenon as complex as the city. Cities are cultural creations whose past is contained within them, and any denial of this past risks disaster of the sort Santayana had in mind when he said, "Those who cannot remember the past are condemned to repeat it."

Here, the organic metaphor may be more useful than its mechanistic counterpart (Move #3). While automobiles can be operated quite well without any knowledge of their history (Move #9), it usually makes sense to try to get some idea of a person's background when meeting him or her for the first time. This is because of the belief that a relationship in the present will greatly benefit from an awareness of the past. And so it is with cities. Streets, buildings, parks, and plazas mark the passage of time by their very persistence, and in an interesting work entitled *What Time Is This Place?* (Cambridge: MIT Press, 1967), Kevin Lynch argued quite persuasively that for the urbanite it was as important to be oriented in time as it was to be oriented in space (Move #17). There *is* something disconcerting about losing one's sense of time, and this may be a result of having been trained to attend closely to time in the crowded urban room (Move #2). But in the larger scale of things, all urban history is relatively recent.

In his book *Basin and Range* (New York: Farrar, Straus & Giroux, 1981), John McPhee gave the big picture:

> . . . geologists will sometimes use the calendar year as a unit to represent the time scale, and in such terms the Precambrian runs from New Year's Day until well after Halloween. Dinosaurs appear in the middle of December and are gone the day after Christmas. The last ice sheet melts on December 31st at one minute before midnight, and the Roman Empire lasts five seconds. With your arms spread wide again to represent all time on earth, look at one hand with its line of life. The Cambrian begins at the wrist, and the Permian Extinction is at the outer edge of the palm. All of the Cenozoic is in a fingerprint, and in a single

stroke with a medium-grained nail file you could eradicate human history.

And urban history is probably less than 1 percent of that. Topics dealt with in this section include the "Neolithic Revolution" and the prehistory of cities (Move #4); important dates and events in leading American cities (Move #5); the gridiron as a way of dividing up space (Move #6); some quick notes on zoning (Move #7); Frederick Law Olmsted and nature in the American city (Move #8); the suburb, the strip, and the mall as three important consequences of the incredible popularity of the automobile (Move #9); and a number of utopian visions that have been extremely influential in shaping the modern American city—those of Ebenezer Howard, Le Corbusier, and Frank Lloyd Wright—the Garden City, the Ville Radieuse, and Broadacre City (Move #10).

MOVE #4

Neolithic Revolution and the Prehistory of Cities

THE EARLIEST CITIES APPEARED BETWEEN 5,000 AND 6,000 YEARS AGO. Compared with the 500,000 to 750,000 years the human species has been on earth, and the roughly 40,000 years that physically modern man, Homo sapiens, has existed, cities are relatively recent developments. Of course, these dates are all speculations made from physical evidence, since written history itself begins with the advent of cities—first a need for the keeping of written records, probably first used by Sumerian priests some 5,000 years ago, to record tax payments and commodity exchanges and then the records themselves transforming the events being described. Even the pharaohs must have complained about how the media handled the building of the pyramids and the departure of the Jews from Egypt.

Three major factors are generally recognized as important in shaping the development of cities.

ENVIRONMENT

First, there's the environment, that is, the degree to which a given climate, topography, and set of natural resources can support the human species. The environment has changed significantly in the recent geologic past, and of particular interest are the climatic changes resulting from the end of the last Ice Age around 7000 B.C. This melting of the vast northern ice sheets not only converted the steppes and tundra of Europe into a temperate forest but also began the transformation of the prairies south of the Mediterranean and in parts of Asia into deserts dotted by oases. Here grew the wild grasses that later under cultivation were to become wheat and barley. Sheep and cattle suitable for domestication also roamed wild. In this type of supportive place, people could successfully adopt an aggressive attitude toward surrounding nature and actively begin to exploit it.

TECHNOLOGY AND THE NEOLITHIC REVOLUTION

This agricultural revolution first occurred south and east of the Mediterranean, in an area known as the Fertile Crescent, and generally falls under the second heading of technology. Only through dramatic technological advances, particularly in areas of agriculture and animal husbandry, could surplus food be generated that in turn allowed for large, dense populations to settle permanently in a fixed location. In earlier pre-urban Paleolithic times, only a concern for the dead and ritual cave sites used to insure good hunting such as those at Lascaux and Altamira brought people together repeatedly to the same place.

A fully Neolithic technology included major reliance for food on domesticated crops and/or animals and only minor reliance on hunting, fishing, and gathering; the making of stone tools by grinding and polishing instead of flaking and chipping; and the development of weaving and pottery. Collectively, these advances are often referred to as the "Neolithic Revolution."

Cultivation of grain, the development of the plow, the potter's wheel, the sailboat, the draw loom, metallurgy, abstract mathematics, exact astronomical observations, the calendar, and writing all came into existence around 3000 B.C., give or take a few centuries.

CIVILIZATION

The third factor usually cited as necessary for the development of cities is a type of social organization termed "civilization." This allowed for the collection and distribution of surplus food and the coordination and choreography that are necessary when large groups of people live in close quarters (Move #2). The emergence of civilization was often under the leadership of a strong central authority. Fustel de Coulanges and Numa Denis, in their classic book *The Ancient City: A Study on the Religion, Laws and Institutions of Greece and Rome* (Boston: Lothrop, Lee & Shepard, 1901; first published in Paris in 1864), cited the importance of religion in this centralizing role, while Lewis Mumford believed that the institution of kingship served this function. He points to a third-millennium B.C. Egyptian hieroglyph that said one of the functions of kings was to found cities.

Mumford also believed that the city

> was the chief fruit of the union between neolithic and a more archaic paleolithic culture. . . . As a result of the union of the two cultures, the widest sort of crossbreeding and intermixture probably took place all along the line. This gave the city potentialities and capabilities that neither the hunter, the miner, the stockbreeder, nor the peasant would ever, if left to themselves in their regional habitat, have been able to exploit. Where the hoe culture supported hamlets, plow culture could support whole cities and regions. Where local effort could build only minor embankments and ditches, the large scale co-operations of the city could turn a whole river valley into a unified organization of canals and irrigation works for food production and transport-shifting men, supplies, and raw materials about, as need dictated. (The City in History; New York: Harcourt Brace Jovanovich, 1961)

In "The Urban Revolution" (*Town Planning Review*, April 1950), Gordon Childe cited ten criteria for a place to be accorded the status of "city." With the exception of the second criterion, the first five deal with the importance of full-time specialists, supported ultimately by the ability of farmers to produce a food surplus: (1) full-time specialists such as draftsmen, transport workers, officials, and priests, (2) larger, denser populations than in Neolithic villages, (3) great art by full-time specialists, (4) writing and numerical notation systems for record keeping, (5) exact and predictive sciences such as arithmetic, geometry, and astronomy invented by literate members of society and used in the planning of major projects.

The remainder of Childe's criteria concern themselves with how the surplus produce was collected and used in ways other than for the support of specialists: (6) tribute or taxes were paid by farmers to a religious or secular administration, thus allowing for the concentration of the surplus product, (7) formation of the state-society organized around residence and not around kinship, (8) the building of monumental public buildings symbolizing the society's surplus, (9) the establishment of foreign trade, and (10) the emergence of a class society, with the privileged leading different kinds of lives than those of less privilege. With minor modifications, these criteria are still quite useful when thinking about contemporary urban America. While it could be argued, for example, that contrary to criterion 9 American cities don't pursue independent foreign trade policy, metropolitan newspapers on an almost daily basis report and usually applaud the efforts of government and business people actively pursuing foreign investment and business. In the last two decades the amount of foreign investment in American cities has increased quite dramatically.

The earliest cities first appeared at the eastern end of the Mediterranean in a region known as the Fertile Crescent. This encompasses areas of the present-day Egypt, Israel, Jordan, Lebanon, Iran, Iraq, and Syria. At the time, these regions had a very different climate and topography than they do now and were heavily forested. A short time later, cities also arose in India, China, and Crete.

DEVELOPMENTS IN THE NEW WORLD

The first inhabitants of the New World crossed from Asia on a land bridge over what is now the Bering Strait sometime between 12,000 and more than 40,000 years ago. The earliest civilization produced in the New World of which there is any information, the Mayan, appeared about 3000 B.C. They lived in the tropical forests and mountainous areas of Guatemala, Honduras, and the Yucatan peninsula of southern Mexico. While they had considerable knowlege of mathematics and astronomy, they had no metal technology except that which produced a few gold and copper ornaments. They developed a form of hieroglyphic writing, but they never got around to using the wheel as anything more than a decorative object. They also used primitive "slash and burn" agricultural techniques at a time when several other civilizations had made significant agricultural advances.

Mayan cities grew to magnificent heights between 300 B.C. and A.D. 300, but there is considerable debate as to whether these were true cities because most of the permanent inhabitants were probably priests and other members of the religious establishment. The rest of the population lived on farms and villages and collected at the temples only for rituals.

A derivative civilization was later formed in the valley of Mexico by the Aztecs, who built true cities. Tenochtitlan, their capital, was established in A.D. 1325 as a mud hut village on an island in Lake Texcoco and grew to an estimated size of 60,000 households with a population of 300,000. The city greatly impressed the Spanish under Cortes, who conquered the Aztecs and their ruler Montezuma II in the 1520s.

Tenochtitlan was the site of present-day Mexico City and developed through the gradual drying of the lake and the formation of intensively cultivated *chinampas*, or floating islands, out of the extreme fertile soil dredged up from the lake bed. During the reign of Montezuma I (1440–68 B.C.), an aqueduct was built to bring in pure water, a dike ten miles in length was constructed to prevent flooding and to counteract effects of increasing salinity on the cultivated *chinapas*, and architects were employed to design suitably impressive buildings.

Bernal Díaz del Castillo, one of Cortes's men, after first seeing the city wrote that he "did not know what to say or whether what appeared before us was real, for on one side in the land were great cities and in the lake, ever so many more, and the lake itself was crowded with canoes and in the causeway were many bridges at intervals, and in front of us stood the great City of Mexico."

The only other major indigenous New World civilization about which there is any bulk of information was that of the Incas in what is now Peru and Bolivia. At its height, the empire of the

Incas extended 2,500 miles along the Pacific coast from Ecuador in the north to midway down the coast of Chile in the south. This tremendous area, five times the size of Europe, was ruled by a centralized governmental bureaucracy under a god king and was held together with a spectacular 10,000-mile system of highways.

Even before the unification of the Inca empire between A.D. 1100 and A.D. 1400, some Incan cities, such as the Chimu capital Chan Chan, reached 50,000 in population. The Inca capital of Cuzco was located at the same site as the present city of that name. All of Childe's ten criteria, with the exception of writing, were developed by the Incans by about A.D. 900. They did develop a system of numberical notation in the *quipu*, a knotted string, but they never developed a system of writing. They were conquered by the Spanish, led by Pizarro, in the year 1532.

ADDITIONAL READING

Morris, A.E.J. *History of Urban Form: Before the Industrial Revolutions.* New York: John Wiley and Sons, 1979.

Mumford, Lewis. *The City in History.* New York: Harcourt Brace Jovanovich, 1961. This is an important book for the lover of cities, with interesting perspectives on a wealth of historical information and an annotated bibliography of classic works on the city. Mumford's work has influenced all students of the city.

Park, R.E., E.W. Burgess, and R.D. MacKenzie. *The City.* University of Chicago Press, 1924. A classic work of the Chicago school of urban sociology, this book emphasized environment, technology, and social structure, along with population increase, as the factors necessary for urban growth. Park believed the basic law of ecology was "competitive cooperation," while MacKenzie utilized the processes of "concentration," "centralization," "segregation," "invasion," and "succession" to account for how people would locate themselves in the space of the city. Many of the classic studies of this school were done on neighborhoods (Move #24) which they considered to be "natural areas."

Wilson, Josleen. *The Passionate Amateur's Guide to Archeology in the U.S.* New York: Collier Books, 1980. This guide lists important museums, digs, and archaeological sites in the United States and is a useful tool for those who want to go and look directly at the past.

MOVE #5

Some Dates and Events in the Early Urbanization of the United States

1492: In December, Christopher Columbus builds a crude fortress, La Navidad, from the timbers of the wrecked *Santa Maria* on the north coast of the island of Española. The settlement doesn't survive the winter.

1493: Columbus establishes the town of Isabella seventy-five miles to the east, but it too is short-lived.

1497: John Cabot seeks out new land briefly on Cape Breton Island. This serves later as the basis of the English claim for all of North America north of Florida.

1502: Santo Domingo rebuilt to the west across the river by the newly arrived governor from Spain, Nicolás de Ovando, and remains the oldest existing city founded by Europeans in America. In 1526, Gonzalo Fernandez de Oviedo y Valdes, a Spanish historian, describes Santo Domingo:

> I wish to point out that with regard to the buildings, no town in Spain—unless it is Barcelona which I have seen many times—is superior in general. The houses in Santo Domingo are for the most part of stone like those in Barcelona, and the walls are strong and beautiful, constructed of wonderful masonry. The general layout of the city is much better than that of Barcelona, because the many streets are more level and wide and incomparably straighter. Since the city was founded in our time, there was the opportunity to plan the whole thing from the beginning. (*Natural*

History of the West Indies; Toledo, 1526. Translated and edited by Sterling A. Stoudemire; Chapel Hill, University of North Carolina Press, 1959)

This ability to plan the "whole thing from the beginning" was to be characteristic of all the new cities in America, in contrast with most of their European counterparts, but in general, the preceding description of Santo Domingo is much more positive than most of the early descriptions of American cities. All of these places were colonial outposts far from the centers of empire, and as such they were, at first, rather primitive places.

Spain was the first nation to establish urban settlements on the North American continent. For the next half century, Spain was effectively unchallenged in the Western Hemisphere.

According to the American urban historian John Reps, "Town life became the basis of colonial development for two reasons: it afforded the best protection against possible hostile attacks, and it represented a continuation of the established system of living with which most colonists were familiar . . . Physical environment, isolation and inadequate resources all acted in different ways to prevent wholesale transplanting of the newer techniques of city design which had evolved in Europe" (*Town Planning in Frontier America*; Columbia and London: University of Missouri Press, 1980).

1519–21: Spain conquers Mexico and places the major emphasis on plundering the wealth of the southern continent because of the disappointing findings of reconnaissance parties in North America in search of gold and the mythical passage to India.

1534–42: Extensive activity of explorer Jacques Cartier fails to lead to permanent settlements by the French in the New World.

1565: *St. Augustine* in Florida is established as a Spanish base of operations against the French in Fort Caroline, which had been set up the previous year. The French are beaten, and in order to secure their victory, Spain populates the coastline as far north as the Carolinas with forts and missions.

(Spanish settlements take three forms: presidios, pueblos, and missions, although often in practice the three functions—military, commercial, and religious—blend with one another. Spanish influence in the east is usurped by the New England colonies from the early seventeenth century onward, but Spain remains the dominant European power in the south and west until well into the nineteenth century.)

1573: Philip II, king of Spain, issues the Law of the Indies (Move #7), which is the first planning code in the New World.

1584: Sir Walter Raleigh is commissioned to find a suitable site for an English colony, and a small fort is established on Roanoke Island in North Carolina, but its commander, Ralph Lane, provokes the Indians, and Sir Francis Drake rescues the settlers from imminent catastrophe. Little is known about the colony after that, but the first English colonial effort in the New World ends in total failure and the mysterious disappearance of the tiny colony.

1604: French settlements are established along the northeast coastline and up the Saint Lawrence, beginning with Sainte Croix on the island of Douchet in what is now Maine.

1607: In May the Virginia Company founds an English colony at *Jamestown, Virginia*. This is England's toehold on the continent, and the start of 170 years of colonial occupation and town building. The early history of Jamestown and other settlements in Virginia is one of repeated misfortune. By the start of fall, almost half of the original settlers are dead. In the winter of 1609–10, the population, which had increased to 500, shrinks to 60 because of disease, Indian attacks, and starvation. In May of 1610, Sir Thomas Gates arrives with supplies but, seeing the sad state of the town, decides to take the survivors and abandon the site. At the last minute, Lord Delaware arrives with 150 new colonists, and Gates returns to Jamestown for a new attempt. From that moment on, the survival of the colony is assured. By 1619, the tobacco plantations of the Jamestown colony extend some twenty miles along the James River, and the colony has a population of about 1,000 people.

1609: *Sante Fe, New Mexico*, is established by Don Pedro de Peralta as the most northerly of the provinces of New Spain.

1620: Pilgrims arrive on the *Mayflower* and establish the *Plymouth* Colony. They survive that first fierce winter, and turkey becomes central to the tradition of national Thanksgiving.

1626: *New Amsterdam* is established by the Dutch as a small, fortified village at the extreme southern end of Manhattan Island. When the British capture the city in 1664, renaming it *New York*, the population is about 1,500. Present-day Wall Street, the line of a 1633 defensive system, is its northern border. By 1775, the population is 23,000, and Chambers Street has been reached in the population's march north up the island. The British occupation during the Revolutionary War and two disastrous fires reduce the population to about 5,000. In 1789, the city is the temporary capital of the new nation. Trade once more flourishes, and by the beginning of the nineteenth century, the city has become the economic capital of the country. By 1820, more than 150,000 people live here, and this figure doubles by 1840 under the stimulation of economic growth aided by the construction of the Erie Canal. By 1850, the population is 515,000, and present-day 42nd Street is the northern limit. In 1858, Olmsted and Vaux win the competition to design Central Park (Move #8), and by 1870, population figures have reached 942,000. In 1883, the Brooklyn Bridge is completed. By 1890, the entire island of Manhattan is populated, and in 1898, the boroughs of Brooklyn, the Bronx, Queens, and Staten Island are added to the city. In contrast to many other American cities, New York started originally without a plan, and it was only after a period of almost 150 years of organic growth that the first continuous grids were laid out (Move #7).

1629: Charlestown is chosen as the future capital for the Massachusetts Bay Company. In 1630, after an outbreak of fever, the capital is moved across the river with the founding of *Boston*. The new site has a much greater availability of water, and according to John Reps in *Town Planning in Frontier America* (Columbia and London: University of Missouri Press, 1980), "men not cows, as legend would have it, created the Boston street system, and by the standards of the 17th. century, it was reasonably well suited to the community. The exact location of the rocky banks, the marshes, the low and muddy sinks of the virgin site were never recorded. The odds are, however, that these minor topographic variations shaped the early street pattern that has so persistently remained to plague the modern driver." By 1772, the population has reached 12,000, and by 1776, it has grown to 16,000. In 1786, the first toll bridge is completed across the Charles River, and this stimulates development on both sides of the river. The State House of Charles Bulfinch appears north of the Common on the slope of Beacon Hill in 1798, and this leads to the residential development of the Beacon Hill slopes to the west. Louisburg Square on Beacon Hill is completed in 1840. Soon after 1850, the Back Bay is filled, and streets are laid out to provide more land for the rapidly growing city.

1666: *Newark* is established as the last Puritan settlement in North America by a band of Connecticut families headed by Robert Treat. Broad Street is the most spacious street in America when laid out in 1667. While first a theocracy, the town soon feels the liberalizing influence of Dutch, Irish, Scottish, and German immigrants. Town is chartered in 1696, and by the time of the American Revolution, the boundaries extend as far west as the farms of Livingston and as far north as Clifton. In the area that makes up the present city there are approximately 1,000 people and 100 structures. In 1796, a bridge is opened up across the Passaic River. By the beginning of the nineteenth century, Newark is a manufacturing center with machines, coaches, and leather goods among its more notable products. With the coming of the railroads and shipping canals in 1830, the city increases its industrial base and is incorporated as a city in 1836. By the time of the Civil War, local products include clothing, jewelry, paint, varnish, beer, precious metal refining, and chemicals. The population jumps from 17,290 in 1840 to 105,000 in 1870, and masses of additional immigrants lead to the building of housing amidst the heavy industry of Down Neck.

1670: *Charlestown* is founded as the capital of the Carolina Territory which Charles II had granted to eight court favorites in 1663. Writing in 1680 ("A Contemporary View of Carolina in 1680," *South Carolina Historical Magazine*, Vol. 55, 1954, pp. 153–54), Maurice Mathews provides the following description:

> The town is run into four large streets. The Court house which we are now building is to be erected in the middle of it, in a Square of two ackers of land upon which the four great streets of 60 feet wide doe center, and to the water side there is laid out 60 foot for a publicke wharf as also for other conveniences as a Churchyard, Artillary ground, etc. and without there is care taken that the front lines be preserved whereby wee shall avoid the indecent and commodious irregularities which other Inglish Colonies are fallen into for want of arre early care in laying out the Townes.

1681: King Charles II of England makes William Penn governor and proprietor of Pennsylvania in return for being freed from a sizable debt to the estate of Penn's father. Penn dispatches a group of settlers and directs them in his instructions to the commissioners:

> let the rivers and creeks be sounded on my side of the Delaware River, . . . and be sure to make your choice where it is most navigable, high, dry and healthy, that is where most ships may best ride, of deepest draught of water, is possible to load or unload at the bank or key side, without boating or lightering of it. . . . Such a place being found out, for navigation, healthy situation and good soil for provision, lay out ten thousand acres contiguous to it in the best manner you can, as the bounds and extent of the liberties of the said town. (S. Hazard, *Annals of Pennsylvania*; Philadelphia, 1850)

In 1683, the basic plan of *Philadelphia* is drawn up by Captain Thomas Holme, surveyor general of Pennsylvania, lots are surveyed, and the first buildings are erected. The city is located on the neck of the peninsula between the Delaware and Schuylkill rivers. Although Holme's original plan only extends about halfway across to the Schuylkill, Penn extends the city over the peninsula to give it frontage on both rivers. Philadelphia is much larger than earlier colonial towns, its dimensions approximately one mile by two miles, and Holme and Penn create America's first designated public parks. By 1775, the population reaches 20,000, and at the outbreak of the war, Philadelphia is the largest American city and in England is surpassed only by London. Philadelphia is the capital of the country until 1800 (except for a short period of time when New York plays this role), and its plan of grids and public squares affect the subsequent course of town design throughout the United States. Raleigh, North Carolina, and Tallahassee, Florida, are two other cities based on the Philadelphia plan.

1701: *Detroit* is founded by the Frenchman Antoine de la Mothe Cadillac to control the key Detroit River link between Lake Erie and St. Clair Lake. The original plan of the town is much like that of the *bastide* towns of southern France in Cadillac's native Gascony. These were planned new towns of thirteenth-century France generally built by Edward I. Several were also built in England and Wales. The fortifications enclosed a space 600 feet wide by 400 feet, and the widest street, Rue Sainte Anne, is less than thirty feet wide. In 1805, Detroit is designated capital of the Michigan Territory, and then a fire destroys the fort and about 300 dwellings in the nearby town. Arriving in town three weeks after the fire, Augustus Woodward, one of the three judges appointed to administer the territory, lays out the new town with a combination of rectilinear and diagonal streets and a variety of open spaces, in a design strongly influenced by Woodward's native Washington.

1706: *Albuquerque, New Mexico,* is established by Don Francisco Cuervo y Valdez, who names the settlement after the viceroy of New Spain. In 1846, the area that is now New Mexico is occupied by U.S. troops, and in 1848, it becomes a U.S. territory. The town is held briefly by Confederate troops during the Civil War and is incorporated as a city in 1891.

1722: *New Orleans* is founded by the Frenchman Bienville, whose interest is spurred by John Law and the Western Company, which received a charter from the French government. The engineer Adrien de Pauger lays out the city with the focal point being the place d'armes, modern-day Jackson Square. Development is slow, and even by 1797 not all the city land has been built on. The city is under Spanish control from 1763 to 1801, returns briefly to French control, and in 1803 becomes part of the United States with the Louisiana Purchase. From this time on, the city begins to prosper and expand, up and down the Mississippi River, with extensive use of the urban square as a major urban element.

1729: *Baltimore* is founded as a trading center for the tobacco farmers of southern Maryland and named after Charles Calvert, fifth Lord Baltimore, governor of the colony of Maryland and a descendant of those who originally started the colony as a haven for English Catholics. In the eighteenth century it becomes a flourishing port and in 1799 is incorporated as a city with a population of some 20,000. During the American Revolution, the Continental Congress temporarily flees from Philadelphia for a period of two months and establishes the city as the capital of the United States. Shipbuilding booms when Congress authorizes the privateering of British vessels, and it is here during the war of 1812 that Francis Scott Key writes the "Star Spangled Banner" while viewing the British attack on Fort McHenry from a ship in the harbor. During the Civil War the city, pro-south in sentiment, is occupied by Federal troops and suffers along with the devastated South during the reconstruction. All of downtown is destroyed during a disastrous fire that breaks out on February 7, 1904.

1733: James Edward Oglethorpe founds *Savannah, Georgia,* as an experiment in prison reform where those confined in English jails by their creditors can start new lives. In 1745, the town has nearly 350 private houses in addition to a number of public buildings. By the time of the American Revolution, the city ranks as twentieth in size in the American colonies, with a population that exceeded 3,000. Oglethorpe's plan for Savannah is somewhat unusual in its extensive use of open space in the center of each gridiron ward and the 125 years of controlled and planned urban growth. This allows Savannah to avoid developing the greatest number of building lots on a particular tract of land, a pattern that characterizes most nineteenth-century urban development in America.

1754: Fort Duquesne is established by the French, later to be called *Pittsburgh* after its capture by the British in 1758. In 1784, John Penn expands the settlement, and the city becomes prominent as a point of departure for settlers going downriver on the Monongahela and Allegheny rivers to settle the Ohio Valley.

1764: The founding of *St. Louis* marks the end of French urban settlement in the United States. The original plan of the town resembles that of Montreal with a rectangular street system and a *place d'armes* opening on to the river. After languishing under the Spanish during their control of the Louisiana Territory, the city grows rapidly with the opening of American exploration and settlement west of the Mississippi.

1769: Father Junipero Serra, a Spanish Franciscan, establishes a mission to the Indians and a presidio near what is now known as *San Diego* Bay. Conflicts between the soldiers and the Indians cause the mission to be moved to its present site in 1774. After the establishment of Mexican rule in 1822, there's a heavy trade of cattle hides between local ranchers and American shippers. In 1834 a Mexican pueblo is built outside the walls of the presidio, and in 1846, the American warship *Cyane* enters the bay, and troops under John C. Fremont claim the outpost. Old Town, as the settlement is called, receives its first U.S. charter in 1850. A San Francisco businessman, Alonzo E. Horton, founds modern San Diego in 1867 when he purchases a thousand acres of brushland in the present downtown area and builds a wharf, lays out streets, gives land to churches, and opens a hotel opposite the new town plaza in 1870. A nearby gold strike during the same year and the arrival of the Santa Fe Railway in 1885 prompt a rapid population increase from 5,000 to 17,000 by 1887.

1776: *San Francisco* is founded by the Spaniards as a presidio, or military base. In 1839, the village of Yerba Buena, some two miles from the San Francisco presidio, is planned as a community of about a dozen houses. In 1846, the Americans take possession of the city, and when gold is discovered in January 1848, the population doesn't exceed 1,000. By 1849, there are more than 5,000 people, and soon afterwards Yerba Buena is encompassed by the growing city. By 1850, the population is around 35,000, and new gridiron districts are platted in 1856.

1778: *Louisville, Kentucky,* is settled by George Rogers Clarke as a military base from which the British and Indians are driven from the Midwest.

1781: *Los Angeles* is established by the Spaniards as the last surviving civil settlement, or pueblo, in the United States. Philippe de Neve, governor of Upper California, was responsible for the original plan, and by 1850, the population numbered 15,000 as the center of a rich agricultural district. Inexpensive fares on the Southern Pacific and Sante Fe railroads, often as low as one dollar, stimulate further growth.

1791: Under congressional mandate, President George Washington picks the site of the first capital near Georgetown. Congress had stated that the president was to select a site somewhere within an eighty-mile distance from the mouth of the Anacostia River, the "east branch" of the Potomac River and three commissioners be appointed to "provide suitable buildings for the accommodation of Congress and the President and for the public offices of the United States" by the first Monday in December 1800. Until that time, the capital was to remain in Philadelphia. Major Pierre Charles L'Enfant begins surveying and design of *Washington, D.C.*

1805: Zebulon Pike gets land from the Sioux Indians for the establishment of a military post for the U.S. Government near the Falls of St. Anthony on the Mississippi River. The area had first been explored in 1680 by a French Franciscan, Father Louis Hennepin, who was the first white man to see the falls. In 1820, Fort St. Anthony is established, and in 1823, a flour mill is built to supply the fort. The fort is renamed in 1825 after Colonel Josiah Snelling, the man who built it, and St. Anthony, a town on the east bank of the Mississippi, is incorporated in 1855.

Minneapolis, whose name is derived from the Sioux word for water, *minne*, and the Greek word for city, *polis*, is incorporated on the west bank in 1867. They join in 1872. The city becomes a center of flour milling and lumber, with logs floated downriver from the northern forests. The late nineteenth century sees a great influx of Swedish immigration accompanied by many of Canadian, German, and Norwegian background. Railroads and meat packing also thrive in the city.

1830: *Chicago* is laid out by James Thompson in section 9, township 39, range 14 of the National Survey, which imposed a grid on the expanding country (Move #6), to help finance a canal between the Great Lakes and the Mississippi River. While the canal does not open until 1848, the promise of trade stimulated growth and extensive real estate speculation. Harriet Martineau, who visits the city in 1836, paints a vivid picture (as quoted in Homer Hoyt, *One Hundred Years of Land Values in Chicago;* Chicago: University of Chicago Press, 1933):

> The streets were crowded with land speculators, hurrying from one side to another. A negro dressed up in scarlet bearing a scarlet flag and riding a white horse with housings of scarlet announced the time of sale. At every street corner where he stopped the crowd gathered around him; and it seemed as if some prevelant mania infected the whole people. As the gentlemen of our party walked the streets, storekeepers hailed them from their doors with offers of farms and all manners of land lots, advising them to speculate before the price of land went higher.

In 1836, there are about 4,000 persons living in the city, and by 1848, the number climbs to 20,000. By the time of the Civil War the canal is obsolete, but the city, a focal point of ten rail lines, has a population close to 100,000. During the next ten years, the city has the most rapid increase in population of any large American city. In 1865, the population is 180,000, which doubles by 1872, in spite of Mrs. O'Leary's cow and the fire of 1871, and quadruples by 1885. The grid seems relentless in its march across the landscape, only to be relieved by the later development of the suburbs (Move #9).

1836: Even before the first streets exist, founders J. K. and A. C. Allen, brothers from New York, begin advertising the new town of *Houston* nationwide as the garden spot of Texas.

1836: Fort Dallas is built near the mouth of the *Miami* River during the Seminole wars. Earlier maps of the area show an Indian village at the site of what is presently Bayfront Park in downtown Miami. In 1844 in Apalachicola, Florida, Dr. John Gorrie invents air conditioning, which is later to figure prominently in the development of many southern cities in the United States and around the world. The city is founded in 1870, and in 1896, Henry Flagler extends the East Coast Railroad to Miami under the urging of pioneer settler Julia Tuttle. Tuttle had first visited her father in the area in 1875 and returned from Cleveland to live there permanently in 1891, upon the death of her husband. At a meeting of 343 people in 1896, the city is incorporated. The name is probably derived from an Indian word, *mayami*, meaning "big water." At the time of its incorporation, there are only two dwellings and one storehouse within the present corporate limits. Shortly afterwards, Henry Flagler begins the construction of the Royal Palm Hotel, prompting the development of the area as a resort and vacation area. In 1909, work is begun on cutting a channel from Miami to Lake Okeechobee and on to the west coast of Florida, providing an inland waterway and draining much swamp. By 1910, the population is 5,471, and this increases to 29,571 by 1920. Much development occurs during the great land boom of the early twenties, which collapses in 1926 as the result of a hurricane and a financial panic. After World War II a great increase in hotel construction further consolidates the area as a tourist and vacation center. A large influx of Cubans in the 1960s and in 1980 add even further impetus for the development of the city as a major link, or gate (Move #2), between the United States and Latin America.

1841: *Dallas* is founded by Tennessee lawyer John Neely Bryan, who builds a cabin at the junction of the three forks of the La Santissimma Trinidad River and sets about advertising the city by word of mouth and circulars. By 1850, 430 people have joined him.

1849: *Fort Worth* founded as a frontier army post by Major Ripley Arnold to provide protection from the Indians. After the Civil War, this is a key stop on the Chisholm Trail.

1851: Five pioneering families from Illinois settle on the south end of Elliot Bay and call their community New York. Within a month, lumber is being shipped to San Francisco where the Gold Rush has stimulated a building boom. In March 1853, most of the settlers move to the east side of Elliott Bay, the present site of the city's business section, because the original location made it difficult to load lumber. The settlement is named for Chief *Seattle* of the friendly Duwamish and Suquamish tribes, and in May a plan of the town is recorded with the territorial government. Henry Yessler establishes the first sawmill, and soon stores, saloons and dance halls spring up along the "skid road" (later corrupted to "skid row" in American urban usage). The settlement is attacked by Indians in 1856, and incorporation of the city comes in 1869. The population numbers 1,107 in 1870. A fire on June 6, 1889, started in a glue pot in a print shop, destroys most of the city's business district. The Great Northern Railway establishes a terminal in 1893, and the Japanese begin using the city as a port of entry in 1896. The discovery of gold in the Klondike the same year also helps to stimulate growth until the city is the largest in the Pacific Northwest.

1858: *Denver* is established by a group of prospectors, led by William Green Russell, looking for gold near the place where Cherry Creek joins the Platte River. Gold isn't located, but the two townships of Auraria and Denver City are founded and join together in 1860 as Denver. The new city serves as a supply point during the Gold Rush, and with the arrival of the railroad, the population grows to 5,000 in 1870, 46,000 in 1880, and more than 100,000 by 1890.

1893: In an essay titled "The Significance of the Frontier in American History," the historian Frederick Jackson Turner writes: "And now, four centuries from the discovery of America, at the end of a hundred years of life under the constitution, the frontier has gone."

While later scholars have questioned many of Turner's conclusions, the end of the nineteenth century in America did herald many significant changes that would have an impact on the establishment of cities in the United States.

ADDITIONAL READING

Glaab, Charles, and Andrew Brown. *A History of Urban America.* New York: Macmillan, 1967.

Reps, John. *Town Planning in Frontier America.* Columbia: University of Missouri Press, 1980. This is a shorter version of the definitive work by the same author, *The Making of Urban America: A History of City Planning in the U.S.* (Princeton: Princeton University Press, 1967).

Tunnard, Christopher, and Henry Hope Reed. *American Skyline: The Growth and Forms of Our Cities and Towns.* Boston: Houghton Mifflin, 1955.

MOVE #6

The Ubiquitous Grid

GRID PATTERNS ARE EVERYWHERE IN THE MODERN WORLD, AND nowhere is this more apparent than in the street layouts of American cities. This Move is unavoidable in urban America. To travel through the American city is to encounter the grid, and this has been true from the beginnings of European settlement (Move #5), but it may make sense to make the Move again in a more self-conscious fashion. In most of our dealings with the grid, we treat it as a "path," or simply a device to get from point A to point B. Little attention is paid to the grid itself and to the relationship it has with the buildings, plazas, and other urban elements around it.

In its capacity as a path, the grid offers a full range of emotional experience. A pleasing trip through light or moderate traffic, whether on foot or in an automobile, where you don't lose your way and all the straights and turns are negotiated successfully, can be a delightful encounter with everything that's orderly and rational in modern city life. And then there are the horrors of those other journeys—stuck in a traffic "jam" (what a wonderfully evocative word for the stickiness of the situation) and late for an occasion where it's absolutely imperative that you be on time (Move #2), perhaps important family or business matters hang in the balance. Wednesday is, after all, Prince Spaghetti day, and on the west coast Tuesday is Red's Tamales day. Everyone is waiting. To be in this situation is to have feelings opposite those of Theseus when he was being chased by the Minotaur in the ancient Labyrinth of Knossos on Crete. He probably would have welcomed a little less movement.

Central to this move is some reflection on the consequences of using the grid as a way of organizing cities compared with using other methods. Experience with the grid suggests a number of questions. Where did the form originate, and under what circumstances has it been used? What are its advantages and disadvantages? How regular is the rhythm of movement in the two situations? And compare the issue of navigation and getting lost in areas with and without grids (Move #17).

And then there are questions about the relationship of the grid to the other urban elements around it. Does the pattern of the streets have anything to do with where the buildings are located? The shape and size of parks?

A final set of questions arises about the motivations of the people responsible for adopting this pattern of streets. Just what did they have in mind when they set things up this way? What kinds of experiences were they trying to provide, and what kinds of messages were they trying to send about the city?

It might help to keep in mind a point that the art critic Rosalind Krauss made when she was investigating the popularity of the grid in modern painting, where it can be seen in the work of painters as diverse as Malevich, Mondrian, Ad Reinhardt, and Jasper Johns. She suggests that the grid evokes both the world of material concerns, the grid of the accountant's ledger, and a higher world evoked by the transcendent qualities of absolute orderliness and symmetry.

NOTES

Contrary to popular belief, the grid pattern as a way of organizing cities goes back in history at least as far as Mohenjo Daro, one of the ancient cities of the Indus Valley. In tracing the history of the grid through its Indian, Greek, Roman, and European phases, the geographer Dan Stanislawski pointed out some important factors to keep in mind when reflecting on the grid.

According to Stanislawski ("The Origin and Spread of Grid Pattern Towns," *Geographical Review*, January 1946), the grid "is possible only in either a totally new urban unit or a newly added subdivision. This pattern is not conceivable except as an organic whole. If the planner thinks in terms of single buildings, separate functions, or casual growth, the grid will not come into being; for with each structure considered separately, the advantage lies with irregularity."

This was certainly the case with all the new cities laid out in the New World. Almost from the beginning, they were planned as comparatively large settlements, given the number of residents actually there at the time. The picture of Savannah, Georgia, in 1734 seems as notable for what isn't present, as for what is (see Figure 4). This empty feeling is typical of many early grids and is a direct physical expression of the tremendous amounts of wilderness that surrounded these new settlements. Whether public relations or utopian vision, one thing the grid expresses is hope.

For Stanislawski there was also some form of centralized control, whether political, religious, or military, and this often indicated colonial status. There was also "a desire for measured apportionment of land." These last three conditions invariably existed when American cities were first established. Although the grid is one of the oldest ways of laying out cities, there's little

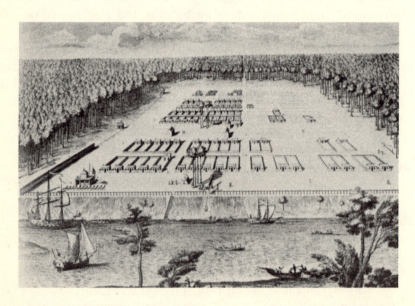

FIGURE 4: A view of Savannah, Georgia, as it stood the 29th of March 1734, by Peter Gordon of London.

evidence that it existed in the New World before it was brought over by Europeans.

The first American city planning code, the Law of the Indies, was issued in 1573 by Philip II of Spain as the basis for city planning in the New World. Many cities, including St. Augustine, Florida; San Antonio, Texas; Santa Fe, New Mexico; and San Diego, San Francisco, San Jose, and Los Angeles, California, were planned around the ideas of this document. Although most of the Spanish influence in American city planning is now gone, one urban feature that this law did emphasize, the grid, is still very much alive. A good deal of time is spent negotiating its long straight streets and avenues with their repetitious patterns of symmetrical intersections. What have architects, planners, and other observers of the American city to say about this way of laying out streets?

Commenting on these early Spanish grids, and on grids in general, in *Building the Unfinished* (Beverly Hills and London: Sage, 1976), the architect Lars Lerup wrote:

> The grid itself is fascinating. Its beginning is no different from its end. It is open-ended, it suggests endlessness. It is laid out with the simple device of ruler and cord. With its strict geometry, it is peculiarly artificial. The grid is undiscriminating in its equidistant pursuit of a landscape; it is unbending, and its required rigor causes it to be unresponsive to its setting and context. Paradoxically though, the grid depends on its context for direction and in fact, only the power of the context can make it stop. Employers of the grid look ahead—they plan. It is with a future orientation that they, with a cord and ruler, lay out the first chalklines of the future town.

Again, there is the picture of the urbanite as one who thinks about the future (Move #2), but here the future is the colonial dream of a European monarch out to overwhelm the local population of Indians. The Spanish ritual of town founding in the Americas began with the planting of a pike, the utterance of a challenge, and the cutting of weeds as acts of possession. For Philip II, the imposition of the grid on the natural landscape that preceded it was another act of possession.

In writing about early city planning in America (*Town Planning in Frontier America*; Columbia: University of Missouri Press, 1980), the historian John Reps pointed out a more positive quality of the grid:

In particular, the Philadelphia city plan materially affected the subsequent course of town design in America. As the first large city to be laid out on the gridiron pattern, Philadelphia has always been identified, usually unkindly, as the inspiration for the great era of town planning during the preceding century. This influence is undeniable, but it was not always unfortunate. Even where the results proved unhappy, part of the blame must be assessed against those who disregarded the good features of the gridiron or who extended an original settlement with mechanical regularity in disregard of topography. . . . If Philadelphia must share the blame for the ubiquitous gridiron, it should also be credited as the source of an occasional square occupied by public buildings or used for park purposes.

The Land Ordinance Acts of 1785 and 1802 laid out the entire westward expansion of the United States in terms of the grid. These were the products of Thomas Jefferson's National Survey and embodied his belief that Americans could best pursue life, liberty, and happiness on family farms rather than the villages organized around a common that were favored in New England. The acts specified that the land starting immediately west of the Ohio River was to be laid out in six-mile rectangular townships, and each township was to be divided into thirty-six square sections of one square mile or 640 acres. Half the land was to be sold by townships and the other half by sections.

The report of the commissioners who laid out New York City above Washington Square in 1811 also cited a number of positive qualities of the grid, pointing out that they "could not but bear in mind that a city is to be composed principally of the habitations of men, and that the straight sided and right-angled houses are the most cheap to build, and most convenient to live in." ("Commissioners' Remarks," William Bridges, *Map of the City of New York and Island of Manhattan*, New York: 1811).

Lewis Mumford wasn't as sympathetic with this way of patterning streets. In *The City in History* (New York: Harcourt Brace Jovanovich, 1961), discussing European city planning from the seventeenth century onward, in places like Stuttgart, Berlin, and London, he viewed the wide usage of the gridiron as having "answered as no other plan did, the shifting values, the accelerated expansion, the multiplying population, required by the capitalist regime."

For Mumford, San Francisco lost a great opportunity when it decided to use this method to lay out streets:

> In paying no attention to topography, the gridiron planner opened the day for fat pieces of honest municipal jobbery, in grading and filling and paving streets. On steep, hilly sites, like that of San Francisco, the rectangular plan, by failing to respect the contours, placed a constant tax upon the time and energy of the inhabitants and inflicted on them daily economic losses, measurable in tons of coal and gallons of gasoline wasted, to say nothing of undoing major aesthetic possibilities of a hillside which is intelligently platted.

A comment from the geographer J. B. Jackson in *American Space* (New York: Norton, 1972) focused on a major quality of the grid which may well help to account for some of its American popularity. With its regular edges and corners, every unit of the grid is the equal of every other unit:

> The grid system of land subdivision is unpopular with many contemporary Americans, chiefly for aesthetic reasons; yet it possessed and still possesses important virtues, political as well as economic, and in the early years of Western (and Midwestern) settlement it served the nation well; it expressed very clearly the general belief in equality of opportunity and in possession of the land as one of the bases of citizenship.

August Heckscher in *Open Spaces: The Life of American Cities* (co-written by Phyllis Robinson; New York: Harper & Row, 1977) also talked about what he perceived as a uniquely American quality:

> Streets laid out on a square grid were adopted almost universally in the East, and in the nineteenth century towns beyond the Alleghenies this pattern was imitated. This was in part because the grid seemed the very image of urbanity (curved roads belonged to the country) and in part because it offered so convenient a means for real estate speculation. But the grid was adopted also because it conformed to the American's preference for spatial openness. A man standing at almost any point within the town could look outward to fields and woods.

ADDITIONAL READING

Jackson. J. B. *American Space.* New York: Norton, 1972. This fascinating book focuses on the transformations of both the environment and the perception of that environment that occurred in the United States during the decade just after the Civil War. The author deals with not only the grid, but also the beginnings of scientific forestry, village improvement societies, bonanza farming, and the landscape movement that was to later produce such city parks as Central Park in New York (Move #8). The author is quite successful in conveying the attitude toward space that has made the grid so popular in the United States.

Stanislawski, Dan. "The Origin and Spread of Grid Pattern Towns," in *Geographical Review,* January 1946.

MOVE #7

Zoning

What It Is and
Where It Comes From

Two quotes reveal something of the complex nature of zoning:

It's a bobtailed term for a long tailed power to control the height, volume and use of buildings, the use of land, and the density or number of people who may occupy land and buildings. (Seymour Toll, *Zoned American*; New York: Grossman Publishers, 1969)

Zoning laws have been for real estate what the Marquis of Queensbury rules were to boxing. (Jonathan Barnett, *An Introduction to Urban Design*; New York: Harper & Row, 1982)

SOME BACKGROUND
INFORMATION

Ever since New York City enacted the first comprehensive zoning legislation in the United States in 1916, American cities have used these kinds of laws to help determine what the overall makeup of the city would be. Although there had been legislation as early as 1656 in New Amsterdam—removing all haystacks, hen houses, and hog pens in an effort to clean up the streets—and the first height control legislation in the United States was passed by San

Diego in 1912, the New York plan was the first comprehensive scheme.

Once the Supreme Court upheld the zoning laws of Euclid, Ohio, in 1926 and gave cities the legal right to exclude certain uses from residential areas, even though they wouldn't ordinarily have been considered nuisances, there was an incredible rush for other cities to adopt similar restrictions. By 1929, 60 percent of the urban population of the United States was living in places that had zoning ordinances.

Zoning is a central component of urban planning that was increasingly endorsed at the end of the nineteenth century as an answer to America's many urban problems. This was a period when many American cities reeled under the difficulties caused by rapid expansion spurred on by intense industrialization and immigration (Move #25). Municipal government was often viewed in highly unfavorable terms. James Bryce, in *The American Commonwealth* (New York: Macmillan, 1919), called them "the one conspicuous failure of the United States." A multitude of new horrors seemed to be captured daily by the words of writers such as Lincoln Steffens, who published *The Shame of Cities* (Garden City, NY: Doubleday, 1904), and the brilliant photographs of Jacob Riis, Lewis Hines, Edward Steichen, and others.

WORLD'S COLUMBIAN EXPOSITION

The World's Columbian Exposition of 1893, popularly known as the Chicago World's Fair, was organized by Daniel "make no small plans" Burnham, the designer of New York's Flatiron Building (Move #12) and one of the most highly regarded architects of his day. (He had been responsible for plans for Manila, Cleveland, Chicago, and San Francisco.) So many major figures in architecture and design participated that the sculptor Augustus Saint-Gaudens called it the greatest assembly of artists since the fifteenth century. While many of the specific details of the City Beautiful Movement were later rejected—Louis Sullivan lamented the stress on classical style and called it "the virus of a culture, snobbish and alien to the land"—the general idea that planning could help solve urban problems *did* receive wide support.

The gleaming white plaster, the grand boulevards, and artfully composed buildings set amidst lagoons of water, which came to be known as the "White City," strongly influenced Daniel Burnham, Charles F. McKim, Augustus Saint-Gaudens, and Frederick Law Olmsted Jr. in their report of the Commission on the Improvement of the Park System for Washington, D.C., in 1902. Many of their recommendations for the Mall and the area around the Lincoln Memorial show the impact of the White City ideas that were first articulated on a large scale at the Chicago World's Fair. Civic centers throughout the country—from Springfield, Massachusetts, to Duluth, Iowa, to Berkeley, California—also reveal this influence.

PLANNING, SOCIAL DARWINISM, AND THE "NEW" IMMIGRANT

The First National Conference on City Planning met in Washington in 1909. Many of those attending, including its organizers, Benjamin Marsh and Frederic Howe (the latter the author of *The City: The Hope for Democracy*; New York: Scribner's, 1909), were extremely impressed by the history of zoning in Germany. There it had long been used as a central component of planning and as a mechanism for shaping urban form and preventing "race deterioration," something like Social Darwinism in reverse.

If, as Charles Darwin and his followers suggested, environment played an important role in evolution, then it could be argued that its intelligent manipulation could insure that evolution would bring improvement of the species—or at least prevent further deterioration of the sort that medical examinations of enlistees for the Boer War revealed when it was found that very few physically fit men were coming from English cities. Some years earlier, in the 1840s, the life expectancy was thirty-six in London and twenty-six in Liverpool and Manchester, whereas in England and Wales as a whole, it was forty-one. According to the historian Oscar Handlin, in *The American People in the Twentieth Century* (Cambridge: Harvard University Press, 1963), facts like these led to the belief that measures such as slum clearance and the provision of free land in the West would bring about a whole host of improvements. These would supposedly include a reduction of crime, the growth of democracy, and the curtailing of the rampant corruption that muckrakers such as Upton Sinclair, Frank Norris, and Lincoln Steffens were continuously uncovering. In a series of articles written during 1902 and 1903, Steffens wrote of St. Louis, "bribery prices for all sorts of grants"; Pittsburgh, "politically it is hell with the lid on"; Philadelphia, "corrupt and contented"; and Memphis, "the government of the city asked criminals to rob the people."

The New York City zoning ordinances of 1916 were concerned with access of sunlight to streets, and in order to achieve this end, "setbacks" on skyscrapers were created. This was one of the major determinants of the early form of these buildings. The access of light and air to building interiors was also a concern. The streets of lower Manhattan had become increasingly dark and canyonlike as downtown buildings grew taller and taller (Move #12).

A strong desire to keep the expanding loft factories of the garment district away from the fashionable shops and homes along Fifth Avenue existed as well. According to the earlier-quoted zoning authority Seymour Toll, "The immigrant is in the fiber of zoning."

In San Francisco in the 1880s, a series of legal encounters came to be known as the "laundry cases." In these cases, the local laws controlling the location of Chinese laundries were enforced as part of a virulent anti-Oriental movement, although the city claimed that it was really concerned with fire safety. In two cases decided in 1885, *Soon Hing* v. *Crowley* and *Barbier* v. *Connolly*, the U.S. Supreme Court upheld the local city ordinances regulating the locations of the shops and severely restricting night work.

The immigrant was also a significant factor in prompting the New York legislation. Describing the situation along Fifth Avenue in New York, which the first zoning legislation was designed to protect, Toll wrote in *Zoned American*:

Immigrants working in the needle trades took to the sidewalks during their lunch hour, mixing there with the carriage trade . . . the things which were the essences of the garment industry— the strange tongues, the outlandish appearance and the very smell of its immigrant laborers, its relentless drive to follow the retail drive wherever it went . . . violated the ambience in which luxury retailing thrives. It demands insulation from gross forms of work and workers, the symbols of wealth and good living and sidewalks inviting the stroll, the pause, the purchase.

Zoning legislation worked as a gate (Move #2) designed to keep certain people and activities at a distance. The period between 1888 and 1920 was one of extreme anti-foreign, anti-Catholic, and anti-Semitic feeling in the United States. The historian Maldwyn Jones wrote in *American Immigration* (Chicago: University of Chicago Press, 1960):

> As the new immigrants grew more numerous and conspicuous . . . the initial repugnance excited by their appearance and habits gave way to a dread of subversive tendencies. Already alive to the existence of a foreign menace nativists came to see a special danger in an influx of Slavs, Italians, and Jews who were associated in the prevailing ethnic stereotypes with disorder, violent crime and avarice, respectively . . . The notion that the "new" immigrants constituted a collective entity, different from and inferior to the old, arose not from popular antipathies but from the theorizing of a handful of race-conscious New England intellectuals. . . .

Among the intellectuals cited by Jones were Richard Mayo-Smith, who questioned the economic value of immigration, and Francis A. Walker, president of the Massachusetts Institute of Technology and director of the U.S. Bureau of the Census, who attributed the declining birth rate of the native population to immigrant competition.

Early in 1894, many of these admittedly racist efforts resulted in the formation of the Immigration Restriction League. About 1906, certain Boston intellectuals began to use genetics as a scientific basis for their claim that immigration restriction was absolutely necessary to preserve the American national character (Move #25). They were most assuredly not sold on the idea of "hybrid vigor." Zoning, it was believed, could be used to help this improvement by keeping the "close stranger" at a distance (Move #2).

And of course, as is inevitably the case in a consumer society, many of these beliefs and values were expressed in terms of protecting real estate investments. In the proceedings of the Sixth

National Conference on City Planning in 1914, one speaker noted, "the tendency of districting is to convert interests in land—which in undistricted cities have proved to be of uncertain and fluctuating value—from speculative to conservative investments. It is like changing a somewhat risky 10% bond or stock into a conservative one. The result is an increase of fully 50% in its value, with no lack of buyers."

In the Marquis of Queensbury rules of real estate, the object is to knock the other person out and win with as much profit as possible while at the same time assuring that things don't get so out of hand (no hitting below the belt or automatic weapons) that people refuse to enter the ring and play the game at all. Zoning can become a central element in urban conflict.

WHAT EXACTLY IS ZONING?

Zoning is the process of dividing a city up into areas, each of which has different legal requirements pertaining to how the land may be used and the kind of structures that can be built upon it. Within each zone, regulations specify the size and shape of the buildings that can be placed on the land and the uses to which those buildings can be put. As you move through the city, a good deal of what you see is the result of zoning.

A quick look at some of the features of the 1916 and 1961 New York City zoning regulations, those of Philadelphia amended on May 15, 1970, and some special zoning legislation passed by San Francisco in August of 1971, should serve to clarify further just what some of the particulars of this type of legislation are.

NEW YORK ZONING
ORDINANCES OF 1916
AND 1961

New York City's 1916 zoning legislation was to some extent a response to such structures as the Equitable Building of 120 Broadway (Move #12), which rose 540 feet straight up from its lot line without any setback at all and had 1.2 million square feet of rentable space. Its huge mass cast shadows for blocks around, and to protect the streets and avenues below from being turned even further into dark, airless canyons, height regulations were established. (Interestingly enough, in a recent zoning battle in New York City some seventy years later, the initial plan for a structure on Columbus Circle was overturned in court in part because it too would cast significant shadows over 40 percent of Central Park.) These limited the height a building could rise in proportion to the width of the street it faced, until it had to "set back." For each foot it set back, it could rise an additional number of feet, depending on the district it was in. The two most common rise to setback ratios in midtown Manhattan were 2½:1 and 3:1. This led to all those "wedding cake" buildings that are so characteristic of parts of midtown Manhattan and a number of other cities of the same time. Another part of this initial legislation allowed a portion of the building, up to 25 percent of the lot area, to rise without setbacks, as long as it was a minimal distance from the street (see Figure 5).

New York zoning was completely revised in 1961 as a reaction to both the style of buildings generated by the 1916 regulations and a somewhat new set of urban conditions. A "sky exposure plane" replaced height districts to govern setbacks, and in order to provide greater amounts of office space, the tower that could penetrate the plane was increased from 25 percent to 40 percent.

The idea of a "floor area ratio," or FAR, was also introduced to govern bulk. This specified the total amount of floor area the building could have in proportion to the lot size. The floor area for the largest buildings was fixed at fifteen times the lot area, or FAR 15. Bonuses of 20 percent were given for including features such as plazas at the base of the building (Move #15), raising FARs to 18. To prevent too many plazas from destroying the dense character of avenues such as Fifth and Madison, bonuses were also offered for interior spaces. These bonuses could bring the FAR up to 21.6 and were examples of what was referred to, in zoning parlance, as "incentive zoning." This allowed additional structure and therefore more salable or rentable space if the owner provided certain amenities for the general public.

FIGURE 5: Two of five drawings of Hugh Ferris's, done in collaboration with Harvey Wiley Corbett, showing skyscraper possibilities under the 1920 zoning laws of New York. (*Courtesy of the Cooper-Hewitt Museum, Smithsonian Institution/Art Resource, New York*)

PHILADELPHIA

Philadelphia's zoning ordinances, which were amended in 1970, also serve to reveal some of the specific characteristics of zoning. They established fifty different zoning district classifications: twenty-eight residential districts, ten commercial districts, eight industrial districts, and four special districts. For each district, the ordinances listed permissable uses and also established regulations on the size and location of structures and surrounding open spaces.

In terms of use, districts ranged from "most restrictive," such as R 1(14-202), which permitted only single-family detached dwellings, to the "least restricted" industrial districts, LR(14-509), where any legal industrial use might be conducted. This included heavy industries that often produce undesirable environmental impacts in terms of smoke, noise, and so forth. The old horrors of the Victorian city that Ebenezer Howard's Garden City proposals were designed to remedy (Move #10) would now be dealt with by zoning.

The Philadelphia ordinances gave maximum building heights for only some of its fifty zoning districts, while other districts were controlled only indirectly through limitations on Gross Floor Area or Floor Area Ratio. The zoning ordinances also included specifications on the maximum and minimum lot size, the maximum percentage of the lot that could be occupied by the structure, and the size of front, rear, and side yards. Taken as a package, these ordinances go a long way in determining what in Philadelphia goes where and the general look of the place.

PUDS, SPECIAL ZONING DISTRICTS, AND SAN FRANCISCO

A number of legal devices have been developed by cities to overcome some of the rigidities of traditional zoning. Planned Unit Development (PUD), or "cluster zoning" as it is sometimes known, can be used in rural or suburban areas that are being intensively developed for the first time. In these cases, the developer submits a master plan for the entire area that is being developed. The plan contains the same overall density but provides for higher density clusters of housing, which then leave significant areas of the tract in their natural state. This type of zoning permits a sensitivity to specific features of the site and allows for departures from the more traditional grid plan (Move #6).

Municipalities have also created "special zoning districts" where additional specific goals have been incorporated into the overall plan. In the first of these in Manhattan, for example, a builder was allowed a 20 percent larger tower if a theater was incorporated into the design of the building. Since the area had been historically associated with the development of theater, and the very name of one of its main thoroughfares, "Broadway," had become synonymous with theater itself in the national vocabulary, this was felt to be a legitimate goal.

Special zoning districts allow the city to exercise more power in deciding the direction development will take. This is often necessary in the United States, where the city itself rarely owns a significant portion of the land being developed. This is in stark contrast to many European cities where zoning first originated, and large portions of the land *were* directly owned by the city. Special zoning districts were found to be effective, and New York instituted a number of others, including Lincoln Square, Fifth Avenue, Greenwich Street, and Lower Manhattan.

The Fifth Avenue District was prompted by the departure of two downtown department stores, Best & Co. and DePinna, whose leaving, it was thought, would have an adverse effect on the rest of the area. This was one of the first zoning laws in the United States that encouraged a mix of residences, offices, and shops in single buildings in a downtown office district. This went against the grain of specialization that has dominated most of urban development (see "American Attitudes Toward Urbanization" in the Introduction).

Incorporating rules about usage, where structures could be located on the lot, and setback guidelines for towers, the special district actively attempted to preserve the existing character of the area. In New York, the need for departures from some of the traditional rigidities of earlier zoning finally resulted in the incorporation of the following sentence in the zoning law: "The Planning Commission shall permit such development as, from time to time, it considers to be appropriate." A frank admission of the fact that no system of rules, no matter how comprehensive, could possibly be appropriate for every urban eventuality.

In 1971, and then again in 1985, San Francisco passed zoning legislation in response to what many considered to be the "Manhattanization" of its skyline. The general reaction to a number of new high-rise buildings was highly unfavorable because of either their bulk—the Bank of America building by Skidmore Owings & Merril with Pietro Belluschi and the Embarcadero Center by John Portman—or their atypical shape—the Transamerica Building and the Holiday Inn. Many people became convinced that new laws were needed to control development if San Francisco was to maintain its unique regional flavor.

The new laws were derived from a number of preliminary reports, including an analysis of the city and an overall design plan, based on much of the work of Kevin Lynch (Moves #1, #17) and Donald Appleyard (Move #20). New height and bulk restrictions were based on an appreciation of the conditions of the surrounding buildings, the "context," which was to become so important in postmodern design (Move #12). Throughout the plan and the subsequent zoning controls adopted to implement it, there was a sensitivity to a broad range of urban design issues that made it somewhat unusual and gave San Francisco a strong tool for guiding future development.

Most people rarely encounter zoning directly, although its consequences surround almost all of urban life in contemporary America—"almost" because Houston is the last major American city that still has no zoning laws, but even here, many of the same objectives are achieved through restrictions on the deeds of property.

On infrequent occasions we do deal with zoning directly—the conversion of a home from a one- to a two-dwelling unit or the search for corporate office space or maybe even involvement in a neighborhood land-use dispute: "There's no way we're going to let them put *that* here!" In general, however, it's something we leave to lawyers and politicians. Like much of the urban environment, it escapes our notice until something goes wrong, and only then do we realize that the legislative decisions have direct impact on our lives. Newspapers bristle with zoning battles, and it can be enlightening to follow one such dispute through its different stages. Pay particular attention to the reasons those involved give for taking the positions they do. How reminiscent are these of some of the motivations that first prompted zoning legislation early in this century?

ADDITIONAL READING

Boyer, Christine. *Dreaming the Rational City*. Cambridge: MIT Press, 1983. This is a scathing attack on city planning as it's been practiced in the United States. Boyer looks behind all the lofty goals expressed by planners. She sees them as essentially defenders of dominant economic interests.

Jacobs, Allan B. *Making City Planning Work*. Chicago: American Society of Planning Officials, 1978. In this book the story of the recent changes in the San Francisco zoning codes is told by the man who was in charge of the planning board at the time.

Toll, Seymour. *Zoned American*. New York: Grossman Publishers, 1969. Toll's history covers the beginning of zoning legislation in the United States.

MOVE #8

Nature and the City
Frederick Law Olmsted

THE FOLLOWING LIST OF SOME OF THE MORE SIGNIFICANT WORK Frederick Law Olmsted accomplished with his partners, particularly Calvert Vaux, in the years between 1857 and 1895 reveals the enormous influence he has had on the American urban scene.*

Urban Parks

Central Park, New York City (1858–ca. 1880)

Prospect Park, Brooklyn, New York (1865–80)

Public Pleasure Grounds for San Francisco, California (1866–68)

Fort Green Park, Brooklyn, New York (1867)

Walnut Hill Park for New Britain, Connecticut (1867–70)

Branch Brook Park for Newark, New Jersey (1867)

City Park for Albany, New York (1868)

Parks for Hartford, Connecticut (1870–95)

Park for Fall River, Massachusetts (1870)

---

*List adapted from Appendix 1 in Julius Fabos, Gorden Milde, and V. Michael Weinmayr, *Frederick Law Olmsted: Founder of Landscape Architecture in America* (Amherst: University of Massachusetts Press, 1968).

South Park, Chicago, Illinois (1871)

Park in Philadelphia, Pennsylvania (1871)

Mount Royal, Montreal, Quebec (1873–81)

Common, Amherst, Massachusetts (1874)

Belle Isle Park, Detroit, Michigan (1882–83)

South Park, Buffalo, New York (1882–93)

Beardsley Park, Bridgeport, Connecticut (1882–86)

Memorial Park, New London, Connecticut (1884)

Park for Trenton, New Jersey (1884)

Franklin Park, Boston, Massachusetts (1886)

Morningside Park, New York City (1887)

National Zoo, Washington, D.C. (1887–93)

Seneca Park, Rochester, New York (1887–93)

Park System, Pawtucket, Rhode Island (1888)

Wood Island Park, Boston, Massachusetts (1889–91)

Charlestown Playground, Boston, Massachusetts (1891)

Washington Park, Albany, New York (1891–95)

Boone Square, Louisville, Kentucky (1892)

Logan Place, Louisville, Kentucky (1892)

Kenton Place, Louisville, Kentucky (1892)

Park for Kansas City, Missouri (1893)

Lake Park, Milwaukee, Wisconsin (1893–95)

West Park, Milwaukee, Wisconsin (1895)

Jackson Park, Chicago, Illinois (1895)

Community Design

Riverside near Chicago, Illinois (1868–69)

Tarrytown Heights subdivision, New York (1871–72)

"Belleview" suburb of Newark, New Jersey (1879)

Providence subdivision, Rhode Island (1882)

Aspinwall Land Company subdivision, Summit, New Jersey (1882)

Providence land subdivision, Rhode Island (1882)

Goddard land subdivision, Providence, Rhode Island (1883)

Chestnut Hill subdivision, Massachusetts (1884)

Newport and Providence, Rhode Island; Yonkers, New York (1884–88)

Newport Hospital subdivision, Rhode Island (1886)

Six subdivisions in Brookline, Massachusetts (1886–88)

Swampscott, Massachusetts, subdivision (1888)

Buffalo subdivisions, New York (1888)

Sudbrook, Baltimore, Maryland (1889)

"World's End" development, Boston Harbor, Massachusetts (1889)

Kirkwood Land Company, Atlanta, Georgia (1893)

Urban Design

World's Columbian Exposition, Chicago, Illinois (1890–93)

Campus Design

Estate of the College of California at Berkeley, California (1866)

Amherst College, Amherst, Massachusetts (1870–85)

Trinity College, Hartford, Connecticut (1872–93)

Yale College, New Haven, Connecticut (1874)

Johns Hopkins University, Baltimore, Maryland (1874–76)

Madison (now Colgate) University, Hamilton, New York (1883)

University of Vermont, Burlington, Vermont (1884)

Smith College, Northampton, Vermont (1884)

Harvard University, Cambridge, Massachusetts (1886)

Stanford University, Palo Alto, California (1886–89)

United States Military Academy, West Point, New York (1890)

Princeton University, Princeton, New Jersey (1893)

Washington University, St. Louis, Missouri (1895)

These places invite a visit, and to be in any one of them is to witness the work of an acknowledged master of urban form—the man who most completely argued for a comprehensive attitude toward nature in the rapidly urbanizing society of nineteenth-century America. How did these places come to be the way they are? And what exactly did Olmsted and his colleagues have in mind when they designed them? Who did they think would be using them? And to what end?

NOTES

Olmsted was the founding figure of landscape architecture in this country and left his imprint on practically every aspect of the national landscape. His influence can be seen in the traditional American placement of houses on gently curving streets set back behind lawns and surrounded by informal arrangements of shrubs and trees, divided parkways with overpasses that permit the uninterrupted flow of cross traffic, and the preservation of Yosemite as our first national park. It was also Olmsted who gave a classic address on "suburban development" to the American Social Science Association in 1870 and who was highly influential in the national move toward suburbanization (Move #9). In addition, he developed plans for a campus community in Berkeley, California, and was instrumental in the design of Riverside, Illinois, and Sudbrook, Maryland.

The years of Frederick Law Olmsted's life, from 1822 to 1903, saw the transformation of the United States from a rural nation with over 90 percent of its population living on farms or in villages of fewer than 8,000 people to a nation of 75 million, where fully a third lived in cities whose increasing size made it more and more difficult to gain easy access to nature. In 1882, no American city was extensively developed more than two miles from its commercial center, but by 1903, "a walk to the country" became an impossibility in the large majority of American urban settings. It's hard to imagine what such a walk would be like today, and even the question of where and what exactly is the "country" has become more than a little problematical.

After time spent as a surveyor, Yale student, bookkeeper, sailor, farmer, journalist, author, and engineer, Olmsted was appointed superintendent in charge of construction of New York's Central

Park in 1857. It was here, in his work with Calvert Vaux and a team of dedicated coworkers, that Olmsted put into practice his many beliefs on the beneficial and ameliorative powers of a close association with nature. In these beliefs, he followed in the tradition of men such as the English Romantic poet William Wordsworth, the New England writer and thinker Henry David Thoreau, who was just beginning his stay at Walden Pond in 1845, the poet and newspaper editor of the New York *Evening Post*, William Cullen Bryant, and, above all, the American landscape designer and theorist Andrew Jackson Downing. Downing brought Calvert Vaux to America as his partner in 1850, and it was Vaux who later worked so closely with Olmsted on many of his major projects that he's generally considered to be as much responsible for them as Olmsted himself was. This, in fact, was one of Olmsted's great strengths. As a result of both his own wide background and powerful administrative skills, he could command an immense breadth of talent and information to deal with urban issues with which he was concerned.

Olmsted was a great believer in what was known as "active" and "passive" recreation. All his parks have places for playing games and settings appropriate for quieter moments of reflection and contemplation. He wrote that natural scenery existed "for the mind without fatigue and yet exercises it, tranquilizes it and yet enlivens it." In the rapidly expanding cities of nineteenth-century America, park development was also stimulated by fears of diseases such as cholera, but Olmsted was one of those who saw parks as the natural places for celebrations of civic virtue. Parks provided settings where the Jeffersonian ideals of a good life for all, and not just the aristocracy as in European society, could be enacted. In his writing on Prospect and Central parks, these sentiments were clearly evident, as were those of a belief in an architecture that would use physical form and design as a means of achieving social goals. His views were similar in this regard to a number of utopian visions (Move #10) and to the zoning incentives that prompted the development of many vest pocket parks and plazas (Move #15).

In 1870, Olmsted addressed the American Social Science Association in Boston on the subject "Public Parks and the Improvement of Towns." In his speech, Olmsted advocated that the American city should be replanned to help encourage friendly associations among poor and rich, female and male, old and young.

This, he thought, was the only way to respond to demands for equality of women and the immense influx of immigrants (Move #25):

> Consider that the New York (Central) Park and the Brooklyn (Prospect) Park are the only places in those associated cities where, in this eighteen hundred and seventieth year after Christ, you will find a body of Christians coming together, all classes largely represented, with a common purpose not at all intellectual, competitive with none, disposing to jealousy and spiritual pride toward none, each individual adding by his mere presence to the greater pleasures of all others, all helping to the greater happiness of each. You may thus see vast numbers of persons brought closely together, poor and rich, young and old, Jew and Gentile.

In the *Art of the Olmsted Landscape* (New York: New York City Landmarks Preservation Commission, 1981), authors Kelly, Guillet, and Hern identified a number of characteristics as typical of Olmsted's work. Among them were, first, roots in the English Romantic style of landscape design, which emphasized the "natural," rather than in the other more formal traditions such as those that came out of French and Oriental landscape practices. How "natural" was the feel of the Olmsted place you visited? It's hard to realize that immense amounts of earth and rock were often moved—almost 5 million cubic yards in the case of New York's Central Park—to create these "natural" places.

The fact that often the very land of the city is a designed creation must be kept in mind whenever you reflect on the relationship between nature and the city. More than one-third of San Francisco Bay has been filled and built upon since 1849, and Walter Muir Whitehill, in *Boston: A Topographical History* (Cambridge: Belknap Press of Harvard University Press, 1968), wrote of the massive addition to the city of Boston, the filling of the Back Bay: "Land fill progressed at the rate of almost two house lots per day, a train of 35 loaded gravel cars arriving in the Back Bay on the average of once an hour, night and day, six days a week for almost forty years."

Miami is another city that comes to mind when thinking about the very topography of the city as a designed object. Landfill projects, the digging of several canals, and the draining of much of the Everglades have totally rearranged the entire configuration of water and land in the area.

Another feature of Olmsted's creations was the way they contrasted with the surrounding city. If cities were places typified by confinement and restraint, then his parks provided settings where movement and freedom could be realized.

Other characteristics of Olmsted's landscapes include the use of bold land forms and extensive vistas that offered the visitor numerous opportunities to look off to some distant sight, whether a particularly dramatic rock, a wooded knoll, or an architectural structure. Olmsted also favored the separation of different types of traffic, with individual systems of paths for horses, pedestrians, bicycles, and automobiles. This pattern was later often repeated in suburban America (Move #9). His designs usually included the presence of artistically composed plantings and at least one formal element, such as the Mall in Central Park. This served as both a meeting place for crowds, which makes it a wonderful place for people watching (see Part IV) and as a transition element between the rigidity of the designed city and the more "natural" informality of the surrounding park.

A question that comes to mind when viewing any of Olmsted's work today is what exactly is their place in the urban America of tomorrow? How will they fit into a culture that has been totally transformed by the automobile (Move #9) and technology (Move #19) and has expanded its view of nature and ecology from the flora and fauna of a particular region to that of the entire planet?

ADDITIONAL READING

Fabos, Julius, Gorden Milde, and V. Michael Weinmayr. *Frederick Law Olmsted: Founder of Landscape Architecture in America*. Amherst: University of Massachusetts Press, 1968.

Fein, Albert. *Frederick Law Olmsted and the American Environmental Tradition*. New York: George Braziller, 1972.

Kelly, Bruce, Gail Guillet, and Mary Hern. *Art of the Olmsted Landscape*. New York: New York City Landmarks Preservation Commission, 1981.

MacHarg, Ian. *Design with Nature*. New York: Doubleday, 1969. MacHarg has developed techniques for site analysis that prevent disruption of the ecological elements of soil, water, vegetation, topography, and geology.

Spirn, Ann Whiston. *Granite Garden*. New York: Basic Books, 1984. This is a comprehensive treatment of urban ecosystems, including earth, air, water, flora, and fauna, and how they can be incorporated into urban design and city life. The author presents valuable data, raises significant issues, and summarizes some ecological success stories, including those of Dayton, Ohio; Woodland, Texas; Washington, D.C.; and Stuttgart, Germany.

MOVE #9

Car Town
The Suburb, the Strip, and the Mall

THE INFLUENCE OF THE AUTOMOBILE ON AMERICAN LIFE AND THE American city has been enormous. Ironically, the word *automobile* was invented by the members of the French Academy after terms such as *autokinet, ipsometer, molectro,* and *motocycle* had been rejected. Although the word itself is French, the great romance with the automobile has been decidedly American. In no other country have so many people owned so many automobiles and has their impact been so great.

In 1900, 4,192 automobiles were purchased in this country. Eighty years later, the Department of Transportation reported 161,614,294 motor vehicles registered, and in 1987, there were more than 176,000,000. In 1910, there was one passenger car for every 44 households in the United States; by 1930, this figure had climbed to one for every 1.3 households, and at present, there are almost enough cars for every single person above the age of sixteen.

In their classic study of Muncie, Indiana, *Middletown: A Study in Contemporary Culture* (New York: Harcourt Brace Jovanovich, 1929), Robert Lynd and Helene Merril Lynd discovered that of the twenty-six car-owning couples sampled, twenty-one had no bathtubs. When questioned on their priorities, a farmer's wife quickly responded, "Because you can't ride to town in a bath tub." In a way, that said it all. "There's no where to go but everywhere" was the way Jack Kerouac put it twenty-eight years later in *On the Road* (New York: Viking Press, 1957).

Think about what the city and city life would be like without the automobile. And consider the American fascination with the highway and the open road. Public transportation is certainly more efficient. With the average car during rush hour carrying between 1 and 1.5 people, a single lane of traffic can move roughly 3,000 people per hour. A mass transit system like the subway can move about 60,000—twenty times that amount—and rail lines, without all the typical discomforts of subway rush hours such as standing and crowding, can move about 30,000 people per line per hour. But efficiency aside, what do we make of all those experiences uniquely related to the automobile?

Automobiles symbolize the privacy of ownership, and obtaining a driver's license is an important adolescent rite of passage. We are accustomed to "drive in" everything—from banks to hamburger stands to movies to mortuaries—and the automobile plays a pivotal position in both the individual and national economies. Nearly one-sixth of the nation's work force is employed in the production and marketing of automobiles. The automobile is typically the second most expensive commodity purchased, and one on which a large percentage of the population makes monthly payments throughout a good portion of their lives.

A glance down at the odometer of your car usually reveals mileage figures well in excess of those covered by the epic travelers of history—Odysseus, Cortés, Magellan, and even Captain Cook. You and I probably cover more miles going back and forth to work and shopping for the groceries than Marco Polo did on all his shopping trips across Europe and Asia in the thirteenth century. Of course, a lot of our movement is quite different from that of those earlier travelers who were directly exposed to a wide range of landscapes and sensory experiences (Move #20). But nevertheless, there is a tremendous amount of geographic scurrying about. In 1980, the Department of Transportation reported that, as a nation, we took some 108.8 billion automobile trips involving 907.6 billion vehicle miles. This geographic mobility has often been associated with social mobility, and "making a move" in one's personal or business life has often been just that.

Commenting on the central place that automobiles occupy in urban life, the French writer Roland Barthes wrote in an essay titled "The New Citroen" (*Mythologies*; New York: Hill & Wang, 1972), "Cars today are almost an exact equivalent of the great Gothic cathedrals: I mean the supreme creation of an era, conceived with passion by unknown artists and consumed in image, if not in usage by a whole population which expropriates them as purely magical objects."

And the American writer Harry Crews clearly saw the need for some sort of reformation in our national automotive theology when he had a character in his novel *Car* (New York: William Morrow and Co. Inc., 1972) eat a 1971 Ford Maverick from bumper to bumper. In trying to explain his actions to a distraught father, the car eater said, "I can tell you. The car is where we are in America. . . . I'm going to eat a car because it's there."

It certainly *is* there, and its presence has reshaped the American city. The three places most strongly influenced by the automobile are the suburb, the strip, and the mall. You can't live in America today without encountering these three places. The suburb, the strip, and the mall are everywhere; frequently we even seem to stop noticing them because they're so much an expected part of the landscape (Move #16). But what are their essential characteristics? And how did they come to be the way they are?

NOTES

Some Significant Moments in the History of the Automobile

According to Stephen Sears, in *The American Heritage History of the Automobile in America* (New York: American Heritage Books, 1977), all the essential steps in the development of the internal combustion engine took place in Europe in the closing decades of the nineteenth century—something of a paradox, considering the United States would eventually be the country so strongly identified with the automobile. How did it come to happen this way?

Sears points out that most investment capital in the United States at the time was channeled elsewhere, not into the development of the car but into exploring the continent. And the relatively good European road systems, which in some cases date all the way back to the Roman Empire, made it easier to imagine road travel abroad than in the United States. The incredibly bad conditions of those early American roads made automobile travel truly something of an adventure—in fact, the state of Tennessee required you give a week's notice before beginning an automobile trip and the Saks and Company Emergency Motorist Kit included bars of chocolate and four pounds of meat. You never knew where you might end up when you started out in one of those infernal machines.

In the "Race of the Century," on Thanksgiving Day of 1895, it took almost eight hours of driving and two hours of repair work to cover the fifty-four miles from Chicago to Evanston and back. Even with all the drama and delay, this race served as stimulus for further development in the automotive industry.

In 1903, Dr. Horatio Nelson Jackson, Sewell K. Crocker, and a bulldog named Bud completed the first coast-to-coast automobile crossing. The trip took sixty-four days over a route that covered at least 4,500 miles and was made to settle a wager of $50 after at least thirty-seven previous attempts had failed. General Motors, which was to become one of the largest companies in the world, was formed in 1908. In that same year, Henry Ford came out with the Model T, and by 1920, half of the 8 million cars on American roads were model Ts. They were called everything from "Tin Lizzie" to "Mechanical Cockroach" to "Bouncing Betty" and came to symbolize an entire era. In 1909, Alice Huyler Ramsey became the first woman to drive across the United States from Hell's Gate on the Atlantic to the Golden Gate on the Pacific. This was also the year of the first Indianapolis Speedway one-hundred-mile race. In three days of action, five people were killed.

Essential to the emergence of the automobile was the development of a good road system that would eventually allow cars to go almost everywhere. In 1927, the Holland Tunnel, the first underwater vehicular tunnel for automobiles in the United States, was completed, and three years later the first limited-access highway was built. It went through suburban areas of Westchester County in New York state. Three of the great bridges initially designed for cars were also finished shortly afterwards. The George Washington Bridge was completed in 1931, the San Francisco Bay Bridge in 1936, and the Golden Gate Bridge in 1937.

Between 1933 and 1941, the mileage of paved roads in the United States more than doubled under Franklin Delano Roosevelt's Public Works Administration, the Works Progress Administration, and the Civilian Conservation Corps. In New York, Robert Moses built an incredible array of roads, bridges, and parks, demonstrating a complete commitment to the automobile. In *The Power Broker: Robert Moses and the Fall of New York* (New York: Knopf, 1974), Robert Caro documents the relentless force with which he pursued this policy. His work was to have national impact. Connecticut's Merritt Parkway, the first limited-access toll road, was completed in 1937, and the Arroyo Seco, which was later renamed the Pasadena Freeway, was completed in 1940. In the same year, the Pennsylvania Turnpike was also opened, and while authorities predicted that the road would carry 715 vehicles daily, within two weeks the actual figure climbed to 26,000—more testimony to the incredible popularity of the automobile and the impossible task of accurately predicting the immense impact it would have on American life.

The Suburb

While usually thought of as a relatively recent addition to the urban landscape, suburbs have been around as long as there have been cities. According to Lewis Mumford, this development may well have explained the ability of the ancient cities to survive the unsanitary conditions that usually prevailed within their walls. In the Near East, there is evidence of suburban development in Ur, one of the first cities, with scattered buildings as far as the temple of al'Ubaid, four miles away. And in 1622, the poet John Donne wrote of England as "the suburbs of the Old World."

City people have always wanted to escape to the nearby countryside, but only relatively recently, with the availability of cheap land and the mobility afforded by the automobile, has this form of living become so widespread. Census figures of 1970 revealed that, for the first time, more Americans lived in the suburbs than either the city or the rural areas of the country. By 1980, census figures showed that in many places even larger proportions of the urban population lived in the suburbs (see Table 5). The city had indeed moved from the ancient Egyptian hieroglyph—the "crossroads within the wall"—to its modern American counterpart—the "crossroads within the sprawl."

Writing in the fifteenth century, the Italian architect Leon Battista Alberti sounded a theme that has become almost synonymous with suburban life, that of informality: "There is a vast deal

Table 5 **Degree of Suburbanization of Major U.S. Cities**

Rank	Metro Area	Central City Population	Outside City Population	Percentage Suburban	Suburban Population/ 100 City
1	Newark	329,248	1,636,056	83.25	496.91
2	Pittsburgh	423,938	1,839,956	81.27	434.02
3	St. Louis	453,085	1,902,191	80.76	419.83
4	Boston	562,994	2,200,363	79.63	390.83
5	Washington, D.C.	637,651	2,422,589	79.16	379.92
6	Atlanta	425,022	1,604,596	79.06	377.53
7	Miami	346,931	1,279,048	78.66	368.68
8	Riverside	377,753	1,179,327	75.74	312.20
9	Salt Lake City	227,440	708,815	75.71	311.65
10	Dayton	203,588	626,482	75.47	307.72
11	Rochester	241,741	730,138	75.13	302.03
12	Syracuse	170,105	472,270	73.52	277.63
13	Sacramento	275,741	738,261	72.81	267.74
14	Cincinnati	385,457	1,015,946	72.49	263.57
15	Detroit	1,203,339	3,149,423	72.35	261.72
16	Anaheim	548,911	1,382,659	71.58	251.89
17	Buffalo	357,870	884,703	71.20	247.21
18	Portland, Ore.	366,383	875,804	70.51	239.04
19	Cleveland	573,822	1,324,898	69.78	230.89
20	Grand Rapids	181,843	419,837	69.78	230.88
21	Minneapolis– St. Paul	641,181	1,473,075	69.67	229.74
22	Flint	159,611	361,978	69.40	226.79

SOURCE: U.S. Department of Commerce, Bureau of the Census, *1980 Census of Population: Standard Metropolitan Statistical Areas and Standard Consolidated Statistical Areas: 1980* (October 1981).

of satisfaction in a convenient retreat near the town, where a man is at liberty to do just what he pleases. I, for my part, am not for having a [villa] in a place of such resort that I must never venture to appear at my door without being completely dressed." (*Ten Books on Architecture*, Florence: 1485, translated into English by James Leoni, 1726)

The original impetus for the suburb was based on *both* an attraction to the countryside *and* reservations about the city itself. This attraction to the countryside may be another manifestation of those anti-urban attitudes that are so much a part of the history of the city (see the Introduction); many of the reservations about the city are often ways of expressing negative feelings toward the racial and ethnic minorities who frequently inhabit them. While earlier suburbs were often built in response to a fear of infection from diseases—for instance, the plague in the cities of medieval Europe—today's suburbs arise to some extent out of a fear of mixing too closely with blacks and Hispanics in the cities of the United States. In 1960, there wasn't a single black among the 82,000 residents of Long Island's Levittown.

There's also been a desire for more space, lower density. People wanted to live in the less formal world Alberti spoke of, a place near the city and, indeed, part of the city itself that didn't have any of the traditional urban characteristics of numbers, variety, and density that can, at times, be so difficult to deal with (Move #16). To avoid these problems, developers often laid out suburban areas according to romantic principles that owed much to the landscape parks of Frederick Law Olmsted (Move #8). Central Park, for example, exhibits two characteristics that were to become quite common in later suburbs: the separation of pedestrian and vehicular traffic, proposed at least as far back as Leonardo da Vinci, and a general avoidance of laying out streets in strict grid patterns (Move #6).

The English planner Raymond Unwin's pamphlet *Nothing Gained by Overcrowding* (London: P.S. King and Son for Garden Cities and Town Planning Association, 1903) was an important document in the modern history of suburban development. Unwin argued that by cutting down on the needlessly large number of streets required by British law, he could provide much-needed recreational space and thereby create more gracious surroundings. The belief that pleasant open space, in the form of parks and playgrounds, wasn't merely a luxury of the aristocracy but could be provided in much more modest housing schemes was a major innovation in modern urban design. This led directly to the creation of the superblock and the cul-de-sac, two features that were to become quite prevalent in suburban America.

Another important planner was Clarence Perry. He developed his concept of the neighborhood (Move #24) after residing in the model suburban environment of Forest Hills Garden on Long Island. Perry's goal was to bring within walking distance all those facilities needed on a daily basis by home and school and to keep outside the pedestrian area all other traffic that really had no business in the neighborhood. He believed that no playground should be more than a quarter of a mile from the children it served. The same principle, with some modifications, was used for primary schools and local shopping areas. For Perry, the heart of the neighborhood was the school and the community center, and he calculated that 5,000 people was a good number for the neighborhood unit.

Henry Wright and Clarence Stein took many of the ideas of Perry and built on them in places such as Radburn in Fair Lawn, New Jersey; Sunnyside, Long Island; Greenbelt, Maryland; Greenhills, Ohio; Greendale, Wisconsin; Chatham Village in Pittsburgh, and Baldwin Hills Village in Los Angeles. These places served as planning prototypes for two of America's most successful new communities, Reston, Virginia, and Columbia, Maryland. Wright and Stein paid particular attention to the separation of vehicular and pedestrian traffic and the neighborhood park. Stein's *Toward New Towns in America* (Cambridge: MIT Press, 1957), first published in 1951, was an important work in American planning. Unwin, Perry, Wright, and Stein were all strongly influenced by Ebenezer Howard and his Garden City proposals (Move #10).

The first modern American suburbs were built along railroad lines between 1850 and 1920, and many of those after 1895 owed their existence to the electric trolley car and the subway. The introduction of the automobile, while making the widespread building of suburbs inevitable, also destroyed the pedestrian scale and the natural separation between communities that the spacing of the railroad stations had imposed. Stations were three to five miles apart, and since houses had to be within walking distance of the station, this resulted in communities of between 5,000 and 10,000 people.

Between 1934 and 1954, the suburban population of the United States increased 75 percent while the overall population increased 25 percent. Much of this increase was in large part a response to the critical need for housing after World War II. The giants of postwar suburban development were Abraham Levitt and his sons William and Alfred, who, before they were done, would build more than 140,000 houses. The first Levittown, originally named Island Trees, was built on some 4,000 acres of potato fields in the town of Hempstead. Using construction techniques reminiscent of Henry Ford's production line, the Levitts divided the task into twenty-seven distinct steps and trained a crew to do each job. They eventually put up 17,400 separate houses sheltering 82,000 residents, the largest housing development ever put up by a single builder.

The sociologist Herbert Gans studied a Levittown built in the 1960s in Willingboro, New Jersey, a town within commuting distance of Philadelphia. Contrary to the many unfavorable reports of the time on suburbia, one of the most widely read being William H. Whyte's *The Organization Man* (New York: Simon & Schuster, 1956), Gans found that the majority of people enjoyed their lives in the community, and any changes that had occurred in the new place were desired and were often the very reasons that prompted the move in the first place. He found little evidence of the alienated, group-dominated, socially striving, transient "organization people" that Whyte portrayed in the suburbs of Levittown and Drexelbrook, Pennsylvania; Park Merced, California; and especially Park Forest, Illinois, a suburb of Chicago.

According to Gans, any changes that did occur when people moved into Levittown were more a function of the population mix than of living in suburbia per se. Throughout his distinguished career of studying urban and suburban settings, Gans has repeatedly argued against a naive "environmental determinism." The way of life that people choose is more often a product of class and stage in the life cycle than it is of settlement pattern such as city or suburb, and, according to Gans, the differences between city and suburb, physical and otherwise, are often rather inconsequential and without much meaning for ways of life. Any attempts to compare urban and suburban ways of life are further complicated by the fact that there is clearly more than one type of city life. Gans talked about "cosmopolites," "unmarried and childless," "ethnic villagers" (Move #24), the "deprived," and the "downwardly mobile."

At the heart of suburban development is a critical paradox. As any suburb increases its popularity, by providing people with the more informal, low-density settings that they seem to want, its very popularity destroys the features that first made the place appealing. This paradox has its urban equivalent in the process of "gentrification": A particular neighborhood becomes popular because of the presence of certain kinds of people and activities, but then its popularity drives up land values and rents, and this in turn drives out the very people and activities originally responsible for the area's popularity.

The Strip

Another favorite whipping boy of the critics has been the commercial strip. But as Grady Clay pointed out in *Close Up: How to Read the American City* (Columbia: University of Missouri Press, 1981), "The strip is trying to tell us something about ourselves: namely, that most Americans prefer convenience, are determined to simplify as much of the mechanical, service and distribution side of life as possible, and are willing to subsidize any informal, geographic behavior setting that helps."

The development of the many commercial enterprises that make up the strip, such as the motel, has been extremely fast. By 1940, there were some 14,000 tourist courts nationwide. Even early on, they had their detractors. Talking about these places, FBI director J. Edgar Hoover portrayed a "new home of disease, bribery, corruption, rape, white slavery, thievery and murder." This is a classic portrayal of sleaze, but not even these widely held sentiments, which to some extent are still expressed today in the word *motel*, no matter how undeservedly, could slow growth. In 1951, Charles Wilson started the Holiday Inn with four motels in Memphis, Tennessee. By the end of the decade, 160 Holiday Inns were operating, and there was one multi-unit motel for every 1,300 registered cars in the United States.

Another staple of the strip has been the fast-food emporium. McDonald's was founded in 1940 in San Bernardino by brothers Richard and Maurice McDonald. In 1954, Ray Kroc started building the restaurants under franchise agreement and in 1956 bought the brothers out. Today, such vast numbers of McDonald's burgers are sold annually that environmentalists claim that large parts of the Central American rain forest are being destroyed to convert land to cattle production to provide the meat for hamburgers. My kingdom for a Big Mac.

In the last several decades, with increasing numbers of architects and planners rejecting the more severe forms of modernism (Move #12), a new respect for the strip has emerged. The architect Robert Venturi expressed it most clearly in *Learning from Las Vegas* (co-written by D.S. Brown; Cambridge: MIT Press, 1972) when he wrote, "In dismissing the architectural value of the Strip, it discounts also its simple and commonsense functional organization, which meets the needs of our sensibilities in an automobile environment of big spaces and fast movement, including the need for explicit and heightened symbolism."

Interestingly enough, in arguing for an architecture of the "decorated shed," Venturi portrays the "ugly and ordinary" design of places such as Levittown as a more legitimate vernacular form for today's times than the monumental symbols in space of classic modernism (Move #12). In presenting the qualities of architectural design appropriate for life today, Venturi contrasted them with those of earlier modern approaches: "applied ornament" instead of "integral expressionism," "mixed media" rather than "pure architecture," "high *and* low art," rather than just "high art," "conventional" rather than "creative," "pretty in front" instead of "pretty (or at least unified) all around," and an involvement with cars instead of public transportation.

Venturi argued that the choice for inspiration for design should be Disneyland, a popular life-style, Broadacre City (Move #10), and a "vital mess," rather than piazzas, a "correct" life-style, Ville Radieuse, (Move #10) and "total design." Just look around on any drive down a commercial strip. For Venturi, Las Vegas serves as a positive example of urban forms that somehow fit the way most people today lead their lives. In contrast, the media critic Neil Postman sees the entertainment values epitomized by this Nevada city as having disastrous consequences for modern life (Move #19).

The Mall

The third setting, in large part a creation of the automobile, is the mall. In 1946, there were eight shopping centers in the United

States; in 1960, there were 3,841. While Market Square in Lake Forest, Illinois, which first opened in 1916, was generally believed to be the first planned shopping center in the country, Austrian architect Victor Gruen, the person most closely identified with the development of the mall, traced its origin back to the Greek agora and through the marketplaces of medieval Europe.

Gruen's pioneer effort was Southdale, which opened in 1956 in Edina, a suburb of Minneapolis. This was the first mall in the United States designed as a fully enclosed, comfort-controlled, two-level setting. Before Southdale, malls were typically long strips, all on one level, with no more than a single major department store. This was based on the assumption that that was all the market could support.

The promotional material for Southdale stressed that while Minnesota generally had only 126 "ideal weather shopping days," in the mall there would be green grass, real trees and flowers, and seventy-degree temperatures even during the blizzards of January. The first pedestrian mall and transitway converted from a traditional street in the United States was constructed on Burdick Street in Kalamazoo, Michigan, from a plan by Victor Gruen and Associates in 1958. One of Gruen's goals was to foster community (Move #22) by providing people with the opportunity for face-to-face interaction and thereby overcoming the isolation of the automobile (Move #20). Eventually, he became bitter over the direction away from the communal toward the commercial that the mall was taking, and in 1968 he returned to Vienna.

A keen observer of malls, William Koswinski wrote in *The Malling of America* (New York: Morrow, 1985) that the essential qualities of the mall were enclosure, protection, and control. This created something of a special place away from the ordinary world and in some ways was similar to the magic of theater (Move #14). "Trees grow out of the tiled floor! Plants flourish without sun or rain! . . . moreover, this continuous flowing environment with no reference to the outside—this sense of a special world—permits a kind of unity of experience within an effortless enclosure that is something like the classical theater's unities of time, place, and action."

The geographer Richard Francaviglia has argued that the mall is sort of an idealized version of Main Street U.S.A., something that you might find in a place such as Disneyland. Everything has been sanitized and tidied up, and all those unpleasant and potentially dangerous inconveniences, such as weather and derelicts and automobiles, have been removed. In many malls, things have been built on a ⅝ scale, similar to the way they are in Disneyland, so that shoppers have a greater sense of power and control. This is one way of hiding from the paradox of the "inhuman human creation" where the city is a collection of settings over which people have no control (Part IV). The word *hiding* is appropriate, because the reduced scale of the mall gives the shopper only the *illusion* of control. It's still a totally designed environment where performers have some say in how they behave, but the stage, props, and sets (Move #14) are managed by other people, and, as such, both strongly suggest and limit what it is people should and can do in the setting.

The magic of the mall is something like television, but now one can intrude upon and move around in the show. As any visitor to the mall can attest, the similarities with television are many (Move #19). Both are primarily visual experiences, whose ultimate goal is the selling of products, and both present a world that seems to have been taken from the small-town settings of shows such as "Ozzie and Harriet" and "Happy Days."

Another similarity between these two creations is that both television and the mall place highly incongruous things side by side. A flip through the channels reveals this transcendence of time and space where things not usually encountered together are suddenly found side by side. First there's a ball game, then a plea for starving children of the Third World, then breakfast food commercials, then an old Bogart movie, then the latest congressional committee investigation of governmental scandal, then a soap opera, and finally a news show. All are regularly interrupted by very brief scenarios with people on beaches, scrubbing floors, drinking wine coolers, and having encounters with Juan Valdez, the White Cloud, the laundry detergent of their choice, and the folksiness of Bartles and Jaymes. The message is always that if we buy the stuff they're selling, we'll all somehow be better people for it; romance, glamour, and fame will be ours. The city has always been the place of incongruous juxtapositions—look at some of those descriptions of early Rome and eighteenth-century London (Move #16)—but television seems to have intensified the rate of these experiences.

Among the more well known urban malls, which have been built to revive the dying parts of the downtown areas of American cities, can be listed Portman's Peach Tree Center in Atlanta; Trump Tower and the Market at Citicorp in New York; Century City Shopping Center in Los Angeles; Pittsburgh's One Oxford Center; the Hyatt Regency in San Francisco; Boston's Faneuil Hall; and The Harbor Place in Baltimore.

The last two, with their historical overtones, seem to aspire to the status of "educational television" by making gestures in the direction of informing as well as selling. Combining education, entertainment, and consumerism can be risky business, particularly for education. Watching "Sesame Street," children can get the idea that the number three really is a curly haired little fellow who seems to have it in for red-haired number two. And maybe even more harmful to education is the notion that if you just sit and watch the television screen, the answer to any question you have will eventually show up—and usually in a very short time, certainly before the next sales pitch. Television conveys the notion that learning is a spectator sport. And then there's the educational confusion that can result from watching *Hamlet* played just before a Cousteau special on the mating habits of sea lions. What exactly can we make of this juxtaposition?

The penultimate mall is in Edmonton, Canada. It has everything from a professional hockey team to a beach with surf on it. Here anything, from a dog sled fully equipped with a canine team to a sleek new Ferrari, is for sale. The West Edmonton Mall cost more than $1 billion to build and contains more than 800 stores, more than 130 bars and restaurants, 19 movie theaters, a $5 million ice rink where the Edmonton Oilers can be seen, four submarines that move through a shark-infested lagoon, and a three-acre ocean with a six-foot-high machine-generated surf. The fierce Canadian climate outside can make the whole thing seem like some sort of space ship moving through the hostile void. Daring to go where no shopper has gone before—that may be the future of the mall: totally enclosed cities. It is ironic that they initially appeared out in the suburbs in an attempt to escape from the older, more traditional city.

ADDITIONAL READING

Gans, Herbert. *The Levittowners.* New York: Pantheon Books, 1967.

Gruen, Victor, and Larry Smith. *Shopping Towns USA.* Reinhold Publishing Co., 1960.

Jackson, K. *The Crabgrass Frontier*. New York: Oxford University Press, 1985.

Koswinski, William. *The Malling of America*. New York: William Morrow, 1985.

Patton, Phil. *Open Road: A Celebration of the American Highway*. New York: Simon & Schuster, 1961.

Venturi, Robert. *Learning from Las Vegas*. Cambridge: MIT Press, 1972.

MOVE #10

Utopian Visions
Howard, Wright, and Le Corbusier

UTOPIA, ACCORDING TO KARL MANNHEIM IN *IDEOLOGY AND UTOPIA* (translated by L. Wirth and E. Shills; New York: Harcourt Brace Jovanovich, 1936), is a meaningful program for action that comes out of thought that "transcends the immediate situation"—something that can "break the bonds" of established society.

Sometimes, to think about the city, you have to turn your back on the city, so that you can reflect on what *should* be there rather than what *is* there, so that the feelings of powerlessness that the city often evokes don't cut off the possibility of imagining change. The city of the "inhuman human creation" is so powerful a presence (see part IV) that it often overwhelms any image of an alternative. The strength of the three men discussed in this Move, Ebenezer Howard, Frank Lloyd Wright, and Charles-Edouard Jeanneret, known to the world as Le Corbusier, was that they had the capacity to see beyond what was right in front of their eyes to what might have been there instead.

And when thinking about change of this magnitude, dreams and imagination have to precede action. Before things can be different, there has to be an image of what that difference is going to be, and this is no less true of cities than it is of any other realm of human endeavor. "What gives our dreams their dreaming is that they can be achieved," wrote Le Corbusier.

What would the ideal city be like? If it were possible to start

127

again from the ground up, which *was* the case with the first American cities (Move #5)—and sometimes even happens today with places such as Reston, Virginia; Columbia, Maryland; and Brasilia, the new capital of Brazil—what would things be like? What *should* things be like? What types of buildings should be built, and how should they be laid out in relation to one another and the surrounding landscape? And what social institutions would exist, and how would people lead their lives in these new settings?

The three utopian schemes that have had the most impact on the twentieth-century American city have been those of Howard, Wright, and Le Corbusier. In the work of all three, there was a realization that architectural plans had to be accompanied by political and economic programs if there were to be any real change in the lives of the inhabitants. None were subscribers to a belief in salvation through bricks alone, and like all comprehensive visions of the future, their plans can be viewed as what the historian Robert Fishman called "social thought in three dimensions" in *Urban Utopias in the Twentieth Century* (Cambridge: MIT Press, 1982).

Although the proposals of Howard, Wright, and Le Corbusier haven't been built anywhere in their entirety, all three men *have* placed their mark on world urbanization and the American city. To move around the urban American landscape is to encounter the dreams and images of these three figures. What were those dreams and images? And exactly what has been their impact on the modern American urban scene?

NOTES

All three men worked between 1890 and 1930 and were strongly impressed by recent technological advances (Move #19). Their writing was filled with the image of the city as a living organism, the organic metaphor (Move #3). They portrayed the city as a life form that had grown so rapidly it became entirely out of scale, a giant destroying everything around it. The evidence was overwhelming. In the nineteenth century, London went from a population of 900,000 to 4.5 million, Paris from 500,000 to 2.5 million, Berlin from 190,000 to more than 2 million, New York from 60,000 to 3.4 million, and Chicago changed from a small village to a city with 1.7 million inhabitants (Move #5). The Industrial Revolution caused an incredible influx of people from the countryside and led to the city of the teeming masses, the tenement, the slum, and the epidemic.

For Howard, these places were like an enlarged ulcer, while Wright wrote that the plan of a large city resembled "the cross section of a fibrous tumor." Le Corbusier regularly portrayed Paris as a body in the last stages of a terminal disease, its circulation clogged and dying of its own noxious wastes. What would be the cure?

Ebenezer Howard and the Garden City

Ebenezer Howard was seventeen years older than Wright, thirty-seven years older than Le Corbusier, and he began his career as a court stenographer. Throughout his life, even after achieving considerable fame, he was to remain a quiet and unassuming man, in strong contrast to the forceful and worldly personalities of Le Corbusier and Wright, neither of whom Howard ever met. It's hard to imagine what these international giants of the art and design worlds would have thought of this mild-mannered man who had even spent an unsuccessful year in Nebraska as a homesteader before returning to London in 1876.

After years as a member of several reading and discussion groups of the Radical Movement in England, Howard came upon Edward Bellamy's novel *Looking Backward* (Houghton Mifflin) shortly after its publication in Boston in 1888. The book had tremendous impact on him, as it had had in the United States on men such as Thorstein Veblen and John Dewey. It quickly became as popular in England as it had been in the United States.

Bellamy portrayed society in the year 2000 organized on principles of cooperative socialism. Industry was grouped into one government-owned cooperative trust, and distribution was handled by a single large department store with branches in every city and village. In Bellamy's utopian society, competition had been replaced by centralized planning, there was no poverty or unemployment, and everyone between twenty-one and forty-five was in the "industrial army" with an equal salary.

Howard opposed the extreme centralization of Bellamy's vision. In this, he was undoubtedly influenced by Peter Kropotkin, the Russian anarchist whose work appeared in several London journals of the time. Kropotkin called for "industrial villages" that were to be twentieth-century equivalents of craftsmen's villages of preindustrial times. Here, set in the countryside, cottage industries would turn out goods more effectively than urban factories could, while at the same time the workers would be able to enjoy the beauty and health of a rural environment.

In a highly influential book known primarily under its 1902 second-edition title, *Garden Cities of Tomorrow* (first published in 1896 in London as *To-morrow: A Peaceful Path to Real Reform*), Ebenezer Howard offered up his image of the ideal city, "Town and country must be married, and out of this joyous union will spring a new hope, a new life, a new civilization."

Howard's plan was for decentralization and a radical reduction of density (Move #16), which he believed to be one of the major ills of the cities. Communities would consist of no more than 30,000 individuals, who were to live in an environment of co-operative socialism on 1,000 acres set in 5,000 acres of a "green belt." The green belt would consist of farms and parks, and these would supply the city with fresh food, clean air, and all those other pastoral pleasures that had become unavailable to the workers of the day in places such as London and Manchester.

The Garden City itself would contain quiet residential neighborhoods and areas for industrial, commercial, and cultural activities. While much of Howard's influence in the United States can be seen in suburban development and in the "neighborhood" concepts of Unwin, Perry, Wright, and Stein (Move #9), his original goal was not to establish a "bedroom community," which many of these places in the United States have become. He was attempting to build a complete city that would meet all its inhabitants' needs. People would be able to live, play, and work without having to go elsewhere. In this "spatial community" (Move #22) it wouldn't be necessary to scurry all over the landscape in the contemporary American fashion (Move #20).

As shown in Figure 6, the neighborhoods—or "wards," as he called them—were slices in the circular pie of the town, with each comprising a sixth of the population, about 5,000 people. The basic neighborhood unit was the single-family detached house surrounded by a garden on a 20 by 130–foot lot—a bit of the "American Dream" (Move #11) in England.

A park located in the center of the community would provide recreation for all within easy walking distance, and a surrounding

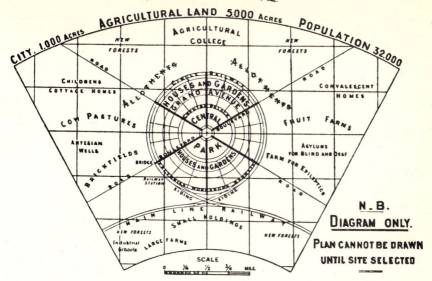

The Garden City surrounded by its agricultural belt. The notation "Diagram only. Plan cannot be drawn until site selected" was added in the second edition (1902). From *Garden Cities of To-morrow*, (1902).

One slice of the circular pie. A typical ward and the center of the Garden City. From *Garden Cities of To-morrow*, (1902).

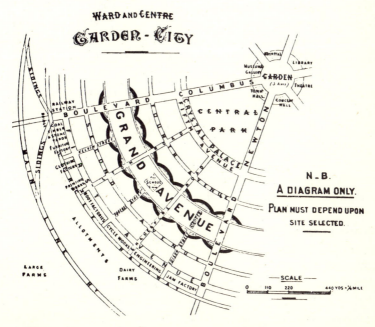

FIGURE 6: Two of Howard's illustrations from *Garden Cities of Tomorrow*.

Crystal Palace housed many of the shops. In the middle of Central Park there would be the town hall, library, museum, concert hall, and hospital. Their strategic location was some indication of the importance they held for Howard, and by placing them literally in the center of Garden City life, Howard hoped they would serve as powerful communal forces, bringing people out of their immediate neighborhoods and into the larger world of the entire community.

As Howard noted on the original drawings, the ideal plan in the diagram was just a general model to be modified depending on the specific site chosen. But throughout Garden City, there was a concern with size and giving the entire population easy access to the countryside. Here, Howard was dealing with some of the same themes developed by Olmsted (Move #8) in his attempts at reconciling the city with nature. But while Olmsted was bringing nature to the city in the form of the many great urban parks he designed, Howard was bringing the city to nature through decentralization.

Ebenezer Howard strongly believed that the land should be communally owned, that utilities be provided on a nonprofit basis, and that there be no domination of a region by a single large city. The idea of the city as a "central place," as described by Harris and Ullman (see the introduction to Part II), was anathema to Howard. Instead, he proposed a series of Garden Cities set around a slightly larger central city, with all being joined by a system of rail lines and canals.

Included among the advantages of combining town and country, Howard listed, "beauty of nature, social opportunity, fields and parks of easy access, low rents, high wages, low rates [taxes and fees], plenty to do, low prices, no sweating, field for enterprise, flow of capital, pure air and water, good drainage, bright homes and gardens, no smoke, no slums, freedom and cooperation."

This was his image of the future, an image that had strong impact on a generation of urban scholars, planners, and designers in both the United States and England and that can be seen, in modified versions, in the English "new towns" of Letchworth and Welwyn and the American planned communities of Reston, Virginia, and Columbia, Maryland. The Crystal Palace never made it into any of these settings, and the perfectly symmetrical circular form was invariably modified to the specifics of the site, as Howard had intended, but much of the spirit of the Garden City is there. Because of his significant influence on such major figures in American architecture and urban planning as Lewis Mumford, Clarence Perry, Henry Wright, Clarence Stein, and Catherine Bauer, Howard's Garden City ideas were reflected in much of their work and through them in the general idea of the suburb as an amalgam of the urban and the rural (Move #9).

Frank Lloyd Wright and Broadacre City

If Ebenezer Howard was concerned with "cooperation," then at the center of Frank Lloyd Wright's image of the ideal city were the issues of individuality and family. (The latter theme was in stark contrast to his own life, where Wright, always ahead of his time, anticipated much of the domestic turmoil that decades later was to become the norm.) In much of the plan of Broadacre City there's a yearning for tranquility and permanence, rootedness, that typically characterizes images of home in this culture (Move #11). In 1935, Wright exhibited a detailed scale model of Broadacre City at an industrial arts exhibition in New York's Rockefeller Center. In this model, he depicted a place so decentralized that many were hard pressed to call it a city at all. Wright felt even more strongly on the subject of density than did Howard, whose Garden City had twelve families per acre:

A human being, from the time he is born is entitled to a piece of ground with which he can identify himself by the use of it. If he can work on his ground, he should do it. But, barring physical disability, he should not eat if he does not work—except when he can fairly trade his right to work for some other contribution to the welfare and happiness of those who do work. Money is today (1937) his immunity from work, a false privilege, and because of it there is insecurity, confusion and loss of quality in all life-values. The philosophy of every form in Broadacres is just this "out of the ground into the light," in circumstances that make a happy thing of man's use and improvement of his own ground.

Wright envisioned a world spread out over a grid (Move #6) system of highways, with everyone's having at least an acre of land, families on their individual homesteads staying in touch through sophisticated transportation and communication systems

(Move #19), and, above all, by use of the automobile. Wright was one of the first to argue that these new machines, which could overcome distance through their speed (Move #21), had made the traditional concentration of people in cities archaic and out-moded. Technology had made it no longer necessary to endure all the discomforts of millions of people piled up one on the other. Wright's designs for houses in Broadacre City accommodated from one to five cars. At the time, this must have seemed excessive, but today it doesn't seem that outlandish. American life *is*, to a large degree, built around the automobile.

Wright proposed a kind of agrarian Jeffersonian democracy, built on developments pioneered by Edison (Move #12) and Ford (Move #9). Like Jefferson, Wright was highly suspicious of the traditional city and the life it bred (see "American Attitudes To-ward Urbanization" in the Introduction). In one of his books, *The Disappearing City* (New York: W. F. Payson, 1932), he presented a historical parable of two human types, the "radical" nomad or Wanderer and the "static" conservative Cave-Dweller: "The Cave-Dweller became the Cliff-Dweller and began to build cities. Es-tablishment was his. His God was a malicious murderer. His statue . . . he erected into a covenant. When he could he made it of gold."

Wright was much more sympathetic to the Wanderer who was an adventurer, and it was only through the survival of some of the original instincts of the Wanderer that the city had retained any of its humanity. The walled city had tamed the Wanderer, but according to Wright, the machine was now coming to his aid. The city of the future, Broadacre City, would be a city without walls and a city with the freedom of mobility.

There was something very American about Wright's vision, from his distrust of the city itself to a love for the Wanderer and the belief that technology and the machine would ultimately pro-vide a solution—"On the Road" with Frank Lloyd Wright. What he didn't seem to realize, along with almost everyone else at the time, was that the very technology he counted on for salvation would create a tyranny of its own. And one of its first victims, according to many of its critics (Move #19), would be the mobility and authenticity that Wright seemed to cherish.

Why go anywhere if you can experience everything in your own living room through television? The nice thing about arm-chair quarterbacking or going down the Amazon on a *National*

Geographic prime-time special is that you don't have to worry about linebackers or unfriendly natives out for your hide. Why do anything at all, if you can watch it being done by other people? The essence of urban leisure, according to the historian Gunther Barth in his book *City People* (New York: Oxford University Press, 1980), is watching other people do things.

And more and more often, the experience of the city itself is being had by people watching other people on television do things in cities. These shows range from the media packages put together for visitors in places as diverse as Colonial Williamsburg, Boston, New York, Chicago, and Los Angeles to all those other television offerings that make "location" a significant part of the package. San Francisco becomes a "Rice a Roni" cable car and Karl Malden chasing criminals up and down hills, Cincinnati is known only as the home of WKRP, and Dallas is forever identified with the evil machinations of J. R. Ewing. (I myself hope to run into Robin Leach if things go well with *City Moves*.) The budget for one episode of "Miami Vice," $1.4 million, is almost as large as the annual budget of the real vice squad of the Miami metropolitan police force.

Broadacre City was to be a nation of independent farmers and proprietors with universal ownership of land and very little concentration of wealth and power. Rigid specialization into farm workers, factory workers, and office workers would also be eliminated. Everyone would engage in physical and mental labor on a daily basis, and this daily variety of tasks would soften the line between work and leisure. It was yet another attack on that specialization and fragmentation that characterized traditional cities (see "American Attitudes Toward Urbanization" in the Introduction) and that Wright felt was inimical to leading the "good" life. In a number of respects, Broadacre City would be organized in the nonspecialist fashion that is more often associated with pre-urban tribal societies (Move #3) and where the theatrics of city life (Move #14) are considerably less complex.

The plan of Broadacre City showed a mix of residential, industrial, and agricultural uses of land, with the accompanying drawings picturing vegetation everywhere and people moving through the landscape on foot, in automobiles, and in helicopters of Wright's design (see Figure 7). It is ironic and tragic that the one large-scale setting, aside from certain mining and construction sites, where this mix of people and machines has been seen is in

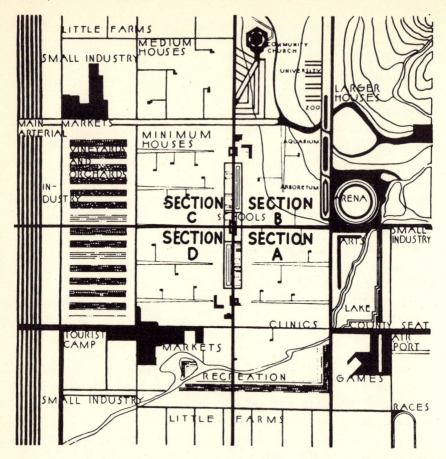

FIGURE 7: Plan of the center of Broadacre City from F. L. Wright, *When Democracy Builds* (Chicago: University of Chicago Press, 1945). *(Copyright © The Frank Lloyd Wright Foundation, 1945)*

warfare situations such as Vietnam. This was the "automobility" he often wrote about. The major meeting places outside the home were to be the Roadside Market and the Community Center. The latter would contain a golf course, a racetrack, a zoo, an aquarium, a planetarium, an art gallery, theaters, and restaurants.

Throughout Broadacre City, there was a commitment to decentralization and severely limiting the size of those few institutions that were thought to be absolutely necessary. "Less is more"—but not quite in the sense Mies van der Rohe and other modern architects meant (Move #12). Government would serve essentially an administrative function and exist primarily on the county level. Most of the major decisions would be made outside the political process, and although Wright wasn't too precise on just how this would happen, he did boast, "No politician as such could make a living in Broadacre City." Schools would also be on a small scale, and the primary school curriculum would include things such as cooking, gardening, and drawing in an attempt to develop the whole individual.

Many inhabitants of Broadacre City probably wouldn't go beyond high school, but there would be small institutes for advanced research should they choose to pursue more formal learning. And then there would be the Design Center, where the creative artists of Broadacre City would create an indigenous style for their community out of the most advanced industrial techniques of local factories. Wright strongly believed that it was the role of the artist to humanize the machine so that it might work for the common good and not in the destructive fashion that had characterized much of the preceding century. Those at the Design Center would also be responsible for protecting the balance between man and nature (Move #8) on which all of Broadacre City was built.

In 1932 Wright recruited twenty-three apprentices and *did*, in fact, organize a design center at Taliesin. The apprentices built their own quarters, farmed, cooked, and spent about half their day in manual labor. The rest of the day was spent in drafting rooms under Wright's direct supervision. Design and the architect played a central role in Wright's vision of the ideal city, and he believed it was absolutely necessary that they be given rigorous training in a wide variety of activities. It would be the architects, after all, who would be responsible for much of the direction of Broadacre City. He was quite explicit on this matter: "The creative artist is by nature and by office the qualified leader in any society, natural, native interpreter of the visible form of any social order in or under which we choose to live" ("Broadacre City, A New Community Plan," *Architectural Record* 77, No. 4, April 1935.)

Le Corbusier and Radiant City

While similar to Wright and Howard in his respect for modern technology, the Swiss architect and planner Le Corbusier stood in opposition to them in his belief that the key to the ideal city was not to reduce but rather to increase density and centralization even further. His Radiant City proposals, first published under this name in 1935 after several similar earlier plans, called for approximately 1,200 inhabitants to the acre. But because of the use of high-rise structures, 85 to 95 percent of the ground was to be left open (see Figure 8).

Born October 6, 1887, in the Swiss town of Chaux-de-Fonds, a community famous since medieval times for the production of fine watches, Le Corbusier moved from the artisan tradition of watchcase engraving to the forefront of modern architecture in a period of a little more than thirty years. He first used the pseudonym Le Corbusier in a journal he coedited with the painter Amédée Ozenfant in the early twenties, and it was at the end of one of these articles that he issued his famous dictum, "Architecture or Revolution, Revolution can be avoided."

Le Corbusier believed that the existing cities of the time offered too much possibility for what he called "anarchistic individualism" and too little scope for planning. In *La Ville Radieuse* (Boulogne: Seine, 1935), he took the reader on an imaginary automobile ride into his new city.

"Suppose we are entering the city by the way of the Great Park," Le Corbusier wrote. "Our fast car takes the special elevated motor track between the majestic skyscrapers: as we approach nearer, there is seen the repetition against the sky of the twenty-

FIGURE 8: Le Corbusier's plan for Antwerp, from *La Ville Radieuse*, which was never built. *(Copyright ARS N.Y./SPADEM, 1988; Fondation Le Corbusier 14198.)*

four skyscrapers, to our left and right on the outskirts of each particular area are the municipal and administrative buildings; and enclosing the space are the museum and university buildings. The whole city is a park."

In their book *Communitas* (New York: Vintage Books, 1960), Paul and Percival Goodman outlined the plan in all its simplicity, "To decongest the centers—to augment their density—to increase the means of getting about—to increase the parks and open spaces." Le Corbusier proposed either demolishing the existing chaos or starting afresh on a new site. First, level highways and tramways radiating from the center would be built, and every 400 meters or so at the subway stations, skyscrapers would be built. And ringing this new opened-out center, there would be large apartment houses for residences, although in the final version of the Radiant City the housing would occupy the center. Industry would be quarantined somewhere "on the outskirts." The Goodmans called it a *Cité Jardin*, a French version of the Garden City.

In a book strongly critical of Le Corbusier, and of Ebenezer Howard for that matter, *The Death and Life of Great American Cities* (New York: Vintage Books, 1961), Jane Jacobs also noted the Garden City as a source for Le Corbusier's Radiant City, even though many of the specifics and details of the two places were strikingly different.

Le Corbusier himself wrote, "The Garden City is a will of the wisp. Nature melts under the invasion of roads, houses and the promised solution becomes a crowded settlement. . . . The solution will be found in the 'vertical garden city.' " Jacobs also noted that many planners out of the Garden City tradition had popularized the ideas of the superblock, the project neighborhood, and as much green and nature as possible, particularly in the form of grass. This helped prepare a climate of acceptance for Le Corbusier's ideas.

In her own work, Jacobs strongly advocated the concept of neighborhood (Move #24), and she accused both Howard and Le Corbusier of being essentially anti-urban in spirit. Among their sins were a denial of the street as an essential urban element and a belief in the virtues of low density at ground level. This, along with an extreme reverence for visual and social order, would eventually destroy the vitality of real cities, which thrive on complexity and heterogeneity. For Jacobs, the numbers, variety, and density (Move #1) make the city a special place, and she blamed many of the problems of American cities on those who have followed the basic tenets of Howard and Le Corbusier. There's almost no curriculum in architecture, city planning, or urban design that hasn't been strongly influenced by the ideas of these men.

The Radiant City was to be a paper city where draftsmen, typists, and administrators would carry on their work in a world of artificial light and conditioned air, settings Reyner Banham called "regenerative" (Move #12) because the environment was managed through the selective use of power and the new machine technology rather than the building of massive structures. Even the walls of Le Corbusier's beloved skyscrapers were thin membranes that would use modern technology to mediate between "inside" and "outside."

Two well-known statements of Le Corbusier's—"the city of the speed is the city of success" (Move #21) and "a house is a machine for living in" (Move #11)—were strong affirmations of his dedication to what he perceived to be the essential qualities of the new age. In keeping with this age, he felt that space should be treated as an undifferentiated whole to be structured without dealing with specific features of the topography. This was reflected in his love of the right angle and the grid. Le Corbusier's characteristic use of pilotis, or above-ground support columns, flattens the landscape and is as much a denial of the local topography as is the grid (Move #6). His feeling was that a good building was a good building was a good building, and it didn't particularly matter where it stood—in the same way that 2 plus 2 is always 4 no matter where one happens to be. Context becomes irrelevant in the face of a universal truth.

One of Le Corbusier's legacies to the modern city was the idea of the high rise in the garden. He was a strong advocate of the skyscraper (Move #12) and was even taken with the visual impact of these buildings. In one of the early appreciations of the skyline he expressed the sentiment that a major determinant of our feeling toward the city would be the silhouette of the buildings against the sky. This was certainly the case when San Francisco introduced new zoning legislation (Move #7) in response to what many in the city considered to be a desecration of the skyline by inappropriately shaped buildings.

The centers of life in the Radiant City were the great residential high rises called *Unites*, each of which would contain 2,700 people. These places were meant to be complete neighborhoods (Move

#24), and many collective services would be provided. Because Le Corbusier's Syndicalism required men and women to work full-time as equals, the *Unite* would provide services such as cooking, cleaning, and day care. In addition, there would be workshops, meeting rooms, cafés, restaurants, and swimming pools in each of the residential skyscrapers.

Interestingly, as early as 1906, the builder Thomas Starret proposed a one-hundred-story building that contained industry, business, residences, public plazas, theaters, shops, and an amusement park, but his plan wasn't as developed or comprehensive as that of Le Corbusier. This part of Le Corbusier's vision can be found in the real estate section of many Sunday newspapers trying to rent and sell high-rise apartments. These special features are frequently offered as added attractions. In this he seemed prophetic, as he did in his general endorsement of the high rise as a modern form.

When looking at the work of Ebenezer Howard, Frank Lloyd Wright, and Le Corbusier, it's important to note not only the specific contributions they made to the contemporary city, but also the whole breadth of issues they raised with their comprehensive utopian proposals. Their work has offered alternative visions of the city and demanded a reexamination of such central urban issues as those of density (Moves #1, #16), dwelling form (Move #11), relationships between home, work, and leisure, and the central concern of nature and the city (Move #8). As much as anything else, this is their interest for readers of *City Moves*.

ADDITIONAL READING

Bellamy, Edward. *Looking Backward, 2000–1887*. Boston: Houghton Mifflin, 1888. One of the more influential nineteenth-century utopian novels, this offered an alternative view of society and served as a powerful stimulus to Ebenezer Howard's thinking. A version edited by Sir Frederic Osborne with an important introductory essay by Lewis Mumford was published in 1965.

Fishman, Robert. *Urban Utopias in the Twentieth Century*. Cambridge: MIT Press, 1982. This is an interesting examination of the work of Howard, Wright, and Le Corbusier that places it in historical context.

Goodman, Paul and Percival. *Communitas*. New York: Vintage Books, 1960. Percival Goodman is a contemporary architect, and Paul Goodman has written with distinction on many facets of modern life. Their highly stimulating work serves as a manual of modern city plans and offers three community paradigms.

Howard, Ebenezer. *Garden Cities of Tomorrow*. London: Sican Sonnonschein and Co., 1902.

Le Corbusier. *La Ville Radieuse*. Boulogne: Seine, 1935. (*Radiant City*, translated by P. Knight, E. Levieux, and D. Coltman. New York: Grossman, 1967.)

Wright, Frank Lloyd. *The Disappearing City*. New York: 1932.

———. "Broadacre City: A New Community Plan." *Architectural Record*, 77, no.4 (April 1935), pp. 243–254.

III

BUILDING
BUILDINGS

THE THREE MOVES IN THIS SECTION DEAL WITH OB-
jects and spaces that range in size from parts of
rooms to groups of buildings: the city on a smaller
scale and in a more immediate sense than those
patterns of time and space that were explored in
Part II.

Move #11 deals with the universal theme of
"home" and some of the things it may mean at the
end of the twentieth century in urban America. If
home and dwelling are intimately involved in human experience—and this experience has clearly
changed, which is obvious when you think about
the way in which you go about leading your life
compared with the way in which your parents went
about leading their lives—then how are these
changes reflected in our ideas of home and dwelling? In today's world of high mobility and changing
family structure, for example, what is the "ideal"
home?

Move #12 deals with a structure that's come to
typify America in the twentieth century, the sky-

scraper. Where did it come from, and where is it going? What exactly were some of the technological breakthroughs that made its development possible and in what locations can significant examples be seen? And finally, Move #13 answers the questions that everyone who has spent any time in the city has asked at one time or another, "What are all those people doing down there in that hole in the ground at that construction site? And why am I so interested in watching them?"

MOVE #11

Home Sweet Home

In 1678, JOHANNES HOFER, A SWISS MEDICAL STUDENT, COINED THE word *nostalgia*. It described an illness whose symptoms included insomnia, anorexia, palpitations, stupor, and, above all, a persistent thinking of home. John Howard Payne wrote, "Be it ever so humble, there's no place like home."

These are still strong sentiments in a world that, in most other regards, has radically changed since those words were first written. And why not? Home is the place where we first encounter the world, and throughout life many of our most significant moments occur there. It's still the place that distinguishes the familiar from the strange, order from chaos, and comfort from adventure. Travel has been one of the traditional vehicles for exploration of home, and this is a Move we all make when we return from a journey—no matter how enjoyable the trip has been—and think to ourselves, it's good to be home. The feelings felt at that moment, the grand occasion of arrival, can almost serve as a catalog of contemporary definitions of home. This experience can take place anywhere, from an airport to a marker on the highway, to your front door. How you feel as you cross the edge into it is critical.

Now imagine for a minute all the different places you've lived. Then pick the three places that meant the most to you, those special settings that always signify "home" for you and still evoke warm memories. If you haven't moved around as much as most Americans, who on the average move between eight and nine times in a lifetime, then just pick the one or two places where you *have* lived. It doesn't matter if they were rooms, apartments, houses, shacks, tents, or trailers. One of the interesting things about a Move like this is that often there's very little correspondence between anything like an objective description of the settings and our feelings toward them. Often the most modest home can call forth the most nostalgia. ("Dallas" and "Falcon Crest" tell us every week that money can't buy happiness—but in the words of one famous comedian, it sure as hell can make misery more palatable.) What exactly are the qualities of the place that comes to mean "home" for us?

As for those special places, what were they like? How were they similar, and in what ways were they different? What did you like and dislike about them? Did they have any qualities that you thought were particularly strong and came to represent the place for you?

Again, it makes some sense to do some writing on these themes. Perhaps it does feel like a school writing assignment, but putting it down on paper does demand a certain amount of editing, analysis, and precision. The first question to ask is, what exactly does home mean to you? Is it primarily a shelter from the elements, or does it also have other meanings? Is it about people, space, security? Does Le Corbusier's famous dictum, "a house is a machine for living in," capture any of your feelings? No one seems to remember the next line in that speech he gave to open worker housing at Pessac, France, in 1926. After talking about a machine for living, Le Corbusier then said, "But since men also have hearts, we have tried to ensure that men with hearts would be able to live happily in our houses."

Or is Gaston Bachelard closer to your sentiments when he argued that what the home was about was providing "shelter for the daydreamer"? Clare Cooper-Marcus talked about the "house as the image of the self," and for Lord Raglan, in *The Temple and the House* (New York: Routledge & Kegan Paul, 1964), the home was a "sacred hut."

Given the realities of modern life, what would the "ideal" home be like? How might factors such as longer life expectancy and, consequently, larger numbers of old people or the high divorce rate be taken into account? Given the latter statistic, perhaps it is fortunate that we now have modular furniture that unhitches when two partners decide to go their separate ways. No tacky arguments about how much the dining room table is really worth.

NOTES

Rootedness and Permanence

Galileo was quoted as saying, "Being rooted is the property of vegetables," and while we know the troubles he got into, given the present mobility figures in the United States, he doesn't seem far off the mark. Today, however, even vegetables aren't particularly rooted. How many miles do you think that salad you had for lunch traveled before it reached your plate?

But even in this age of almost universal movement, in most cultures "home" is traditionally associated with feelings of permanence and rootedness. Of course, there *are* exceptions, particularly in hunter-gatherer and herding societies such as those of certain Mongol tribes, the Plains Indians of an earlier era in the United States, the Bedouins of Asia Minor, the Pygmies of equatorial Africa, the Bushmen of South Africa, and the Aborigines of Australia. In urban cultures such as the United States, the overwhelming sentiment is for permanence and rootedness. Simone Weil wrote of a need for roots even while admitting that "her proper niche in the world was the bare waiting room of a train station." Robert Southey, the poet laureate of England, said it less equivocally when he wrote in *The Doctor* (cited in *Magill's Quotations in Context*; New York: Harper & Row, 1969), "Beware of those who are homeless by choice! You have no hold on a human being whose affections are without a tap root. The Laws recognize this truth in the privileges which they confer upon freeholders. . . . Vagabonds and rogues are convertible terms, and how much with propriety anyone may understand who knows what are the habits of the wandering classes, such as gypsies, tinkers and potters."

In the Soviet Union, the word for Jews is "rootless cosmopolites," a phrase similar to the expression the Nazis took from Spengler in their persecution of Jews and Gypsies. Without a fixed home, one is suspect, and there tends to be a general abhorrence of individuals and groups that move around. This close association of home with something that stays fixed in place also accounts for the dismay most people feel when first presented with a mobile home. Somehow the very idea of a house with wheels seems self-contradictory, even though the only journey the large majority of these structures ever make is from the factory to the site. Once they arrive on the site, every effort is made to dig them into the ground as completely as possible, but just the knowledge that they've been moved and the possibility of more movement in the future make them unwelcome intruders for the large majority of municipal planning authorities.

It may well be the case that these feelings of rootedness and permanence are particularly needed in an age of considerable movement, where the competitive nature of the marketplace forces regular encounters with highly unstable conditions. The one thing we *do* know today is that we're not really sure what's coming tomorrow. Everything moves and changes, often quite quickly (Move #21). And if that's so, then it's nice to come home to a bit of stability and permanence—more than nice, maybe even necessary. But just how long can our images of home include this element of rootedness if the urban culture itself is becoming more mobile? Traditional nomadic cultures view fixed dwellings and those who occupy them with as much disdain as urban cultures direct toward "rootless cosmopolites." In his *Universal History*, the fourteenth-century Islamic historian and philosopher Ib'n Khaldun gave the nomadic perspective and argued that desert nomads were better then city people because they were "more abstemious, healthier, braver, more free, less craven, less bloated and less liable to submit to unjust laws." In an interesting use of the organic metaphor (Move #3) the gypsy word for *settler* is the same as the word for *meat*—the image of the city as a place of nourishment and the place where the beef is.

A number of media scholars, including Marshall McLuhan and Joshua Meyrowitz, have argued that this change has already begun, with a shift on how we think about "place" (Move #19), and that in many ways, we've already become like the Neolithic hunter-gatherer (Move #4). Nomads in search of information can now be found everywhere and not just in those settings that in the past were labeled "educational." It's inevitable that this will have consequences for the way we think about "home." Is there any significant evidence that even today we're becoming more and more like a nation of nomads?

The historian Clifford Edward Clark Jr., in *The American Family*

Home: From 1800 to 1860 (Chapel Hill and London: University of North Carolina Press, 1986), raised the related issue of status:

> To a great degree, therefore, the strong and persistent popularity of the reformers' ideal of the single family home as a peaceful retreat can be understood as a reaction to basic features of the American social system. Ownership of the single family home not only provided a useful way to separate the private from the public dimensions of one's life, but it also represented a financial asset of considerable value that could testify to the individual's position in society itself.

Housing Preferences and Family

Almost every study of housing preference in the United States has reported that the overwhelming choice is the single-family detached house with a bit of land around it. This is true for people of all incomes and backgrounds and is such a strong desire that it's become an essential part of the national aspiration, the "American Dream."

Apartments and rentals are generally viewed as transitions up the "ladder of life." In a work on social order and land use in America, *Everything in Its Place* (Princeton: Princeton University Press, 1977), Constance Perin reported on what those involved in municipal development—mortgage bankers, appraisers, developers, planners, architects, and politicians—had to say about "owners" and "renters." "Renters" were seen as young, having no housing choices, and wanting a carefree situation; they were not the best types of persons, not as likely to maintain property, and lived differently. In contrast, "owners" were viewed as having the ability to decide where they would live and what they would do, functioning better, being nontransient in nature, and having higher values than other kinds of people.

The single-family housing choice, the "ideal house" that almost every child has drawn, has a front yard and door, some windows, and the almost ubiquitous peaked roof. Flat roofs have long been suspect by a wide range of groups, including the Nazi party, the Federal Housing Adminstration (which was reluctant to grant mortgages for this type of construction in the 1950s, even in those areas where the climate might have suggested it), and the workers of Pessac, France, many of whom rejected the flat roofs that were provided for them by Le Corbusier (Move #10). They tended to associate the flat roof with what in their eyes was the low-status world of Arab North Africa. This incredibly strong attachment to a specific design feature illustrates a more general theme that appears again and again—the absolute love of tradition and continuity in the realm of the home.

A break from tradition is almost never welcomed in regard to the dwelling place. It would be almost like redesigning the face of one of your parents. Familiarity is what we want from these people. And as for the rest of the world, it's O.K. for plastic surgeons and other physiognomic designers to help someone more closely approximate an ideal—that "perfect" nose or those wonderful breasts—but anything really new or innovative, three breasts or a nose that runs sideways, no matter how well justified in terms of either theory or function—it "works" more efficiently or "if two are nice, wouldn't three be better"—would be viewed as stigmatizing and treated as such.

This is another outcome of treating cultural choices, such as the preference for a peaked roof, as if they were natural "givens," somehow determined by biology or some objective reality out there in the world—climate or the availability of a particular building material, for instance. Cultures tend to do this around many significant issues, and the opening quote of Johannes Hofer on nostalgia treats thinking about home itself in this manner. This is a mistake that both simplifies human behavior to the point of parody and gives everything the feel of inevitability. It just isn't so, as anyone who has ever pondered the choices when designing, building, or redecorating a dwelling will testify. The element of choice is always there, and it's the availability of these choices that adds to the significance of the activities.

Even in urban America, a good deal of life is lived at home. In a major study of activity patterns, 1,476 people in forty-three American metropolitan areas were asked by researchers F. S. Chapin and R. K. Brail to detail their time and space budgets for a single weekday. One general finding was that if all obligatory activities were excluded from the typical adult twenty-four-hour day, then only about five hours remained for discretionary activity, 80 percent of this time usually spent at home.

Of the 80.4 million occupied housing units counted in the 1980 census, 53.9 million were single-family detached homes. Herbert Hoover captured the spirit of the nation when he said, "Those immortal ballads, 'Home Sweet Home,' 'My Old Kentucky Home' and 'The Little Gray Home in the West' were not written about tenements or apartments. . . . They never sing songs about a pile of rent receipts." What are the contemporary equivalents of these songs? And Franklin Delano Roosevelt was also reflecting widely held sentiments when he said, "A nation of home owners, of people who own a real share of their own land, is unconquerable."

At President Herbert Hoover's Conference on Home Building and Home Ownership in 1931, where many of today's tax incentives favoring home ownership began, home ownership was called a "birthright" and an "epochal event" in the life of a family. One realtor present at the same conference was quoted as saying that the awful alternative was to be "condemned to die in a rented house." This reads almost like the plot for a soap opera or a realtor's advertising slogan.

In his landmark study of 1830, *Democracy in America* (New York: Vintage, 1954), Alexis de Tocqueville described the American family home as one of the most powerful stabilizing forces in the democratic society: "When the American retires from the turmoil of public life to the bosom of his family, he finds in it the image of order and peace. . . . While the European endeavors to forget his domestic troubles by agitating society, the American derives from his own home that love of order which he afterwards carries with him into public affairs."

This interchangeable use of the terms *family* and *home* is not unusual and runs throughout much thinking about these two institutions. Pronouncements about the nature of the home are almost invariably ways of also talking about the nature of the family, since in this case, the character and layout of the stage strongly influences the kind of performances that can be given upon it (Move #14). The Victorian house, with its many rooms and rigid separations between different areas, is saying something quite different about the relationship between activities and people than is the more open plan of the 1950s suburban ranch style (Move #9) or Le Corbusier's Villa Savoye, for that matter.

A home can be "read" in the same manner that a city can (Move #1). The questions to ask are what *kinds* of space, how are they divided, and how are they used? It's also important to observe which people and activities are given quite a bit of room and which aren't. Then there are the "gates" between the different areas (Move #2) and the props and sets (Move #14).

In *House Form and House Culture* (Englewood Cliffs, NJ: Prentice-Hall, 1969), Amos Rapoport developed the thesis that houses in pre-urban societies reflected the values and dominant themes of the societies that built them. While these relationships are very complex in urban societies and are even further complicated by the fact that design and building tasks are turned over to full-time specialists who are *not* the same people as the building's occupants, a number of Rapoport's categories *are* useful.

How does the form of the dwelling reflect attitudes toward basic needs, the relationships between men and women, the significance of certain family activities such as food preparation, consumption, and leisure? What is the status and definition of the family itself? How is the issue of privacy handled? Is this a home that invites the outside community in, or does it keep it at a distance?

Given the present state of marriage and the nuclear family and today's high building costs, it may soon make more sense to talk about the "starter spouse" than it does to talk about the "starter house." As Dolores Hayden documented in her book *Redesigning the American Dream: The Future of Housing, Work and Family Life* (New York: Norton, 1984), feminists such as Charlotte Gilman Perkins recognized quite some time ago that any changes in women's roles would have to be accompanied by changes in the setting where many of those roles were enacted: home. "Home sweet home has never meant housework sweet housework" was the way she put it in the 1890s.

Grieving for a Lost Home

In a classic study done in the early 1960s, "Grieving for a Lost Home" (in *The Urban Condition*, edited by L. Duhl; New York: Basic Books, 1963), Marc Fried made a number of insights that are useful when thinking about the general theme of "home." In this case, the dwellings were apartments in three- and four-story attached row houses in the West End, a somewhat down-at-the-heels working-class neighborhood in Boston. Although the "American Dream" *is* a single-family detached home, many people still find themselves living in multifamily dwellings. This has been true throughout much of the history of American cities. Manhattan in 1870, for example, consisted of single-family homes, boarding houses, and tenements, but by 1900, a year when only ten single-family houses were built, large multifamily apartment houses were the dominant dwelling form.

After interviewing 250 women and 316 men of Boston's West End, who were forced to relocate because urban renewal was slated to knock down their neighborhood, Fried found that 46 percent of the women and 38 percent of the men suffered fairly extreme feelings of grief. Among their reactions were "the feeling of painful loss, the continued longing, the general depressive tone, frequent symptoms of psychological or social or somatic distress, the active work required in adapting to the altered situation, the sense of helplessness, the occasional expressions of both direct and displaced anger, and tendencies to idealize the lost place." How many of these reactions are typical of any change in dwelling or loss of home, even when this loss is less extreme than that experienced in "urban renewal"?

When Fried more closely analyzed the nature of the grief reaction, he found that it had two components. The first was spatial (Move #22), or a positive relationship to the West End as a physical place and a specific location:

> It is the sense of belonging someplace, in a particular place which is quite familiar and easily delineated, in a wide area in which one feels "at home." And this applies for many people who have few close relations within the area. Even familiar and expectable streets and houses, faces at the window and people walking by, personal greetings and impersonal sounds may serve to designate the concrete foci of a sense of belonging somewhere and may provide special kinds of interpersonal and social meaning to a region one defines as "home."

Fried and a number of other researchers believe that a sense of spatial identity is fundamental to human functioning and absolutely necessary for people to carry on. "Everybody's got to be somewhere" is the way the old joke had it.

The second component of the grief reaction was social. It consisted of the loss of other people: neighbors, friends, and family. Many West Enders had significant numbers of friends and family in the neighborhood (Move #24) with whom they interacted on a daily basis. To lose the West End for them meant the loss of these relationships, because no matter how hard one tries, it's never quite as easy to drive twenty miles as it is to walk two blocks. All too often, there's too little time and too much traffic to make the automobile trip possible. The West End was a spatial community (Move #22) for many of its inhabitants, in strong contrast to traditional middle-class scenes where friends, colleagues, and family are usually scattered over a much wider landscape. Interestingly, those West Enders who were more middle class *did* seem to suffer less grief.

For many of the displaced inhabitants of the West End, "home" was both a specific place and a collection of particular people. And the more the West End was known, the more likely there was to be a severe grief reaction. To know it was to love it, or perhaps to love was to get to know it.

Protection, the Self, and Home

The Pruitt-Igoe housing complex in St. Louis was lost in a somewhat different way than the West End of Boston. Designed in the mid-1950s by Minoru Yamasaki, it was demolished July 15, 1972, at 3:32 P.M. because it had become an unlivable place. According to the architectural critic Charles Jencks, this was the precise moment when modernism as a style in architecture died (Move #12), because it was at this moment that it was realized (or perhaps the word is *should* have been realized) that architecture alone couldn't solve social problems.

Before the Pruitt-Igoe project was built in 1954, the inner city of St. Louis contained dilapidated slums. Approximately 12,000 people were relocated into 43 eleven-story-high structures that stood on fifty-seven acres. Initially integrated, the project soon became a black ghetto, with many of the families having little money and often subsisting on various public assistance programs.

As a dwelling place, Pruitt-Igoe became a total failure, and in 1970, sixteen years after it had been opened, twenty-seven of the forty-three buildings were vacant. Ironically, shortly after they were designed, the same buildings had been praised by *Architectural Digest* as containing no "wasted space." But unfortunately, the way the buildings were designed discouraged any semblance of control, support, or confidence on the part of its tenants. Long, narrow hallways and corridors within the buildings discouraged interaction and promoted anonymity. Sealed-off staircases created dangerous situations where anything could happen because no one was watching. There were no "eyes on the street" in the Jane Jacobs sense (Move #24), and mothers couldn't supervise their children playing outside because of the height of the buildings.

The sociologist William Yancey noted that there was a minimum of semiprivate space and facilities around which neighboring relationships might develop—that lack of "wasted space," which earlier had been seen as such a virtue. The open space that *did* exist at Pruitt-Igoe was too open and public, so that people couldn't congregate in it or recognize outsiders. As a consequence, there was no sense of ownership, and no one felt obligated to protect the place. Most people retreated to their apartments, which satisfied fully three-quarters of them, while only 49 percent were satisfied with project living in its entirety. This was just the opposite of the case in an adjoining neighborhood, where 74 percent of the people expressed satisfaction with the neighborhood, while only 55 percent were satisfied with their apartments. In the sociologist Lee Rainwater's terms, the apartments in Pruitt-Igoe were serving as a "haven from fear." When physical safety is a major issue, then the dwelling can't function as a means of self-expression the way it can for those people who live in safer circumstances, and safety can generally be equated with affluence. It's one of the things bought when a dwelling is purchased. Along with more space and a greater number of amenities, more money usually buys more protection from danger.

Using the work of the psychologist Carl Jung and that of the phenomenologist Gaston Bachelard as a point of departure, Clare Cooper argued that an important part of home was that it allowed for those expressions of the self that made life fuller and more enjoyable, another way of dealing with the "inhuman human creation" (see Part IV). In "The House as Symbol of the Self" (in *Designing for Human Behavior*, edited by Jon Lang; Stroudsburg, PA: Dowden, Hutchinson and Ross, 1974), Cooper explained:

> The house both encloses space (the house interior) and excludes space (everything outside it). Thus it has two very important and different components; its interior and its facade. The house therefore nicely reflects how man sees himself, with both an intimate interior, or self as viewed from within and revealed only to intimates who are invited inside, and a public exterior (the persona

or mask, in Jungian terms) or the self that we choose to display to others.

Among the data Cooper cited was work by the anthropologists Edward Laumann and James House on affluent white home dwellers in Detroit and how their living rooms were decorated as a reflection of their selves. Traditional decor of French or Early American furniture, with wall mirrors, small potted plants and artificial flowers, paintings of people or still lives, and many clocks (Move #2), was usually chosen by white Anglo-Saxon establishment types with occupations and status positions similar to their fathers. More "modern decor"—typified by modern furniture, wood walls, abstract paintings, and solid carpets—was generally chosen by upwardly mobile non–Anglo-Saxon Catholics whose families had migrated from southern and eastern Europe after 1900.

In another study (*The Social Meaning of the Physical Environment*, unpublished doctoral thesis, University of California at Berkeley, 1968), Carl Werthman concluded that many people bought houses of a particular style to bolster their image of self. In one suburb south of San Francisco, extroverted self-made businessmen tended to choose mock colonial display homes that Werthman believed were characterized by a certain amount of ostentation while people in the helping professions tended to go for quieter, architect-designed styles that seemed to meet current standards of "good design."

The fact that the house often *is* a symbol of self can be further demonstrated by just looking around the place in which you presently reside and noting the ways in which the setting can be said to reflect you, the ways in which you've gone about making it yours. These undoubtedly range from particular objects placed in it—home as the place where you keep your "stuff" in the words of the comedian George Carlin—to decorating and architectural transformations that can radically transform the setting. This identification of self with dwelling also accounts for a wide range of phenomena, including the earlier-mentioned resistance to change in dwelling form, the tremendous feelings of violation victims report when their homes are broken into and robbed, and, probably, many of the failures of public housing. These types of dwellings are clearly more collective in orientation than those free-standing homes of our dreams, and if the dominant image the culture has taught us to have of ourselves is more one of a separate autonomous individual than it is of a member of a group or community, then somehow group housing doesn't seem quite right. This ideology of the individual, with its failure to value interdependencies and at times to even notice them, is also played out in the traditional American anti-urban bias (see "American Attitudes Toward Urbanization" in the Introduction). While it's clear that the city is a collective activity, in our disdain of multifamily dwelling, and public housing in particular, we seem to be saying that there's no need to make "home" one also.

In *Defensible Space: Crime Prevention Through Urban Design* (New York: Macmillan, 1972), Oscar Newman offered a number of suggestions on how to reduce crime in settings such as the Pruitt-Igoe project. His basic strategy was to help people establish more appropriate feelings toward the physical setting than those sentiments of fear and anger that many people often have in public housing.

According to Newman, "defensible space is a model for residential environments which inhibit crime by creating the physical expression of a social fabric that defends itself." Get people to care for the place by creating spaces that they feel responsible for. "Perceived zones of influence" were established by subdividing and articulating certain areas of the environment so that people could react to parts of the place rather than to the whole thing. It was important to create situations where surveillance occurred naturally. The place would be safer because other people could observe what was going on, not because they were personally nosy or vigilant, but rather because of a design feature such as a window overlooking the setting they couldn't help but look out when they were in the kitchen. Or maybe the potentially dangerous place itself would have something—a tree whose shape and color change through the seasons or a billboard with different messages—that naturally invited and even commanded attention.

Newman has been extensively criticized for advocating what, at times, appears to be an overly simplistic environmental determinism, and clearly, the relationship between people and their physical settings is much more complex than it is for any other species—you won't wither with quite the same inevitability as a sable palm if you're removed from the sun. But his insights *did* shed some additional light on the nature of home and dwelling —particularly in regard to ways in which designers could help people cope with the paradox of the "inhuman human creation" (see Part IV). How can situations be created in multifamily dwellings where people can generate the necessary sense of control to engage in some of those expressions of self that Clare Cooper and others feel are so important?

Protection for the Dreamer

The concluding note of this Move brings us back to the dream house, but now the dreams aren't about the house itself but are rather protected by the house. For Gaston Bachelard, in *The Poetics of Space* (New York: Orion Press, 1964), the chief function of the house is to protect the daydreamer. And it is in the daydream that the thoughts, memories, and dreams of mankind are integrated: "The house thrusts aside contingencies, its councils of continuity are unceasing. Without it, man would be a dispersed being. It maintains him through the storms of heaven and through those of life."

Again here are the themes of permanence and protection, but now the focus is on the world of thinking and imagination. Not only does the house allow the activity of dreaming to take place —perhaps the ultimate filter (Move #16) is necessary to turn inward and not remain vigilantly on guard against some external threat—but its very form also suggests themes of verticality and centrality that help in the structuring of those dreams.

And a final quote from *The Poetics of Space* on that most ubiquitous form, which is encountered everywhere in and around the dwelling, the corner. "To begin with, the corner is a haven that ensures us one of the things we prize most highly—immobility." And this is one of the quintessential elements of home, whether a room, apartment, house, neighborhood, or even a much beloved favorite booth in a local tavern. Home is not the place you're going to, but rather, the place you are. This is the tragedy of being homeless. You are nowhere.

ADDITIONAL READING

Bachelard, Gaston. *The Poetics of Space.* New York: Orion Press, 1964. First published by Presses Universitaires de France, Paris, 1958.

Fried, Marc. "Grieving for a Lost Home," in *The Urban Condition,* edited by L. Duhl. New York: Basic Books, 1963.

Hayden, Dolores. *Redesigning the American Dream: The Future of Housing, Work and Family Life.* New York: Norton, 1984.

Rapoport, Amos. *House Form and House Culture.* Englewood Cliffs, NJ: Prentice-Hall, 1969.

MOVE #12

The Skyscraper

Its Beginning, Middle, and Now, Postmodernly Adorned, End

To think about the American city is to think about buildings that reach for the sky, and to be in the American city is to be surrounded by extremely tall buildings (Move #1). In his book *Skyscraper* (New York: Knopf, 1982), the architectural critic Paul Goldberger wrote, "The most significant or interesting skyscrapers have been designed by American architects and built on American soil."

While this comment is open to some debate, the "skyscraper," a word that was first heard in New York in the 1880s, has become almost synonymous with the twentieth century in general and the American city in particular. Skyscrapers have so changed the sense of urban scale that it's easy to forget that not until the turn of the century did these buildings outgrow what until then had been the tallest city structures—church steeples. In New York, for example, it wasn't until 1892 that George B. Post's 309-foot Pulitzer Building on Park Row surpassed the 284-foot Trinity Church spire. This marked a clear shift in dominance from the religious to the secular world of business.

A good deal of American city life is led in and around these tall buildings. The vest pocket parks and plazas often found at their bases provide both respites from the intensity of downtown (Move #16) and wonderful places for people-watching (Move #15). And there seems to be widespread fascination with their construction site beginnings (Move #13) and with their lofty ends which offer such wonderful vantage points from which to look down on the city (Move #1), views that in the past were available only through prodigious exercises of the imagination. This democratization of condescension, giving everyone the chance to look down on everyone else, has probably done as much as anything to change the way we think about the city (Moves #1, #17).

As has been the case with the city itself (see "American Attitudes Toward Urbanization" in the Introduction) there's been a good deal of ambivalence exhibited toward these structures. They're both loved and hated. Zoning legislation was an attempt to diminish their overwhelming presence (Move #7); at the same time they're regularly portrayed as an embodiment of everything noble in the human spirit and the answer to every urban dilemma. When Le Corbusier first saw the New York skyline in 1925, he thought the buildings were too short, although he did concede that perhaps there were too many of them. In *The Autobiography of an Idea* (New York: Dover Publications, 1957; originally published in 1924), Louis Sullivan, beloved "Der Meister" of Frank Lloyd Wright (Move #10) and one of the major influences on early skyscraper design, had the following to say, "The appeal and the inspiration lie, of course, in the element of loftiness, in the suggestions of slenderness and aspiration, the soaring quality as of a thing rising from the earth as a unitary utterance, Dionysian in beauty."

What exactly are those structures that are seen every day in the cities of America and that in many ways have come to symbolize those cities? What were the factors that led to their development, and who were the figures who played a role in their history? And why is it that suddenly the era of the "glass box" seems to be at an end, and there are all those new, much more complicated forms dominating the skyline?

NOTES

In the *Penguin Dictionary of Architecture* (Harmondsworth: Penguin Books, 1972), a *skyscraper* is defined as "a multi-story building constructed on a steel skeleton, provided with high speed electric elevators and combining extraordinary height with ordinary room spaces such as would be used in low buildings."

In trying to account for the tremendous popularity of the skyscraper in the American city, August Heckscher wrote in *Open Spaces: The Life of American Cities* (New York: Harper & Row, 1977):

> The skyscraper may be attacked on many grounds, aesthetic, ecological and humanistic. But for one simple reason it has helped preserve a compact city. Basically this is because vertical transportation is swifter and better organized than horizontal transportation. So far as the individual is concerned, the ride is also free. Where skyscrapers are clustered it is possible to go easily on foot from one urban destination to another.

Early Skyscraper Development

The first period in the development of the skyscraper was a functional one in which architecture can be thought of as in many ways still subservient to engineering. Rapid increases in building height were made possible by a number of engineering feats, including advances in fireproofing and the development of metal framing (Moves #1, #13). This allowed the bearing walls on the lower floors to be narrow enough to leave enough room for a significant amount of rentable office space.

New York's first steel-frame building was the Tower Building, built at 50 Broadway some four years after the pioneering example of William LeBaron Jenney's Home Insurance Building in Chicago (Move #1). A number of other significant factors in the development of the skyscraper have also taken place in Chicago, giving the city a prominent position in the history of these types of structures. While New York probably has a greater number of skyscrapers than any other city in the world, it was in Chicago that Louis Sullivan developed the first style that was appropriate for buildings of this height. And it was also in Chicago that the *Tribune* competition of 1922 was held. This turned out to be one of the more important architectural events of the first half of the twentieth century, but even before it was held, a number of technological breakthroughs had to be made before the skyscraper could become a popular form.

It's been pointed out that if the usual masonry walls had been used in the Tower Building the lower floors of the ten-story building would have lost more than 25 percent of their twenty-foot lot-size width. What made the traditional masonry construction an even less appealing economic venture was the fact that the lower floors were also those that could command the highest rents. Not only would the thick masonry walls eat up space, but they would consume the most valuable space. And given the economic motivation of the builders, this was no small matter. But then came steel and steel-frame construction, and the elevator (Move #1).

The elevator was important in allowing the new construction technique to be used to its fullest potential. So much so, that the skyscraper historian Winston Wiseman credited the Equitable Life Assurance Building of 1870 as the first skyscraper, even though it wasn't the first steel-frame building. But it *was* the first business building that fully utilized the elevator, and because it rose to a height of 130 feet, it was twice as tall as the average five-story building of the time. Other important technological innovations that figured in the history of the skyscraper included the revolving door, flush toilets, plate glass, the telephone, the electric light, and rapid transit to serve the extremely large numbers of people who would use the new buildings.

In 1890, about 70 percent of street railways relied on horses or mules, but by 1902, 97 percent used electricity. Chicago employed the first multiple streetcar units in 1897. Electric trains quickly replaced existing steam elevated lines, and beginning with the Boston subway in 1898, Boston, New York, and Philadelphia built underground rapid transit systems. Between 1883 and 1913, the large majority of streets in Manhattan were provided with electricity. It's hard to imagine what skyscrapers would be like without the systems developed by Thomas Alva Edison that helped provide light, heat, and communication networks with other buildings. There also had to be windows for a view of the outside and to provide natural light for interiors. Plate glass, which was essential for strong, high-altitude windows, went into mass production in 1881. Telephones, which were also a necessity, were widely available by the 1870s, and New York was averaging 150,000 calls a day by the mid-1890s, with long-distance calling already a possibility.

And that most ingenious of "gates" (Move #2), the revolving door, was first perfected by Theophilus van Kannel, who received the John Scott medal of the Franklin Institute in Philadelphia in 1889. His company's slogan was "Always Closed." Without this relatively simple device, skyscrapers would have been plagued by a host of problems due to the strong air currents that moved throughout the buildings. Significant losses of heat, problems with opening and closing doors, and air currents playing havoc with office paperwork would have created serious problems. Developments in air-conditioning by another American, Willis H. Carrier, were also of great importance.

Taking note of these technological advances, the architectural critic and historian Reyner Banham, in *The Architecture of the Well-Tempered Environment* (London: Architectural Press, 1967), argued that the North American building tradition and particularly skyscrapers used technology to manage environments in ways that had never been done before on this scale. He labeled it the "regenerative" mode. By this he meant a strategy of manipulating power to create desired environmental conditions, rather than the more traditional architectural approach of building buildings—something like the difference between using wood to build a house to stay warm as opposed to using this same wood to build a fire to stay warm. The heating, lighting, and ventilation systems that skyscrapers invariably used were all examples of this "regenerative" mode.

Ironically, the genius who made much of this possible, Thomas Alva Edison, had his own reservations about the skyscraper. In an interview conducted in 1926, he was quoted in the *Literary Digest* as saying, "If . . . New York keeps on permitting the building of skyscrapers, each one having as many people every day as we used to have in a small city, disaster must overtake us."

Root, Sullivan, Holabird & Roche and Chicago

Many of the earliest skyscrapers were built in the last two decades of the nineteenth century in Chicago, a city that was trying to rebuild itself after the disastrous fire of 1871. The two giants of the Chicago School were Louis Sullivan and John Wellborn Root.

Root was Daniel Burnham's (Move #7) partner and chief designer until his early death in 1891 at the age of forty. Along with Sullivan, Root believed that skyscrapers should express the nature of their construction and the spirit of the new age. Together with Burnham, he was responsible for a number of notable buildings. Among them were the Rookery, in 1886, and the Monadnock

Building, in 1891, which, although it didn't have a steel frame, qualified as a skyscraper in every other respect.

The latter building, known for the simple, smooth, flat surfaces of its sixteen-story brick walls and its monumental silhouette, was a good example of how a practical concern based on economics could, in the hands of a brilliant architect, be turned into an aesthetic asset. In a letter to their Chicago lawyers, one of the owners of the building, Peter Charndon Brooks, expressed the opinion that the building should have no projecting surfaces or indentations, which he believed would only serve to attract dirt, pigeons, and sparrows.

In the hands of Root, even with the use of traditional brick masonry techniques, walls were created whose very lack of ornamentation and surface complexity added to their "soaring quality."

Louis Sullivan, also of the Chicago school, was a monumental figure in the world of architecture. He not only created the first complete skyscraper style but in a number of ways anticipated much of what "modern" architects were going to say years later. In a series of brilliant buildings—including the Auditorium Building (1889) in Chicago, with partner Dankmar Adler; the Wainwright Building (1890) in St. Louis, also with Adler; the Guaranty Building (1895) in Buffalo, New York (see Figure 9); the Bayard Building (1899) in New York; and the Carson, Pirie, Scott store (1901) in Chicago—Sullivan boldly illustrated his belief that "form ever follows function." It should be pointed out that Sullivan meant this in a somewhat different way than many of those who followed and often interpreted it quite literally. Many of Sullivan's buildings were remarkable for their integration of ornamental, floral motifs with structural elements. Sullivan would never have endorsed Adolf Loos's dictum, "All decoration is criminal."

Loos was reacting to the excesses of European traditions at the turn of the century that smothered the designed object—whether it was an ashtray or a building—beneath so much lush decoration that it was often difficult for the viewer to make any sense out of what it was he or she was looking at. The spirit of this aesthetic was captured years earlier when the great chef Careme wrote, "The fine arts are five in number, to wit: painting, sculpture, poetry, music, architecture—whose main branch is confectionery." Building as pastry—it was in rebellion against these kinds

FIGURE 9: Sullivan's Guaranty Building, Buffalo, New York. (*Courtesy of Buffalo and Erie County Historical Society*)

of sentiments that modern architects expressed an extreme distaste for the decorative.

Louis Sullivan believed that the form of the building should reflect what it was the building was doing. And in the case of the skyscraper, this meant singing the praises of modern times and, above all else, soaring to the sky. Although many of his buildings were organized in three parts, with a base, then a shaft, and finally a capital on top, reminiscent of a Greek column, Sullivan strongly resisted the pull toward historical precedents that so many other architects of his time were following.

This was a time in the history of the skyscraper that has been labeled the "eclectic period," and architects were drawing on every possible European source in their search for a skyscraper style. An examination of the buildings of the time, from approximately 1895 to the onset of the Depression in 1929, reveals everything from Gothic, in the case of such buildings as Cass Gilbert's Woolworth Building of 1913 in New York, to the Metropolitan Life Tower designed by Napoleon LeBrun and Sons, which drew its inspiration from the Campanile in St. Marks Square, Venice. The Custom House Tower in Boston, done by Peabody and Stearns in 1915, also used this as a source, while many of the works of McKim, Mead and White seemed to reach back to Greece. Bertram Goodhue's State House in Lincoln, Nebraska, built between 1921 and 1931, made allusions to ancient Rome, the Middle East, Byzantium, and native America. If the city is indeed the place of tremendous variety (Move #16), then it's from much of the work of this time that it's now possible to see in many American cities examples drawn from the entire history of architecture.

Louis Sullivan didn't think much of these developments. In a March 1896 essay entitled "The Tall Office Building Artistically Considered" (originally published in *Lippincott's* and reprinted in *Kindergarten Chats & Other Writings*; New York: Wittenborn, 1947), he argued passionately against what he considered an overdependence on historical European sources. This suspicion of history was to be even further emphasized later by modern architects who went so far as to drop history courses from the architectural program of study when they became established in a number of leading American learning centers. According to Sullivan the skyscraper should express "American impulses," and in many ways, his own work was the embodiment of an even earlier statement on the art of skyscraper design.

In an 1894 article in the widely read architectural periodical, the *American Architect and Building News*, John Moser, a Fellow of the American Institute of Architects, wrote, "the office building of the future will be useful and practical. It will tell exactly what it is and pretend to be nothing else. It will be elegant by virtue of its proportions, its refined simplicity and a skillful handling of its few ornamental forms." This is a good description of the work of Sullivan and even more prophetic in terms of what was to come. "Elegance" and "refined simplicity" seem highly appropriate descriptions of many of the skyscrapers built in American cities in the 1950s and 1960s.

Other important buildings of the Chicago School were the Reliance Building designed by Charles B. Atwood of Daniel Burnham and Company in 1894 and a number of structures by Holabird and Roche. The Reliance Building contained one of the first examples of the "Chicago window," a three-part protruding bay which, while designed to capture more space, light, and rental income, through the design skill of Atwood became a central component in a facade of extraordinary lightness and transparency. In many ways this building anticipated such glass skyscrapers of the mid–twentieth century as the Seagram Building and Lever House.

William Holabird and Martin Roche also helped Chicago lay claim to being the premier city of the skyscraper. Among their notable structures were the Marquette Building of 1894, the Gage Building on South Michigan Avenue, whose facade was done by Sullivan in 1899, and the Ayer Building done in 1900, with the steel frame reflected in the grid pattern of the facade, also remarkable in its resemblance to the later International Style.

Chicago Tribune Competition

The *Chicago Tribune* Competition of 1922 was a seminal event in twentieth-century architecture. More than 250 architects from around the world entered in search of the $50,000 prize money and the chance to design a skyscraper that would stand in downtown Chicago. The winning design, by John Mead Howells and Raymond Hood, was a Gothic tower topped by a circle of buttresses that still stands on North Michigan Avenue. The incredible range of proposals submitted for the competition fully justified the label "eclectic" for this period in the development of the sky-scraper.

The second-place design by Eliel Saarinen evoked such strong positive responses that the architect emigrated from Finland to the United States. It consisted of a stepped-back central tower that had some of the characteristics of Hugh Ferris's drawings exploring the possibilities of the massing of skyscrapers under New York's 1920 zoning laws (Move #7). Other entries included many Gothic-style buildings and several by Walter Gropius, Adolf Meyer, and the Dutch architects B. Bijvoet and J. Duiker, which were of a decidedly "modern" bent. There was even a building by Adolf Loos whose central tower was literally in the shape of a Doric column. Heinrich Mossdorf of Germany proposed a vertical structure topped by the torso of an Indian with arms and tomahawk held high as something of a light tower. So much for American pretensions of moving up in the world.

Modern and Modernistic

The next period in the development of the skyscraper was the era of the glass box, although it has been pointed out that the buildings put up in this time can be divided between "modern-istic," Art Moderne or Deco, and "modern."

"Modernistic" was a richly decorative style attached to conservative and hedonistic values, according to Ada Louise Huxtable. Among the modernistic buildings of note are the Irving Trust Building, by Voorhees, Gmelen and Walker, completed in 1931; the Chanin Building by Sloan and Robertson done in 1929; the Richfield Building by Morgan, Walls and Clement, which was built between 1928 and 1930 and has since been demolished; and that ultimate Art Deco object, the Chrysler Building, done by William Van Allen in 1930. Except for the Richfield Building which was in Los Angeles, the other three structures are located in New York City. This trend pretty much came to a halt with the onset of the Depression and cleared the way for modern architecture to dominate the next era of construction. For many observers of the architectural scene, this commitment to the skyscraper was one of the central characteristics of this movement.

Modern architecture was largely brought to the United States from Europe by people such as Mies van der Rohe and Walter Gropius, although a number of Americans, particularly Louis Sullivan and Frank Lloyd Wright, made significant contributions and anticipated many of its later developments. It's been characterized by a minimal aesthetic and a belief in mass production, functionalism, and social progress through architecture. Le Corbusier exemplified these beliefs in works such as Radiant City (Move #10).

Early modern, or International Style, was first introduced in the United States by a show at New York's Museum of Modern Art, where the curators were Philip Johnson and Henry Russel Hitchcock. Two examples of this style were the McGraw-Hill Building by Hood, Godley and Fouilhoux built in 1931 and the Philadelphia Society Building. At the heart of many of the buildings that followed these early efforts was an aesthetic that has been summarized in the words of Mies van der Rohe: "Less is more."

The Seagram Building (Move #15), which was done in collaboration with Philip Johnson in 1958, and the Lever House (see Figure 10), done by the firm of Skidmore, Owings and Merrill in 1952, are generally considered two of the finest examples of this sentiment. However, the American architect Louis Kahn was fond of saying he thought of the Seagram Building as a beautiful lady in corsets, because while its architects were always proclaiming the virtues of structural honesty and openness, in reality so much of the structure was hidden.

Postmodernism

According to one of its chief advocates, Charles Jencks, postmodernism in architecture began on July 15, 1972, with the destruction of the Pruitt-Igoe housing complex in St. Louis (Move #11). While it's certainly something of an oversimplification to try to pinpoint precisely the beginnings of any complex trend or movement, it definitely *is* the case that modern architecture came under increasing criticism in the late 1960s and early 1970s. Both its social program and its aesthetic were attacked. Mies van der Rohe said, "less is more," and Robert Venturi (Move #9) offered the rejoinder, "less is a bore," in an important book published in 1966 entitled *Complexity and Contradiction in Architecture* (New York: Museum of Modern Art, 1966).

Postmodern architects reintroduced decorative elements, historical references, and context as important features in skyscraper design. They argued that in their reformist zeal modern architects

FIGURE 10: The Lever House. *(Museum of the City of New York)*

had filled the cities of the world with sterile glass boxes that in no way met people's emotional needs. There was also an attempt by postmodernists to deal with issues of meaning when critics argued that architects had to recognize social needs and not just concern themselves with formal issues such as Le Corbusier's trinity of light, space, and air.

In *Complexity and Contradiction in Architecture*, Robert Venturi (Move #9) expressed some of the spirit of these new developments. "As an architect, I try to be guided not by habit but by a conscious sense of the past, by precedent thoughtfully considered. . . . I am for richness of meaning rather than clarity of meaning, for the implicit function as well as the explicit function."

And Robert Stern wrote, in "Doubles of Post Modernism" (*Harvard Architectural Digest*, Spring 1980):

> Traditional post-modernism recognizes both the discursive and the expressive meaning of formal language. It recognizes the language of form as communicating sign as well as infra-referential symbol: that is to say, it deals with both physical and associational experience, with the work of art as an act of "presentation" and "representation." It rejects the idea of a single style in favor of a view that acknowledges the existence of many styles . . . each with its own meanings.

Richness rather than clarity, a conscious sense of the past, physical and associational experience, and the acknowledgment of the existence of many styles has characterized postmodern architecture.

Significant postmodern skyscrapers, such as the A.T.&T. Building in New York, completed by Philip Johnson in 1984, and the Portland Public Services Building, finished by Michael Graves in 1982 in Portland, Oregon, have typically emphasized a much greater range of colors, textures, and profiles than their more austere modern predecessors. Both buildings also make abundant use of historical details and decorative elements in contrast to the "moderns" for whom "history" and "decoration" were taboo (see Figure 11).

If you look up at the skyscrapers around you, and instead of the traditional rectangular form with a flat top, you see almost every possible variation on this theme, including pyramids and,

FIGURE 11: Architect's drawing of the Public Services Building in Portland, Oregon. *(Courtesy of Michael Graves, Architects)*

in the case of the A.T.&T. Building, what has been called a Chippendale highboy top, then you're almost certainly viewing examples of postmodernism. This is the "postmodernly adorned end" that the title of this Move makes reference to. In his book *Skyscrapers, Skycities* (New York: Rizzoli, 1980), Christopher Jencks pays particular attention to this element of design.

Among the many important examples of these types of skyscrapers in American cities are the Pennzoil Building in Houston, designed by Johnson and Burgee; the United Nations Plaza Hotel in New York, by Roche Dinkeloo; 101 Park Avenue, by Eli Attia Architects; City Center in Fort Worth, by Paul Rudolph; the Embarcadero Center in San Francisco, by John Portman; the I.D.S. Center in Minneapolis, by Johnson and Burgee; One South Wacker, by Helmut Jahn in Chicago; the Fountain Plaza Project in Portland, Oregon, by Zimmer, Gunsel, Frasca Partnership; Kohn Pedersen Fox's headquarters for Proctor & Gamble in Cincinnati; and the Humana Building in Louisville by Michael Graves.

Postmodern skyscrapers often take into account context by the stance they take toward the surrounding streets and buildings. Rather than set themselves apart by being raised on Le Corbusier's pilotis or ignoring the street entirely through the use of small parks and plazas (Move #15), they often orient themselves directly toward the street and make reference to nearby structures in both their overall form and specific details.

"Form ever follows function," wrote Louis Sullivan, and Mies van der Rohe went even further when he said, "without function there is no such thing as form." With the advent of the pluralism of postmodernism, the form of the contemporary skyscraper now, more than ever before, follows a whole host of factors. With the work of such groups as Arquitectonica and the completion of the Metro-Dade Cultural Center by Philip Johnson, with its Spanish motifs of tile roof, stuccoed walls, and wrought iron balconies, it can even be said once again some 320 years after the founding of St. Augustine by Spain (Move #5) that "form follows, among other things, frijoles."

ADDITIONAL READING

Goldberger, Paul. *The Skyscraper.* New York: Alfred A. Knopf, 1982.

Huxtable, Ada Louise. *The Tall Building Artistically Reconsidered.* New York: Pantheon Books, 1982.

Jencks, Christopher. *Skyscrapers, Skycities.* New York: Rizzoli, 1980. In this interesting photo essay, Jencks examines high-rise structures through an analysis of three metaphors—"skyprickers," "skyscrapers," and "skycities."

Stimpson, Miriam. *Field Guide to Landmarks of Modern Architecture in the U.S.* Englewood Cliffs, NJ: Prentice-Hall, 1985. In this directory of hundreds of significant structures in American architecture of the last hundred years or so are many of the most important skyscrapers. Important information about location and times when the structures can be visited is also provided for many of the examples.

Venturi, Robert. *Complexity and Contradiction in Architecture.* New York: Museum of Modern Art, 1966.

MOVE #13

Construction Site

"What Are All Those People Doing Down There in that Hole in the Ground?"

THIS MOVE HAS BECOME SO COMMON THAT IT'S AN INTEGRAL PART of the American city scene, a group of people standing around looking down into a construction site at all the activity going on in a hole in the ground. These "sidewalk superintendents" are such regular parts of city life that they're even accommodated by portholes and windows cut through the fencing that surrounds the site. It's ironic, especially for the architects and engineers responsible for its design, that this is often the only time in its life when the building attracts significant amounts of attention from the general public. Once the construction has been completed, it's rare that anyone except someone with particular personal or professional interests, potential tenants, or perhaps architectural critics will examine the building with any of the intensity that is evident at hundreds of construction sites in American cities on any given day.

The only exception to this is that form of urban deconstruction that was favored long before the word became popular in philosophical and literary circles. Estimates of viewers range well up into the thousands for those occasions when major city buildings are being dismantled. In his book *Unbuilding* (London: Hamish Hamilton, 1980), David Macaulay develops the fantasy of taking apart the Empire State Building after it's been purchased by Middle Eastern oil interests who want to rebuild it in the desert as

175

their world headquarters. This interesting work both reveals a good deal about the structure of skyscrapers (Move #12) and suggests a number of other strategies for understanding these kinds of structures, not the least of which are taking the thing apart and imagining it within a totally different context.

Why do people feel so compelled to look at these construction sites? Psychologists have labeled this behavior "stimulus seeking," which simply refers to curiosity and a liking for the visual action and movement that the workers generate as they begin excavating and laying the foundation. Even newborn infants, when given the choice, prefer looking at drawings that are more complex and asymmetrical than those that are simple and regular.

People also desire to have impact on the city and somehow change it through their own action. These are the same impulses that motivate the suburbanite to cultivate a lawn (Move #9), the entire nation to love its automobiles (Move #20), and people who change dwellings to make "nesting moves" when they occupy their new home (Move #11).

"If I hang a picture on the wall and even change some of the colors with paint, then the place is somehow different as a result of my being there, and I possess it in a way I didn't before I made the changes" is what many people engaged in these activities seem to be saying. It's one way of dealing with the paradox of the "inhuman human creation" (see Part IV)—the city as all powerful—even though we know that in reality, other people, just like us, created it.

The city of what the psychologist Robert Sommer has called "hard architecture" rarely affords an opportunity for direct manipulation or modification. Materials such as steel and reinforced concrete can't be changed by the average person without bulldozers, dynamite, cutting torches, and so on, and the rules that govern the operation of most public places generally forbid making these changes. Even with the advent of some participatory design procedures where users have some input into the design process, most desires to modify places such as parks, plazas, streets, and subways are not usually indulged in by the average citizen unless he or she is in the role of architect or designer called in to participate professionally.

That individual impulses and whims cannot be catered to is an understandable but lamentable situation. It seems that the impulse to affect one's surroundings is a strong and deep one.

In a classic article titled "Motivation Reconsidered: The Concept of Competence" (*Psychology Review*, 1959), the psychologist R. W. White argued that if people didn't have enough of these kinds of interactions with the world, where somehow their presence in the situation made a difference, they were later more likely to encounter psychological problems. In conversations, for example, people certainly want to believe that those with whom they're conversing are actually modifying their talk as a result of what it is they're hearing, and once they believe that this isn't true, and what is going on are two independent monologues rather than a dialogue, there's a tendency to end the encounter. Perhaps we're intrigued with the worker at the construction site because it's clear that they're having an impact and engaging in something of a dialogue, but in order to more completely understand the nature of this dialogue, there's some additional information you should have about that construction site.

NOTES

A Quick Word on Soil

On the most basic level, people are digging a hole in the ground. Since in a short time—anywhere from one to two years in the case of most high rises—this soil will help support a tremendously heavy building, the question is, what kind of soil is it and how much weight can it support?

In nature there are rarely soils of a single composition. They generally appear as mixtures and in layers of varying thickness. Engineers grade soil according to their particle size, and this size increases from silt to clay, to sand, to gravel, and finally to rock. In well-graded mixtures, the spaces between the larger particles are entirely filled by smaller particles. Sand fills the gaps between particles of gravel, clay between particles of sand, and silt between particles of clay.

"Rock" will support anywhere from seven to one hundred tons of weight per square foot, depending on whether it's a hard and sound substance like granite or something softer like broken bed rock or compaction shale. A gravel-sand mixture will support from three to seven tons per square foot, with fine sand supporting one to three tons per square foot, and clay supporting a half to four tons per square foot. Sometimes the carrying capacity of soil can be altered through chemical means. The soil under the twin Trade Towers in New York was consolidated by a special chemical process that was devised by an Italian company so that it could more easily carry the weight of the structures above it.

Why Foundations at All?

Foundation costs may reach 10 percent or more of the building, and according to Mario Salvadori, a renowned scholar of building structure, "from the viewpoint of economy and usage, foundations are a necessary evil." What they're basically trying to do is maintain rigid body stability and minimize motions of the building as a whole. When a tall building is acted upon by a strong wind and is not properly rooted in the ground or balanced by its own weight, it may topple over without breaking up. Engineers use the phrase "unstable in rotation." This is particularly true of tall, narrow buildings, as can be demonstrated by setting a slim cardboard box on a rough surface to prevent it from sliding and then blowing on it. The danger of rotational instability is also present when a building isn't well balanced and is supported on soil of uneven resistance. If the soil under the building settles unevenly, the building may rotate, as the Leaning Tower of Pisa still does, and may eventually topple over.

Excavation

Before construction can begin, a good deal of soil at the site must be removed. This process of excavation serves several purposes. It enables the foundation to be built on soil below the surface, which is usually more stable, and it reduces the distance that any required piles or piers have to be driven or drilled.

When the soil to be excavated isn't hard—clay, sand, or weathered rock—big front-loaded shovels can scoop it out and load it on trucks for removal. Solid rock must be dynamited. The drilled holes in which the sticks of dynamite have been embedded are covered with mattresses of heavy chain mesh to contain the flying debris.

If the excavation is to be deep, and its sides are vertical, then the entire site has to be first enclosed by a retaining wall to make sure that the sides of the excavation won't cave in. This is usually done by driving steel piles, called "soldiers," into the earth at ten-foot intervals around the boundary of the excavation and then

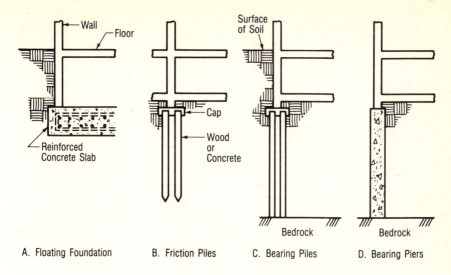

A. Floating Foundation   B. Friction Piles   C. Bearing Piles   D. Bearing Piers

FIGURE 12: Four types of foundations.

placing "breast boards" horizontally behind them to keep the earth from falling back into the excavation.

Types of Foundations

There are essentially four different types of foundations (see Figure 12): floating foundations, those on friction piles, those on bearing piles, and those on piers. A floating foundation is a continuous spread foundation where the entire building sits on a reinforced concrete slab. This type of foundation is used when soil conditions are unstable and when the area of the site is large enough to carry the weight of the structure and any additional live loads—such as occupants, furniture, equipment, and so on—that will be found in the completed building. Because of the tremendous weights involved, floating foundations are almost never used for high-rise buildings.

Friction piles consist of vertical shafts of steel, reinforced concrete, or, in earlier times, even trees stripped of their bark, which are driven into the ground by pile drivers. The weight is supported against the entire length of the shafts as they sit in friction against the soil that holds them. Since there are often hundreds and on occasion even thousands of piles, this has the same effect as distributing the weight across a much more extensive horizontal area.

It's hard to imagine that friction itself can exert such pressure, but to get some idea of the forces involved in this situation, try pushing your fingers down into sand while keeping them vertical and rigid.

Bearing piles are those that go all the way down to bedrock or another substance such as clay, which is capable of supporting the weight of the high rise. While a friction pile transmits the load along its length, a bearing pile is intended to transmit its load through the bottom to firm soil. Bearing piles are therefore much longer, some of them reaching lengths of more than 200 feet. They usually consist of either hollow steel tubes that are filled with concrete and called "pipe piles" or steel beams whose cross sections resemble an H. Both friction piles and bearing piles are generally driven in groups that are then capped by reinforced concrete slabs. They can be thought of as continuations of the building's structure beneath the ground.

Piers operate like bearing piles by transmitting most of their load through the base onto a firm bearing material, but they're constructed by removing a column of earth and replacing it with concrete. Because a single pier is used in place of a cluster of piles, it requires no cap.

Developments above the Ground

The interesting thing about the structure of the modern sky-scraper, most often a steel-frame construction (Move #1), is that the system designed to carry the gravity loads to earth and the system designed to provide resistance to wind forces are two separate structural systems. According to Mario Salvadori (*Why Buildings Stand Up: The Strength of Architecture*; New York: Norton, 1980), "this simple concept gave rise to buildings with relatively flexible exterior frames and an inner core of stiff wind bracing frames, inside of which ran the elevators and many of the pipes and ducts of the mechanical systems."

The strength of the structural materials needed to build a floor is the same whether the floor is the first or the hundredth, since each floor carries more or less the same loads, but the columns must carry the weight of all the floors above them. As the building increases in height, the wind forces on it increase with the square of the height. The Sears Tower, twice as high as the Woolworth Building, must resist wind effects four times as large as those that hit the Woolworth Building (Move #12).

In most high rises, columns are made of steel elements bolted together, while floors consist of reinforced concrete slabs poured on ribbed steel plates resting on steel beams. The skeleton of the building, column and slab, usually grows at the rate of a complete floor every three or four days.

There are two final things to keep in mind as you watch the amazing erector-set drama of modern high-rise construction. First, since all such buildings today are constructed using "fast track" (Move #21) methods, often the design of the building hasn't been completed at the start of construction. And second, construction sites, by presenting the building unadorned without its outer skin and thereby giving you direct visual access to its growth process, are unique opportunities for gaining a greater understanding of how the thing works.

In the early 1920s, Mies van der Rohe sought to explore the aesthetic possibilities of this fact by proposing two skyscrapers sheathed entirely in glass. These were among the first such proposals and allowed Mies to articulate further a concern for structural expressiveness that was to become one of the credos of modernism (Move #12). According to this school of thought, a building should visibly reveal its structure, and by looking at it, you should be able to tell how the thing is put together.

The Image of Clay

The observations made at a construction site, particularly at the beginning of laying the foundation when the earth itself is being excavated, strongly suggest an image that can be quite helpful in a wide range of situations in urban America. Think of the city as something made of malleable stuff like clay, that allows and even invites touching, handling, and manipulating. Change becomes an immediate possibility, and suddenly a broad range of people are given an opportunity to engage in a direct dialogue with the city in a manner similar to that of the bulldozer at the beginning of this Move. The image of clay focuses on the plasticity of the city, the possibility of change, and the processes with which that change can be accomplished.

ADDITIONAL READING

Macaulay, David. *Underground*. Boston: Houghton Mifflin, 1976. This is a wonderful visual guide to the world which exists beneath the streets of the modern city.

Mackay, Donald A. *The Building of Manhattan*. New York: Harper & Row, 1987.

Salvadori, Mario. *Why Buildings Stand Up: The Strength of Architecture*. New York: Norton, 1980.

Salvadori, Mario, and Robert Heller. *Structure in Architecture*. Englewood Cliffs, NJ: Prentice-Hall, 1963.

IV

THE
URBANITE

THE EIGHT MOVES IN THIS SECTION ARE DESIGNED TO help the reader gain a greater understanding of how and why people do what they do in cities. Consider this a field guide for looking at other members of the species in their natural habitats. The numbers and density of the city (Move #1) and the fact that American cities in particular are generally made up of people from a wide variety of racial and ethnic backgrounds (Move #25) make these places wonderful settings for people-watching. It's an activity we all seem to enjoy and any reflection on why this is so generally reveals three different kinds of concerns.

"Interest," "safety," and "identity" can serve as convenient labels. What is meant by "interest" are those situations where the principal motivation is a direct concern with the person or persons being watched. That is, all those occasions where we find ourselves looking at people because somehow the way they look or what it is they're doing interests us. It amuses, intrigues, captures, and captivates in a way that absolutely demands that we keep looking. Looking at sporting events is almost a pure case of this kind of motivation, but there are also many city scenes that have something of this quality. Consider the patron of the sidewalk café or the worker on a lunch break sitting on a park bench, both of whom are observing the passing flow of traffic for no other reason than it interests them to look at it. They don't believe they'll find out anything useful about themselves or the world by people-watching, but this doesn't diminish the pleasures of looking. The city as much as television (Move #19), by providing so many opportunities to just look, has made voyeurs of us all.

And then there are those scenes where "safety" is a concern. Cities are often perceived as dangerous places in both a physical sense—the place of violence and aggression—and a psychological sense. Psychological danger can range from the minor discomforts of social embarrassment (you wear the wrong costume to a particular event because you've misinterpreted the invitation) to the terrors of a complete psychological breakdown. We watch other people to protect ourselves from both these kinds of danger. This is "people-watching" to avoid the suspicious stranger and not be mugged and also to understand what other people are doing so that we can coordinate our behavior with theirs and thereby avoid behaving inappropriately and somehow get into trouble. From a social psychological perspective a good deal of mental health is doing the right thing in the right place—waiting for the bus at the bus stop and not at the family breakfast table in the kitchen—and watching other people can often help in this process. People provide us with clues on how to behave in specific situations and thereby make them psychologically safe for us.

Finally there is the self-knowledge to be gained by looking at others whom most of us regard, in many essential ways, as similar to ourselves. I look at you to find out about me because, just like me, you also eat, sleep, and worry about taxes. George Herbert Mead, one of the founding figures of modern sociology, pointed out that in some ways looking at other people is really the only way we have of looking at ourselves. He believed that these kinds of observations were essential in forming a self-concept. The *looking glass self* was the term he used to describe this process. Using the term *identity* to label one set of motives or reasons people have for watching other people is not meant to imply that whenever someone is just hanging out looking, what's really on his or her mind is some great quest of self-discovery. What the term *is* meant to imply is that somewhere in much of the activity of people-watching is an awareness that we're observing beings similar to ourselves, and as such, this activity can be self-revelatory.

Central to this section of the book are two images—that of the crowded room (Move #2) and the theater with performances being given on a stage (Move #14)—and three paradoxes. First there's the paradox of "the close stranger and the distant friend." In the city we're often surrounded by strangers, while our friends can be some distance away (Move #2). A lot of urban behavior is devoted to distancing the close stranger (Moves #15, #16, #18) and getting closer to the distant friend (Moves #19, #20).

Second, is the paradox of "the known and the unknown." While the city is traditionally the place where knowledge is gathered and stored—in museums, libraries, research facilities, and universities—many of the everyday things that comprise city life are themselves often not understood by large segments of the urban population. Certainly more of us know less about how our homes were built and where our lunches came from than did all those earlier people who built their own dwellings and hunted and gathered for lunch (Move #4).

Why do I need to know how my tuna fish sandwich arrived on the scene if I wasn't in any way involved with the process? I didn't catch the fish, can it, or ship it. I'm not even sure what the damn thing looks like, or how they caught it—hooks and lines, nets, or harpoons? And that's just the sandwich I had for lunch. What about all those incredibly complex electrical and electronic systems (Moves #12, #19) that aren't open to direct visual inspection no matter how hard one tries to look? It's certainly easier to figure out how the gears in a mechanical clock work than it is to understand the functioning of electronic chronometers. The complexity of modern images of time (Move #2) is more than matched by the complexity of the instruments used to measure it.

In a society dominated by specialists who invariably know more and more about less and less, a lot of urban activity is devoted to trying to understand the surrounding objects and events (Moves #16, #17). In a sense, all of *City Moves* is an attempt to deal with this paradox and make the unknown known. For thousands of years, philosophers and social scientists have argued that this search for meaning and comprehension is a basic human motive.

It is *the* basic motive, according to those of the cognitive tradition. Life is a search for order and understanding, and while this knowledge clearly has some survival value, many would argue that as a species we have a fascination for knowledge and information for its own sake. Even when we're not sure how, or if, the stuff is going to be used, it rarely ceases to interest and intrigue. Many of those in the cognitive tradition believe that the human central nervous system was designed to process information in just as unequivocal a fashion as the respiratory system has been designed to process oxygen. "More input" is the way the robot hero of the movie *Short Circuit* put it.

And finally, there's the paradox of the "inhuman human creation." While we know in our heads that the city was designed and built by people similar to us, we often experience it as if it were some monumental fact of nature, something like an ocean or a chain of mountains that seem to say, "I was here before you, I'll be here after you, and there's no way you can ever really influence or control me." On occasion, things like mountains and oceans (Move #3) are even used as metaphors to describe the city as viewed from above (Move #1). A lot of Moves in the city are made with the goal of generating a feeling of control over that which is often experienced as all-powerful. These include a fascination with construction sites (Move #13), driving that wonderfully responsive machine, the automobile (Move #20), and using the dwelling place as a means of personal expression (Move #11).

In his study of people's behavior in small urban parks and plazas (Move #15), William Whyte observed that people often moved their chairs, even if it was only an inch or so, just so they could somehow have impact on the setting and participate, even if in a very minimal sense, in somehow creating their own place.

These two images and three paradoxes can serve as the beginnings of a theory of urban behavior, a framework that can be useful in helping the reader integrate different observations and steer decisions about such important people-watching matters as what, where, when, and how to look. As the noted social psychologist Kurt Lewin once commented, "There's nothing as useful as a good theory." Without one, we'd be overwhelmed by the complexity of most people-watching situations.

Before making any of the Moves in Part IV, it's probably best to take another look at Move #2, and then, because of its central place in thinking about urban behavior, look at Move #14. Move #15 deals with people in small public parks and plazas, and Move #16 concerns itself with some of the dynamics of behavior on a downtown street. These Moves deal with two of the readily accessible public places that make the city such a good setting for people-watching: streets and plazas. Move #20 suggests a drive through the city as a method for understanding certain aspects of urban life, while Moves #17, #18, #19, and #21 invite reflection on the themes of "navigation," "eyes in the city," "technology, friendship, and place," and the role of "speed" in the city.

MOVE #14

Show Time, Role Changes, and the Theatrics of City Life

THE IDEA OF LIFE AS THEATER HAS BEEN AROUND AT LEAST SINCE the time of William Shakespeare, and the popularity of the metaphor has increased in direct proportion to the status of the acting profession itself. In the Elizabethan England of Shakespeare's time, performers were held in very low esteem and were relegated to the bottom of society. They were generally regarded as rogues and knaves, unfit to associate with decent society. In twentieth-century America, from 1981 to 1989 a former actor occupied one of the most powerful positions on the planet, that of the presidency.

In a society that has so totally integrated performance into everyday life (Move #19), a blurring of the line between reality and its theatrical representation seems both inevitable and lamentable. Witness the confusion inherent in trying to feed starving Africans and Americans with rock concerts and hand-holding marathons or having actors who portray narcotics detectives in television series sharing their insights on drugs with us on late-night television talk shows. Which is the more "real" performance? Is it Robert Blake the actor or Barretta the detective? Mike Hammer the detective or Stacy Keach the concerned citizen? David Toma the narcotics detective or David Toma the television personality? And think about Oliver North and Senate investigating committees. What are the implications of President Reagan's comment that the American people were getting tired of the show

189

and were switching to other channels? Should these performances be viewed as education, entertainment, or news? And are there any differences among these categories?

While confusion between life as it is portrayed on television and life as it is lived out in the world often contributes to the very problems the people who orchestrate the events described above are trying to solve, the strategy of thinking about city life as if it were theater can be a useful one. This is particularly true in urban America, where strangers don't have ready access to "back stage" and other performances, and it's easier to engage in what Erving Goffman (Move #15) has called "impression management," the structuring of a given performance so that a desired impression will be created in the eyes of others.

In the language of social science, a "role" is a set of behaviors that go along with occupying a position in a social structure, all those things we think, say, feel, and do in the many parts we play in life—that of "man" or "woman," "daughter" or "son," "worker," "commuter," "friend," and on and on. One thing about modern city life is that there are so many of these performances, and they're often quite different from one another.

Robert E. Park, one of the founding figures of the Chicago school of urban sociology, believed that this would create a situation where people belonged to so many different groups and therefore had so many crossed loyalties that it would be impossible for any central authority to enforce uniform standards of behavior. This in turn would lead to the behavioral innovation and social change for which cities are so well known.

Quite a bit of what might be called "psychological nimbleness" is needed to make the move from one performance to another. Think of some of the shifts required to move from the role of "tenant" or "homeowner" to that of "commuter," to one of the occupational roles that most people spend a good part of their day in. What would the consequences be of treating coworkers at an employment scene with the same blend of detachment and assertiveness that is usually displayed when commuting between home and work? Or of speaking to a close friend in a tone of voice similar to the one taken when giving directions to a stranger on a city street?

This Move requires concentrating rather directly on some of the many performances all urbanites give on a regular basis. If city life is theater, then what would a list of the different roles you play in the course of a week look like, and even more significantly, what are the different performances composed of? That is, when you're in a particular role, what sorts of actions, thoughts, feelings, and attitudes are expected of you? And what about the scripts, props, and costumes? Where do the scripts come from, and exactly how are the props and costumes used?

NOTES

In his *Ten Books on Architecture*, the Roman architect Vitruvius proposed some interesting parallels between the actual physical stage and the kinds of behaviors that took place on it. According to him,

> There are three kinds of scenes, one called tragic, second the comic, third, the satiric. Tragic scenes are delineated with columns, pediments, statues and other objects suited to kings; comic scenes exhibit private dwellings, with balconies and views representing rows of windows, after the manner of ordinary dwellings; satiric scenes are decorated with trees, caverns, mountains; and other rustic objects delineated in landscape style.

While these relationships don't always strictly hold, there usually is some attempt to match the stage with the type of performance to be given on it. Even today, some 2,000 years after Vitruvius, officials responsible for staging the dramas of government seem to have a penchant for columns, pediments, and "other objects suitable for kings"—witness the traditional state capital and large sections of Washington, D.C.

Some Ways to Classify Roles

Performances people are forced to give because of inexorable fate, such as those associated with age and gender, are called "ascribed" roles, while those engaged in because of some sort of accomplishment are called "achieved" roles. In this culture, occupational roles are a good example of the latter. It's also useful to distinguish among roles devoted to family and kinship, those involved with gathering provisions, recreational roles, those concerned with neighboring, and traffic roles. This last set is made up of those performances given as we move from place to place. The three that come most readily to mind are those of "tourist," "pedestrian," and "commuter."

Although tourists are usually disdained by locals and often by the performers themselves (being a tourist is a clear indication that "you're not from around here," and hence everything is a mystery, even something as trivial as where to go for a good meal), it's not a bad strategy to adopt the role of tourist occasionally, even in those cities with which you are familiar. The subsequent dropping of "filters" (Move #16) and openness to experience can be both enjoyable and informative. This is exactly opposite to the tack that many of us take when we really *are* tourists and do our utmost to blend into the context and seem like a native. Because of the immense popularity of the automobile (Move #9), the role of the "pedestrian" may be dying out. In some relatively affluent urban and suburban neighborhoods to be on foot is to invite at least cursory interest by the police of the same sort as any other ancient creature such as a dinosaur or an alligator would command. At the same time, the role of "commuter" is burgeoning.

Entrances and Exits

Generally, achieved roles are separated from one another in time and space, and as a consequence, those architectural elements that mark the edges of areas (Move #1) are quite important for their behavioral significance. It's here that exits and entrances are made, whether to an indoor room or an outdoor plaza (Move #15). Not only does the lobby of a large public building serve as the transition place between inside and outside, but it also assists the performers in making the changes required from those behaviors needed on the street to those necessary for the roles to be played inside. The tradition of carrying the bride across the threshold is testimony to the importance of these places. In *The Temple and the House* (London: Routledge & Kegan Paul, 1964), Lord Raglan noted that Teutons, Finns, Syrians, Egyptians, and Persians considered the threshold of the home a special place not to be stepped on, but, over.

Organismic Involvement

Different roles require different amounts of focus. *Organismic involvement* is the technical term. It refers to the amount of energy thrown into a given performance. The range required is quite wide. Some performances can be given in a fashion so automatic it's frightening. Everyone has had the experience of driving a much traveled route, totally caught up in a fantasy world far removed from the actual scene. What's amazing is the safe arrival at the intended destination without ever having once consciously registered any of the signs and landmarks with which one usually navigates (Move #17). Then there are those performances that require such high levels of involvement that at the end of the scene it's often difficult to slip out of the role. The performance doesn't quite seem to be over when it's over—so there's a stop for a drink before going on to other roles.

Front Stage and Back Stage

A giant of American architecture, Louis Sullivan (Move #12), wrote, "A building is an act, a staging of life." "Role theory" is an elaboration of this sentiment, and in his book *Presentation of Self in Everyday Life* (New York: Doubleday, 1959), Erving Goffman made extensive use of the ideas of "front stage" and "back stage." As in traditional theater, the former refers to places where roles are actually played, while the latter designates settings where these roles are prepared—those less visible places where props are gathered, lines rehearsed, and performances polished. In *Down and Out in Paris and London* (New York: Harcourt Brace Jovanovich, 1933), George Orwell described the movement from one traditional back stage, the restaurant kitchen, to the front stage of the dining room:

> It is an instructive sight to see a waiter going into a hotel dining room. As he passes the door a sudden change comes over him. The set of his shoulders alters; all the dirt and hurry and irritation have dropped off in an instant. He glides over the carpet with a solid priest-like air. I remember our assistant maitre d'hotel, a fiery Italian, pausing at the dining room door to address his apprentice who had broken a bottle of wine. Shaking his fist above his head he yelled (luckily the door was more or less sound-

proof), *"Tue me fais*—do you call yourself a waiter you young bastard? You a waiter! You're not fit to scrub floors in the brothel your mother came from. *Maquereau!"* Words failing him, he turned to the door, and as he opened it, he delivered a final insult in the same manner as Squire Western in *Tom Jones.*

Then he entered the dining room and sailed across it dish in hand, graceful as a swan. Ten seconds later he was bowing reverently to a customer. And you could not help thinking, as you saw him bow and smile, with that benign smile of the trained waiter, that the customer was put to shame by having such an aristocrat to serve him.

"Front stage" and "back stage" can also refer to the same place at different times. The literal front stage of the theater is transformed into a back stage between acts by lowering the curtain, just as the front stage of a public plaza is transformed into a back stage when the police cordon it off to prepare for an important civic ceremony. Or the back stage of the bedroom is converted to a front stage when a guest is invited to inspect the new wallpaper or etchings.

In some settings there's a fairly complete separation between front stage and back stage, while in others, the separation is less severe. The classic French restaurant where the preparation and consumption of food are treated as if they had nothing to do with each other, and patrons are rarely invited back stage, compared to sushi bars and pizzerias where part of the product being purchased is access to the visual drama of food preparation, a concern for both the process and the product.

In a like manner, much traditional architecture hides service elements such as air ducts, elevator shafts, and electrical conduits, while a number of recent structures, generally designated as postmodern (Move #12), often use these typically back stage elements as prominent features of the design. The Pompidou Center by Piano and Rogers in Paris and the Hyatt Regency Hotel in Atlanta by John Portman are two prominent examples of this approach.

And it has also been argued by a number of media scholars that the profound effect on society that television has, is caused to a large extent by the breaking down of traditional separations between front and back stage areas (Move #19). It's harder to have heroes and somehow easier to believe that the Queen of England must use the bathroom just like the rest of us, in an era when people such as Robin Leach and Barbara Walters actually bring the fixtures into our living rooms through the magic of television.

Props and Costumes

And then there are the props and costumes. One of the implications of the dramaturgical metaphor, thinking about city life as if it were theater, is that whatever other function an object may serve, whether it's a watch to tell time or a building to shelter thousands of workers, it's also a communication device that sends messages out about appropriate behaviors and perceptions. Props, sets, and costumes support performances by sending out messages about how to interpret what is going on.

Why exactly do city people dress the way they do? What function does a pair of shoes serve beyond protection from the elements, other people, and the surface of the ground? And what sorts of messages are sent out by a particular style or fashion?

The same Doric column that holds up the entablature of the Greek Revival municipal courthouse also tells the citizen how to go about reflecting on the nature of the law and city government. The size of the column, the materials from which it's made, and even the historical origins of the shape are all codes people learn to read. And while some of these readings may be quite simple and direct, almost on the order of "If that thing is so damn big, I must be pretty small," messages are conveyed, and the appropriate reaction is elicited. The performances go on, and city people rarely misinterpret the definition of the situation.

A brief cautionary note: The language of theater used in this Move is not meant to convey any element of sham or duplicity, as is usually implied when it is used in everyday language. When using the metaphor of drama, there's little to be gained in asking if a specific performance is "real." The more interesting questions are about the nature of the performances given. Just how does the city help people slip into and out of appropriate roles, achieve the proper levels of organismic involvement, and generally support the city scenes urbanites want to play?

ADDITIONAL READING

Goffman, Erving. *Presentation of Self in Everyday Life.* New York: Doubleday, 1959.

Sarbin, T. R., and U.C. Allen, "Role Theory." In *Handbook of Social Psychology.* 2d ed., edited by G. Lindzey and E. Aronson. Reading, MA: Addison-Wesley, 1968. Sarbin and Allen offer a definitive exploration of the implications of the dramaturgical metaphor.

MOVE #15

Urban Adagio

or,
Life in Small Parks and Plazas

ONE SETTING THAT IS ALMOST LITERALLY A STAGE IS THE SMALL urban park or plaza. Interestingly enough, at the beginning of urban history, the agora *did* serve as a place for the mounting of theatrical productions. When Greek theater first moved out of the citadel and temple, where it had been housed since the origins of the Greek city, one of the first places it went was to the agora. Here at the secular center of the city, where everything and everyone could be found, dramatic productions were often given. Today the many small parks and plazas found throughout American cities still make good vantage points from which to watch people.

People-watching is a popular activity. In an interesting series of studies in which William Whyte and his colleagues filmed the movement patterns of people in New York's many vest pocket parks and plazas created by zoning incentives (Move #7), people-watching was found to be the single most important factor in determining the success or failure of these places. The most widely used parks and plazas were those that gave people the opportunity to watch other people go about their daily lives in the city.

Among the settings looked at were 77 Water Street, Greenacre Park, Paley Park, and the plazas in front of the Time-Life Building, the Exxon Building, General Motors, Seagram, Penney's, 345 Park Avenue, the Burlington Building, 227 Park Avenue, 630 Fifth Avenue, the CBS Building, the Pan Am Building, I.T.T., Lever House, and 280 Park Avenue. Comparative observations were also made in other cities, including Minneapolis, Philadelphia, Chicago, Los Angeles, Detroit, Boston, Houston, Atlanta, and Salem, Oregon.

Imagine the following scene or go to one of these places to have a look. It's an early afternoon on a sunny spring day, and you're sitting on a ledge in that little plaza you sometimes visit when you have some free time. There are people all over the place alone and in groups. Some are sitting, some standing, and some walking. Are there any patterns to this movement or any regularity as to where people locate themselves in relation to other people? And the plaza itself: Why is it so crowded when others just like it in the same part of town always seem to be so empty?

NOTES

Proxemics

Deciding exactly where the performers will stand on a stage in a theatrical production is called "blocking out a scene." In social science, the word *proxemics* is used to designate the study of how people utilize the small spaces around them. It can be thought of as something like choreography. As every fighter and lover knows, these spaces can be used to structure possibilities, whether a right cross to the head or the caress of a shoulder, and by reading this information, the viewer in the plaza or in any public place in the city such as the street can learn more about exactly what's going on in the situation.

In an early classic, *The Hidden Dimension* (Garden City, NY: Doubleday, 1966), E. T. Hall presented some observations that he regarded as norms for white, middle-class American society. The precise membership of this group is somewhat open to question, but when making observations in places dominated by other ethnic and cultural groups (Move #25), it should be remembered that, all other things being equal, people from Asia and northern Europe prefer greater distance between themselves and others than do people from the Middle East, Latin America, and southern Europe. Much of the perception of the southern European as "pushy" and the northern European as "aloof" is based on these cultural preferences and the "dance" that many members of these groups get into when they interact. The southerner is always advancing to establish the appropriate conversational distance, while the northerner is retreating for the same reason.

According to Hall, "intimate distance" occurs when people engage in activities such as wrestling, making love, and physically comforting each other. In this phase, there is maximal physical contact, and visual detail is blurred. Olfactory sensations increase, and the muscles and skin participate in the act of communication. This is the distance for lovers, and they're often found in these plazas. The interesting thing about them is that rather than seeking out the less visible places they seem to prefer being out on front stage playing to a larger audience, as if this somehow enhances the performance being given.

In 1897, in one of the first social psychological experiments, Norman Triplett found that boys could ride a bicycle and wind a fishing rod faster in the presence of others than when alone. The psychologist Floyd Allport was later to label the phenomenon "social facilitation," and subsequent research has demonstrated that it happens only when the task is simple and well learned. Clearly this is the case for the billing and cooing of plaza love.

In the far phase of "intimate distance," six to eight inches, vision is still distorted, voices are kept to a whisper, and the heat and odor of bodies can be detected. This area lies well within the personal space boundaries of the individual. "Personal space" refers to a bubble of space around people which they consider extensions of themselves. Invitations, often involving ritual gestures, are usually required before these spaces can be entered.

The next category is called "personal distance," from eighteen to thirty inches, and this is the best distance for appreciating the three-dimensional qualities of an object such as the human face. Fine details of the face are readily apparent, and holding the other person is still a possibility. At the far phase, thirty to forty-eight inches, the periphery of "personal space" is reached. In Postscript, "Prologue: The Birth of Architecture," *About the House* (New York: Random House/London: Faber & Faber, 1965), W. H. Auden put it quite succinctly:

> *Some thirty inches from my nose*
> *the frontier of my Person goes*
> *And all the untitled air between*
> *Is private pagus or demesne*

Stranger, unless with bedroom eyes
I beckon you to fraternize
Beware of rudely crossing it
I have no gun but I can spit.

Other people are now at arm's length, and this can be thought of as the limit of immediate physical domination. Voice level is now moderate, head size is perceived as normal, and odor can't usually be detected, except among those people who use colognes or eat strong-smelling foods.

At the close phase of "social distance," four to seven feet, performers on the urban stage are no longer violating one another's personal space. The eye now takes in a far greater proportion of the other person, and there's a tendency to scan the entire face, taking in one feature at a time. This is the distance most generally used by people working together or socializing. According to Hall, attention and interpersonal feelings of comfort are greatest when interaction between strangers takes place at this distance, just beyond the boundary of personal space.

More formal business is transacted at the far phase of "social distance," seven to twelve feet, where the full figure of the partner can be seen, but visual details are lost. "Public distance" is typically encountered only where a literal performance is being given, and the distance is used to mark the boundary between players and audience.

A glance around the plaza during any busy afternoon will reveal examples of all these distances. The lovers sitting on that ledge wrapped around each other are as close as they can get. Next, there are friends and acquaintances standing around conversing, and then strangers trying to maintain greater amounts of distance between themselves and others. Here, the distance serves as a filter to diminish the impact of the "close stranger" (Move #16). "You're not close to me, so don't get close to me."

Tales of Goffman

The sociologist Erving Goffman has been a leading student of behavior in public places. In a series of brilliant works (the one to begin with is *The Presentation of Self in Everyday Life*; Garden City, NY: Doubleday, 1959), he's added many cogent insights to the literature of urban behavior. For Goffman, these performances consist primarily of "impression management," where the actor is trying to influence how he or she is being perceived by others in the situation.

The information people provide about themselves can be divided into that which is intentionally disclosed and that which is unintentionally revealed or, in Goffman's language, the expression one "gives" and the expression one "gives off." This is the difference between clothing, consciously chosen to present a particular image on a date or in a job interview, and those inadvertent facial expressions that reveal another aspect of the same situation. Even this distinction doesn't always hold because people may intentionally offer information in a manner that makes it appear unintentional. The street vendor who *accidentally* lets it slip out that those earrings you're interested in are really worth five times the price originally marked. This strategy is based on the fact that people usually have greater confidence in information that doesn't appear to be fully controlled by the other person.

And then there are the "tie signs," the many different ways that people signal they are with other people. Around the plaza, these signs range from the simple and conspicuous, such as holding hands, to the more subtle, such as particular patterns of eye contact (Move #18).

The Good Plaza

What exactly is it that makes some of these vest pocket parks and plazas so successful, while others seem to languish from extreme underuse? The answers to this question also reveal a good deal else of interest about urban behavior in general.

Whyte found that the single most important factor determining the success of these places was an "orientation to the street," which gave people a chance to look at other people. Not only is this a popular activity, but the presence of people also attracts others to the scene. "Self-congestion" is what this has been called. In cities where more than 3,000 people an hour pass a place, it's much easier to create an exciting place than it is in those cities of 100,000 to 200,000 people where it's common for fewer than 1,000 people an hour to pass a particular site. And when they do gather, people tend to locate themselves either right on or very close to the traffic lanes that intersect the site. That's where the action is.

The availability of good seating was also important. Seats are major props on this part of the urban stage. Whyte and his colleagues found that people who sat tended to gather in pairs about 65 percent of the time, in groups of three 20 percent of the time, and in groups of four or more 20 percent of the time. He concluded that what worked best was seating with a lot of choice so that people could sit either alone or in groups. In the most used plazas, sitting space ran between 6 percent and 10 percent of the total open space. A conversation with Philip Johnson, who along with Mies van der Rohe, was one of the designers of the Seagram Building, revealed the inventiveness and tenacity of people when dealing with these plazas:

> We designed those blocks in front of the Seagram's Building so people could not sit on them, but you see, people want to so badly that they sit there anyhow. They like the place so much that they crawl, inch along that narrow edge of a wall. We put water near the marble ledge because we thought that they'd fall over if they sat there. They don't fall over; they get there anyhow. . . . It never crossed Mies' mind. Mies told me afterward. "I never thought that people would want to sit there."

In those plazas that were observed, ledges and steps seemed to work better than benches. These were usually too few, too small, and too isolated. Movable chairs were also good because people seemed to want to move them. This was one way of dealing with the "inhuman human creation," where feelings of having impact on the situation are all too rare an occurrence (see the introduction to Part IV). By moving a chair even an inch or two, the person has a sense of creating a new place rather than passively accepting the situation as given.

People preferred sun and trees, the absence of wind, and water as something to touch and listen to. At approximately seventy-five decibels, water served very well as white noise, screening out many of the surrounding city sounds. In a number of plazas in West Coast cities, including San Francisco and Portland, Oregon, the landscape architect Lawrence Halprin had been particularly inventive in using this element.

In her book *The Granite Garden* (Move #8), landscape architect Ann Whiston Spirn wrote of the importance of the waterfall in New York's Paley Park for creating what she called a "shady haven." Subtle use of a dozen honey locust trees for shade and ivy walls that block both reflected sunlight from the walls and the emission of radiant heat also contributed to the creation of a pleasant microclimate in the typical heat and glare of midtown high rises (Move #12).

"Triangulation" was also a regular occurrence in the successful plazas. This is the process by which something external such as a juggler or an outdoor wall mural provides a link among people and prompts strangers to talk to one another as if they were momentarily acquainted. The joys of reducing, if just for a brief moment, the psychological distance from the "close stranger" is similar to another phenomenon that researchers have labeled the "familiar stranger."

This is a person who is visually observed for a long time but isn't approached in any other way. On the average, commuters to New York City had four individuals at their train station whom they recognized but never spoke to. And 85 percent of those commuters questioned had at least one "familiar stranger" who was thought about a great deal and was often the center of a fantasy. Both "triangulation" and the phenomenon of the "familiar stranger" point to some of the traditional uses of these plazas. Here on the small stages scattered throughout the city it's possible both to be with other people *and* to utilize the relative anonymity of the situation as a stimulus for imagining possible alternative scenes, individual utopias (Move #10) that we can all create in our own minds.

ADDITIONAL READING

Goffman, Erving. *Relations in Public.* New York: Basic Books, 1971.

Hall, E.T. *The Hidden Dimension.* Garden City, NY: Doubleday, 1966.

Morris, Desmond. *Manwatching: A Field Guide to Human Behavior.* New York: Abrams, 1977.

Whyte, William. *The Social Life of Small Urban Spaces.* Washington, DC: The Conservation Foundation, 1980.

MOVE #16

Street Scenes
Downtown Walk and Help!

THE TWO STREET SCENES IN THIS MOVE ARE QUITE COMMON AND, in many ways, the diametric opposite of Move #1, the bird's-eye view.

First, imagine a walk on that downtown street in the middle of all that frenzy that can often be the city. The numbers, variety, and density, which were relatively abstract qualities when viewed from above, are suddenly up close, and while it *can* be exciting at times, it *can* also be quite overwhelming. Cities seem to have had this quality from their very beginnings. In examining photographs of archaeological sites of ancient cities, one can almost see the crowds of people who must have lived and worked in these places. Here is Jerome Carcopino talking about the ancient Roman street just after daybreak as the tabernae opened for business (*Daily Life in Ancient Rome: The People and the City at the Height of the Empire* [translated]; New Haven: Yale University Press, 1940):

Here barbers shaved their customers in the middle of the fairway. There the hawkers from Transterina passed along, bartering their packets of sulphur matches for glass trinkets. Elsewhere, the owner of a cookshop, hoarse with calling to deaf ears, displayed his sausages in their saucepan. Schoolmasters and their pupils shouted themselves hoarse in the open air. On the one side, a money changer rang his coins . . . on a dirty table, on another a beater of gold dust pounded his shining mallet on his well worn stone. At the cross roads a circle of idlers gaped around a viper tamer; everywhere tinkers' hammers resounded and the quavering voices of beggars invoked the name of Bellona or rehearsed their adventures and misfortunes to touch the hearts of passers-by.

And Rosamond Bayne Powell wrote on eighteenth-century London in *Eighteenth Century London Life* (London: John Murray, 1937):

The apple woman or the tart woman set up their stalls where they pleased, the bandbox man with a pole slung with bandboxes slung over his shoulder cluttered the narrow street, the bellows-mender and the chair-mender did their repairing on the pavement. Men and women hawked taffety tarts and brickdust, doormats and watercresses, hot spiced gingerbreads, green hasteds, crying their wares as they went. The bear ward, with his unhappy performing beast, came lumbering down the street. He would often stop at the street corner and give an entertainment, blocking the roadway and terrifying the horses. The puppet-show man too would come, and set up where he would collect a crowd to witness the antics of Mr. Punch.

While details of these scenes differ dramatically, the urbanite on the downtown walk, whether in ancient Rome, eighteenth-century London, or the contemporary American city, faces a number of similar dilemmas, how to cope with the vast numbers of sights and sounds that seem to be almost continuously bombarding the pedestrian. And is density really as bad as most people make it out to be, or does it have some positive qualities?

For that second scene, you're a little farther down the street, and suddenly there's a figure lying on the ground. From the way it's dressed, and the way it's positioned, you're not sure exactly what's going on. Who is it and how did it get in the present situation are questions that will have to be answered before any action is taken. A drunk sleeping it off who wants to be left alone, a heart-attack victim, a mugging, or maybe even a setup to lure some unsuspecting person so he or she can be mugged all seem to be possibilities. How does the urbanite decide what's going on in the situation, and what, if anything, should be done about it? And even more broadly, what is the general status of urban mystery and the definition of "emergency" in American cities of today?

NOTES

Screens and Filters

In an interesting article titled "The Experience of Living in Cities" (*Science Magazine*, 1970), similar in many ways to the earlier work of the sociologist Georg Simmel in "The Metropolis and Mental Life," the psychologist Stanley Milgram presented a cognitive view of urban behavior. At the center of this view are the images of people as thinkers and the city, because of its tremendous numbers, variety, and density, as a very difficult place within which to think.

Picture someone in front of a file cabinet trying to put every incoming piece of paper into the appropriate file so that it can be properly dealt with. What happens in the downtown walk is that too much comes in too quickly. This is called "cognitive overload," and as a result, it's difficult to make any sense out of the experience. One way of dealing with cognitive overload is through the judicious use of screens and filters—in the words of Milgram's article, "disregard low priority inputs," "diminish the intensity of inputs through the use of filtering devices," and "block reception off prior to entrance into a system" (an image similar to that of the "gate" discussed in Move #2).

The first of these strategies refers to paying attention only to that which is of particular significance at a given moment. Certainly, the things seen when driving around the block looking for a parking space are different from the things seen when walking through the same streets searching for a friend with whom one has an appointment. Perceptual experience is remarkable in the degree to which it can vary depending on the beliefs and expectations being held by the perceiver.

If low-priority inputs are going to be disregarded, then hierarchical thinking becomes necessary. One must develop criteria for deciding what is and what is not worth paying attention to. Think of all the services offered that essentially consist of ranking large numbers of particular places and events so that the urbanite can avoid dealing with all of them and somehow get only the best. Restaurant ratings, movie reviews, and all those service magazines that evaluate everything from pizzerias to toasters to institutions of higher learning clearly fall into this category. Even cities themselves have been regularly ranked (Move #23) in attempts to help in the making of planning decisions on both the personal and communal level. Where should the federal government locate a new defense facility so that workers will be both numerous and content? Given a particular individual's values and style of life, where should he or she consider living?

Waiting in line is in some ways the spatial analogue of ranking. In a series of studies on the social rules and behavioral regularities associated with waiting in lines, the psychologist L. Mann has made some interesting discoveries. When there are a limited number of items available, say one hundred tickets for a football game or a concert, usually many more than one hundred people line up. By asking every tenth person how many people he or she thought were ahead on the line, Mann found that people toward the beginning of the line generally estimated more people than there really were, whereas people toward the end of the line consistently underestimated the numbers ahead of them. The investigators called this the "wish fulfillment hypothesis." It was also found that the longer the line, the greater its drawing power, and a rapidly growing line tended to draw bystanders into it. This is self-congestion and demonstrates the appeal of action on the urban stage.

Screens and filters can be anything from technological devices such as portable radios and answering machines (Move #21) to patterns of eye movement (Move #18), to verbal communication itself. It's hard to imagine saying good morning to everyone on a walk—no matter how friendly one might be feeling—if the numbers of people passed every ten minutes are up in the thousands because of the extreme density. The screen and filter are found everywhere in the American city as both behavioral strategies and architectural elements.

Density

In much of the literature on urban America, high density has been portrayed as an unequivocal evil resulting in a host of ills that range from environmental pollution to psychological stress. A good deal of this negative portrayal resulted from overgeneralization from a number of classic animal studies. In one such study by John Calhoun (a researcher), it was discovered that all kinds of individual and group pathologies emerged when the overcrowding of Norwegian rats exceeded a certain limit. The term he used to describe the situation was *behavioral sink*. Other authors have found somewhat similar results with Sika deer. Unfortunately, the jump from these animals to people in cities has been made with little regard for the vast complexity of human behavior and the wide range of individual and cultural mechanisms that people have for dealing with density and the "close stranger" (Move #2). It's a vast oversimplification to view high density as directly leading to individual or group pathology.

For example, Hong Kong, considered to be the most dense city in the world, has thirteen census tracts with more than 2,000 people per acre. In terms of room density, many Hong Kong residents have only twenty-four square feet per person. The fact that the mortality rate, number of psychiatric disorders, and amount of serious crime in Hong Kong is considerably lower than in many cities with much lower density figures argues strongly against extrapolating from these animal studies. Authors such as the noted urban scholar Jane Jacobs, in *The Death and Life of Great American Cities* (New York: Vintage Books, 1961) (Move #24), have argued that for American cities to sustain the variety and intensity of activity that is their major attraction, they must have high densities. And rather than this being the problem, low density is the enemy of the city. Once people and their activities are spread too thinly across the landscape, the city loses those kinds of interactions that make it a special place. Now the crowded room of the city (Move #2) becomes the huge auditorium where only thirty-seven people show up for a performance or the large hired hall that is only filled up to 10 percent of its capacity for the special occasion. We know how grim that can be.

In what he labeled a "density-intensity" theory, the social psychologist Jonathan Freedman argued that high density just intensified whatever the dominant mood of the place already was. If a group of people were having a good time at a concert or a sporting event or on a downtown street, then the crowding intensified this feeling. On the other hand, if they were miserable in a doctor's waiting room or on that same city street, then the high density would make them even more unhappy.

As a final word on this theme, here are some figures for comparison when thinking about density. The standard amount of space that's supposed to be available in American prison cells is 38.5 square feet per person, a typical nightclub has 10 square feet, a theater 7 square feet, London slums in the nineteenth century were estimated at 9 square feet per person, the Black Hole of Calcutta and New York subways at rush hour have about 2 square feet per person.

Help!

Response to a rather chilling event that took place in New York City in 1964 helped throw some light on what factors determine whether people will help others, and how city people in general deal with mystery in a city street scene where things are often far from clear. Late one night while returning home from work, Kitty Genovese was stabbed to death outside her apartment. Subsequent investigation revealed that at least thirty-eight witnesses had viewed the crime over a period of more than a half hour from the vantage points of their apartments, and none had tried to render any aid or even to phone the police. In the ensuing furor and outrage that this case caused, a number of researchers became interested in just exactly what was going on in the scene.

In a series of rather ingenious studies, two psychologists, John Darley and Bibb Latane, uncovered several factors that seemed strongly to influence the way people behaved in these situations. They discovered that a common tack many people took when presented with something they didn't really understand—why exactly is that person lying there on the sidewalk?—was to look around and use other people's reactions to help them interpret what was happening. Something like this happens when you're not sure whether or not the joke in the movie is funny or whether it's even a joke or not, and you wait to see if other people in the audience laugh before you commit yourself. While this strategy can be a sensible one in most circumstances, in emergency situations such as the one concerning the stabbing, it often leads to what has been labeled "pluralistic ignorance."

I look at you looking at the prone body trying to decide what to make of it, while at the same time you're looking at me looking at the prone body deciding what to make of it. This short-circuits any impulse either of us may have toward action. And this inactivity is even further encouraged because we've both been taught to look as competent as possible, particularly when we're surrounded by strangers, especially when we don't really know what's going on, because that's when we're at our most vulnerable and most likely to be taken advantage of. So, not only am I confused about what to make of that person stretched out on the street, but I also have a strong vested interest in acting as if I'm not confused and everything is really quite clear. (Maybe *City Moves* should have a plain brown cover.) This is the face that people see on each other when they look for cues, and this often leads to a misinterpretation of what exactly is happening in the situation. "Things can't be that bad because that person over there doesn't seem to be that concerned." And they're looking at you thinking the same thing.

"Pluralistic ignorance" and another phenomenon labeled the "diffusion of responsibility"—a belief that if you don't help, someone else probably will—led to the paradoxical discovery that people are more likely to intervene if they're by themselves than if they're with other people. If there are others around, then there's greater likelihood of both pluralistic ignorance and diffusion of responsibility.

In another series of studies, it was found that a person walking on crutches and wearing a bandage on his leg was helped on the subway 83 percent of the time and at an airport 41 percent of the time. After interviewing bystanders, Darley and Latane speculated that the helping behavior had less to do with socioeconomic class and more to do with the familiarity of the setting. People were more likely to help in situations they felt familiar with, as in the subway.

In summarizing their research on "bystander intervention," Darley and Latane pointed out that in order for someone to help in an emergency situation, he or she first had to notice that something out of the ordinary was happening, then classify it as an emergency, decide that he or she had a responsibility for intervening, and then know what to do. All of these things were less likely to happen on the downtown walk than in other settings because of the complexity of the situation and the numbers of strangers around. It's not that city people are less helpful than others, but rather that the very nature of the downtown situation and the screens regularly used to deal with it diminish the likelihood of correctly interpreting the situation and then feeling responsible to help remedy it.

ADDITIONAL READING

Darley, John, and Bibb Latane. *The Unresponsive Bystander: Why Doesn't He Help.* New York: Appleton-Century-Crofts, 1970.

Freedman, Jonathan. *Crowding and Behavior.* New York: Viking, 1975.

Milgram, Stanley. "The Experience of Living in Cities." *Science Magazine* (1970): 167.

Simmel, Georg. "The Metropolis and Mental Life." In *The Sociology of Georg Simmel*, edited by Kurt Wolff. New York: The Free Press, 1950. In this classic work, the German sociologist argued that the intensity of nervous stimulation would eventually take a toll, and urbanites would defend themselves by not reacting emotionally and participate in reasoned, functional relationships. Responses would be made with the head and not with the heart, and people would become sophisticated, intellectual, and blasé. For Simmel, the only way that urban man could escape this fate and become free would be to learn not to feel tied to job, home, family, or friends and to turn inward on himself somehow for growth and sustenance. The image is that of the meditating monk, and here the screens and filters are quite sophisticated.

MOVE #17

Getting Lost (and Maybe Even Found)

OFTEN, WHEN PEOPLE TALK ABOUT "KNOWING" A CITY WHAT THEY are referring to is some knowledge of how the place is laid out so that it can be traveled through, navigated from point A to point B without getting lost. Maps are an essential tool for this activity, and a look at some of the older specimens reveals many of the vicissitudes of the human spirit. Early maps depict monsters lurking at the world's edges, while the classic routes are marked with an assurance entirely uncalled for, given how little was actually known about the places being depicted.

This Move has two parts. First, make a quick map of the central district of a city you're quite familiar with. Draw it just as if you were making a rapid description of the place to a stranger, covering all the main features. Don't hesitate to include labels. Just make a rough sketch of the sort you carry around in your head to figure out where things are in the city. What parts of the map do you feel confident about in terms of their accuracy, and what parts aren't quite as easy to recall?

Then reflect on the experience of being lost. Think back to those times when you were literally lost. You may in fact want to get lost again for this Move. What was the experience like, and how did you react in this situation? What would a list of your thoughts and feelings in the situation be like? And can you imagine a situation where you might actually *choose* to have this experience, where you actually pay in time, money, or effort for the privilege of getting lost? Consider the delights of a maze in a formal garden or the joys of aimless wandering in a new part of the city where you don't carry around a picture of the place in your head. Certainly much of the appeal of amusement park rides such as the roller coaster or bobsled is that their movement causes a good deal of spatial disorientation.

How are those experiences, which are often sought out, different from the more usual ones where there's a strong effort made to stay on the path chosen to get from one place to another? Perhaps this is somewhat comparable to the difference between not understanding four or five words in a ten-word sentence and having no idea what the entire sentence is about or even whether it's really a sentence at all.

Of course, there's the metaphorical use of the word *lost*. If you're not quite sure what that last sentence in *City Moves* means, then you're "lost" in a similar sense to that described in the second street scene of Move #16, where lack of comprehension of the situation resulted in bystanders' doing nothing or doing the wrong thing.

NOTES

In 1960, the urban planner Kevin Lynch published a landmark book entitled *Image of the City* (Cambridge: MIT Press). This work was a major force in stimulating research and thinking in the areas of cognitive mapping and urban imageability. Lynch thoroughly examined these issues and investigated the consequences of being lost in the urban environment.

"Cognitive maps" are those internal representations people carry around in their heads to help them know a place and how to navigate through it. The sketch you were asked to do in this Move is an attempt to get at a representation of this cognitive map. Edward Chace Tolman made extensive use of the concept in experimental psychology, and Kenneth Boulding wrote an important book on the subject in 1956 called *The Image* (Ann Arbor: University of Michigan Press, 1956), but it was Kevin Lynch who first developed the idea in the world of urban design.

Children as young as five years old can form cognitive maps, and these maps are affected by the familiarity they have with the place and the extent to which they've traveled through it. A study by J. Douglas Porteous found that it was easier to form cognitive maps of cities with hilltop views than those without these views—which is another way of talking about the advantages of the bird's-eye view (Move #1). Other researchers have cited closeness to population flow and architectural and social distinctiveness as the important factors that determine whether or not a particular element in the city can be pictured accurately.

For Lynch, the good city was one in which people didn't get lost. That is, it had "legibility." The parts could be recognized and organized into a coherent pattern, and as a result, the city was "imageable." "Imageability" is "that quality in a physical object that gives it a high probability of evoking a strong image in any given observer." Lynch was primarily interested in what it was that made a city imageable and, to a lesser degree, in how people went about forming cognitive maps.

In his initial study, Boston, Los Angeles, and Jersey City were investigated. Lynch asked a number of residents to make a sketch map of the city and to provide detailed descriptions of a number of trips through the city. He then analyzed these maps and descriptions using the concepts of edges, districts, paths, nodes, and landmarks (Move #1). For most people, paths were the central element in the formation of their cognitive maps.

Lynch found that Boston was the most imageable of the three cities, with Jersey City at the low end of the scale and Los Angeles falling somewhere in between. Although people can develop strategies for navigating through extremely homogeneous environments, such as desert sand and Arctic snow, Lynch made a strong argument for ordering the urban environment so that it was easier to read and make sense of, so that a cognitive map could be readily established.

Among those characteristics an urban element should have if it is to be more imageable, Lynch listed singularity—that is, the feature should stand out from its background—simplicity and clarity of geometrical form, a dominance of one part of the setting over other parts, and the capacity to increase the range of vision, in either the literal or the symbolic sense. It should place the viewer in a situation where he or she can either visually inspect things not ordinarily open to inspection or make mental connections that are new and "see" things in a different way. The former can be accomplished by providing a new vantage point from which to view the world, as in the case of the tall building (Move #1), or by uncovering something that is ordinarily hidden from sight, as was the case of Mies van der Rohe's proposal of a glass high rise that would reveal the mysteries of structure to the viewer. Those urban elements that were linked to others in a temporal sequence and had a name also tended to be more legible.

In follow-up work done in Venezuela, Donald Appleyard found that the maps drawn by residents were dominated by either sequential elements—mainly roads—or spatial elements—landmarks, districts, and nodes. The most primitive sequential maps consisted of fragments of paths or lists of elements unconnected to one another. Fifteen percent of the sample responded this way, while fully one-third drew what Appleyard called "chains." These maps were also simple but more schematic in that they showed relationships among elements though all the bends and turns were treated as straight lines.

In another study in Venezuela, Appleyard had 200 buildings in Ciudad Guayana rated by trained urban designers for the presence of particular characteristics of form, visibility, use, and significance. Then 300 ordinary citizens performed an array of Lynchean tasks, including map drawing, verbal recall, and trip description. In answering the question of why a particular building was imageable, Appleyard found that movement, sharpness of contour or boundary, shape, and size insofar as it contrasted with surrounding buildings were all attributes of the form of the building which tended to make it more imageable. The tops of many recent postmodernist skyscrapers (Move #12), which seem to come in every form and shape except that of the glass box beloved by modern architects, is also testimony to the significance of the contour of the building in making the place imageable. This trait is often sought by the corporate owners of the structure to give their product or service a unique identity and can also serve the designer as the vehicle for individual architectural expression. The brightness or complexity of the surface, the "quality" of the building, and the use of signs were less important in imageability. Appleyard also found that buildings that were located at important intersections and used by a lot of people tended to be highly imageable.

Lynch viewed the issue of being lost, both literally and metaphorically, as a design problem. If you can't find your way in the city, then it wasn't designed properly, and if you can't find your way in this book, then *it* wasn't designed properly. You should be able to "read" both settings to figure out where you've been, where you are, and where you're going. Being lost is inefficient in terms of time wasted (Move #2) and is often experienced as unpleasant because of the feelings of confusion and dependence that regularly accompany the experience.

What happens when you're suddenly faced with a page in a book that doesn't make any sense at all? Or in a city where you're not only uncertain whether you're on the correct street, but even uncertain about whether you're in the right part of town? There's a significant difference between the delight of a small amount of loss of orientation—and with that loss the possibility of experiencing something new and exciting—and the extreme discomfort of being totally disoriented.

While willing to admit the possibility that a certain amount of environmental mystery could be exciting and stimulating, Lynch argued strongly for design clarity and imageability. The city of mystery and the city of complexity and contradiction (Move #9) weren't emphasized by him. In many ways, much of the spirit of Lynch's work seems reminiscent of modern architects and their call to clarity and honesty (Move #12), but Lynch is operating on a larger scale than that of the single building, and certainly the qualities he admired in a place such as Boston are very different from those in a place such as Le Corbusier's Ville Radieuse (Move #10), where everything was pared down to an extreme simplicity, and history was treated like a bad dream.

The Argentinian writer Jorge Borges wrote a story titled "Of Exactitude in Science." In this tale, the people of one of Borges's mythical places gradually increase the size of the map of the kingdom until it is larger than the place it was representing. It then entirely covers the kingdom so that nothing at all can be seen, and its destruction is necessary if the landscape is to be experienced at all.

ADDITIONAL READING

Downs, R. M., and D. Stea, eds. *Image & Environment: Cognitive Mapping and Spatial Behavior.* Chicago: Aldine, 1973.

Lynch, Kevin. *The Image of the City.* Cambridge: MIT Press, 1960.

MOVE #18

Eyes in the City

THE WAY WE USE OUR EYES IN THE CITY IS A GOOD EXAMPLE OF behavior which, although quite complex, has become habitual to the point of being almost automatic. Most people will answer any question on how we use our eyes in a fashion similar to a question on the functioning of the kidney or any other organ of the body. These processes are not open to our direct inspection through introspection. We can't simply "turn inward" and figure out what it is we are doing; our body parts just go on working without our paying any attention to them unless something goes wrong.

Any violation of the rules that every culture imposes on its members about when to look and when not to look is unmistakable. When we talk to someone who maintains eye contact for an inappropriately long or short period, we're almost immediately aware that something isn't quite right. While we probably won't be able to specify exactly how much eye contact *should* be maintained in this situation, we *will* know when things feel wrong. And the same holds for that strange fellow in the plaza (Move #15) who's always staring up, unfocused, into the sky. We've been taught the rules of eye usage so completely—psychologists call this process of internalizing group values and rules for behavior "socialization"—that they become part of us almost the way our biology is part of us.

A possible dilemma of making such habitual behavior more

conscious is that it may alter our behavior so that our actions aren't quite as smooth as they are when done automatically. Try driving a standard shift car while focusing on what it is your right arm, left foot, and right foot are doing at any given moment. You'll probably convert what was a smooth ride into a series of missed shifts and grinding gears. The same can be said about the use of eyes in the city. It's very difficult, if not impossible, to use them and be aware of what it is you're doing at the same moment. Because of this, the instructions for this Move are not quite as specific as those for most other Moves.

Do whatever you can to gain a sense of how people use their eyes in the city. You can examine your own behavior (again with the cautionary note that this is very difficult to do) and may well introduce a certain awkwardness into social behavior that is typically quite smooth when done automatically. Or you can observe other people in a variety of urban situations, alone, with friends, with strangers, in public and private places.

What exactly is it people look at? What don't they seem to attend to? Under what circumstances is eye contact established with other people? Why? And what does the eye contact mean in different scenes? For instance, what happens in a crowded subway or elevator? Do friends see a different set of eyes than strangers? And in those situations where we don't have the use of our eyes is anything else lost in addition to large amounts of visual information?

NOTES

Eyes are used to collect messages and information about the world and to send information about ourselves and our situation in the world. Pupil size is influenced by both the amount of light in the air and the interest in the subject matter being observed. Direction of gaze serves as a very effective filter (Move #16), by determining what will and even more importantly what won't be seen at any given moment. It can serve as a signal to others that it's legitimate to initiate interaction and can also influence the intimacy level.

From time immemorial, the eyes have been thought of as the windows of the soul. And at those times where we don't want others to be aware of our thoughts and feelings, we hide them behind masks of one kind or another. This is as true for the twentieth-century state trooper as it was for the nineteenth-century Chinese jade dealer. It's also one of the things behind the commuter's masking his or her face with a book or newspaper. None of these people want others to know where they're looking, nor do they want their interest and excitement given away by the enlarged pupils that often accompany these emotions. Italian courtesans of the eighteenth century were trying to send another message. They used extract from the deadly nightshade plant, known as belladonna, to dilate their pupils and thereby signal excitement to potential customers.

Even more revealing than pupil size is the direction of gaze. The social psychologist Michael Argyle, a prominent researcher in this area, has shown that vision and gaze are neither arbitrary nor accidental. They follow definite rules, some of which we're born with and others which we acquire from our culture.

As a filter in those situations where the individual might be flooded by too much information, the eye can be quite effective. "What I don't see I don't have to deal with." Investigators reported that while direct eye contact was relatively rare in a post office and store in downtown Philadelphia—about 14 percent—the figure increased to approximately 45 percent in the same types of establishments in a suburb of Philadelphia. In a small town in rural Pennsylvania, direct eye contact was reported 80 percent of the time. Since direct eye contact is also a nonverbal invitation to initiate further interaction (those famous "bedroom eyes" and perhaps even more famous "Bette Davis eyes"), it's understandable why there'd be less of eye contact in the big city of strangers than in the small town of acquaintances. All our quirks and problems with relationships aside, we *do* talk more with people we know than with those we don't, although there are certainly vast numbers of people employed in the counseling and therapy professions who make good money dealing with the exceptions to this rule.

As a social signal, gaze emerged before the evolution of man. Several different kinds of fish, birds, moths, and butterflies have patterns that resemble eyes on their bodies. These serve to scare off predators. In much of the animal kingdom, direct gaze signals threat and often comes just before aggression. Ralph Exline and Absalom Yellin found that if a caged monkey was stared at, it attacked or threatened to attack 76 percent of the time, but if the stare was quickly broken off, this was seen as a sign of appeasement, and the caged monkey responded aggressively only about 50 percent of the time. People in the city frequently behave in a similar fashion. To the extent that the city is perceived as a dangerous place, and given the traditional anti-urban bias (see "American Attitudes Toward Urbanization" in the Introduction) that is considerable, we all learn to use our eyes with the same discretion and care with which we might treat a loaded gun. We often read the direct stare as potentially threatening and consequently prepare for "flight or fight." Phoebe Ellsworth and her researcher colleagues found that when motorcyclists or pedestrians stared at automobile drivers paused at an intersection, the drivers drove off from the stoplight more rapidly than they ordinarily did. Like a loaded gun, the eyes can be used to secure an advantage at both the traffic intersection and the business meeting.

The higher up the evolutionary ladder the species is, the greater the range of significance of the eyes. Only primates (monkeys, apes, and human beings) use gaze to attract as well as to threaten. It has been hypothesized that the origin of the use of the gaze for affiliative purposes lies in the fact that primate infants and mothers can look at each other during breast feeding. Human babies, for example, are able to focus at a distance of approximately twenty to thirty centimeters, roughly the distance from the mother's face when she holds the infant to nurse. Primates are the only animals where nursing fosters eye contact, and because of this, warm feelings come to be associated with mutual gaze.

Studies with monkeys indicate that an additional effect of a direct stare is arousal. Various measures of physiological arousal—galvanic response, EEG, brain stem activity—show that organisms can tolerate a certain amount of stimulation and find it interesting, but that overstimulation becomes unpleasant. As Argyle said, "Too much arousal is unsettling and causes the animal—wolf, bird, or human being—to avoid the prying eyes by fleeing, fighting, or threatening. This is true whether those prying eyes are those of one's natural predator or those of a stranger on the subway."

This is one of the reasons we feel so uncomfortable when someone is pressed up against us in a crowded elevator or subway, and they look us right in the eye. Part of our discomfort has to do with overstimulation, and part of our discomfort has to do with the situation's having an inappropriately high level of intimacy. Since in those crowded situations other factors that help to determine the level of intimacy, such as physical distance, cannot be regulated, attempts are made to compensate for this by diminishing the amount of direct eye contact. When this can't be done, there's an uncomfortable feeling that things are getting entirely too cozy for an interaction between complete strangers in a public or semi-public urban space.

While the exact meaning of a look may change from culture to culture, people everywhere know that a direct look means that the other person is attending and therefore requires some reaction. That long glance at the end of an utterance in a conversation serves as a full stop signal to the listener and is also used to collect feedback. It lets the speaker know what the listener thought about what was just said. The lack of this element in telephone conversations makes them essentially different experiences from face-to-face interactions.

The experience of being looked at has a particular subjective quality, which is a major part of city life and is often found to be quite enjoyable. How much time is spent preparing ourselves to be seen by others? And how do those city scenes where we feel like the part of the audience that is doing the observing differ from those scenes where we feel like the performers who are being observed? (Move #14).

Different ethnic groups engage in varying amounts of eye contact. Among male foreign students at the University of Colorado, it was found that those from non–contact cultures (Move #15), where people liked more space around them and engaged in very little touching when they talked, such as Asia and Northern Europe, spent much less time gazing at one another when conversing than people from contact cultures such as the Middle East, Latin America, and Southern Europe. This tended to happen no matter how much time had been spent in the United States. Apparently, it's easier to learn a new language of the tongue than a new language of the eyes.

Within a particular culture, a person who gazes too much is generally regarded as threatening, insulting, or disrespectful; while a person who looks too little is thought of as inattentive, impolite, dishonest, or submissive. In the public areas of the city, we often face the dilemma of not wanting to see much that is around us (Move #16) while at the same time presenting a vigilant image to the world, to send the message that we can't be taken advantage of. This requires a delicate balance between looking and not looking. For example, a waiter can't establish direct eye contact with a patron until he or she has the time to respond immediately to that eye contact and therefore must use peripheral vision to monitor the surrounding situation. In certain scenes, the shifty eye becomes adaptive, and the ability to create corners around which you can peer becomes a valuable urban skill.

ADDITIONAL READING

Argyle, Michael, and M. Cook. *Gaze and Mutual Gaze*. Cambridge, England: Cambridge University Press, 1976.

Henley, Nancy. *Body Politics: Power, Sex, and Nonverbal Communication*. Englewood Cliffs, NJ: Prentice-Hall, 1977.

MOVE #19

"Reach Out and Touch Someone"
Technology, Friendship, and Place

TECHNOLOGY HAS BEEN DEEPLY INVOLVED WITH THE CITY AND CITY life from its very beginning. It was only a series of technological advances in agriculture and animal husbandry in Neolithic times that generated the surplus food that made cities possible at all (Move #4). And in modern times this involvement with technology has, if anything, increased.

The literary critic Hugh Kenner, in his book *The Mechanic Muse* (New York: Oxford University Press, 1987), described the period at the end of the last century "when every thinkable human activity save perhaps the reproductive was being mapped onto machinery." And today, even that realm has been mechanized with the advent of techniques such as artificial insemination, in vitro fertilization, and phone fantasy sex. In their classic study of human sexuality, Masters and Johnson gathered data by watching women copulate with machines. One is reluctant to say "make love," even in an age where peoples' most intense relationships are often with automobiles (Moves #9, #20), telephones, and the world of television, and all those other wonderful tools and devices with which we surround our lives.

We live in a sea of machines, and on a daily basis there is increasing evidence that even those distinctions between organic and mechanical, alive and dead, are becoming more and more difficult to make. Few of us regularly mistake the food processor

223

or even *Robocop*, for that matter, for dear, old Aunt Mabel, but technological advances have tremendously complicated what had been much simpler issues in earlier times such as those of birth and death. Maybe the volume of status in the coming centuries will be *Who's What* rather than *Who's Who*, and people will point with as much pride to the make of their artificial joints and implanted electronic wizardry as they do today to their automobiles and watches.

The American love affair with technology began quite early. In *The Machine in the Garden* (New York: Oxford University Press, 1964), Leo Marx recorded that early in the nineteenth century the country was taken with the idea that technological progress would lead to the "annihilation of space and time." In some senses, this *has* already happened (Move #2), and the fact that these changes are so dramatic and obvious has convinced many people that the answer to every problem, whether social, economic, or psychological, is the development of a new technology. This sentiment is understandable given the remarkable successes and the relative ease in believing in ideas such as "improvement," "progress," and "refinement" in the realm of technology compared with other areas of human endeavor. These are areas where the products and processes aren't quite as tangible and therefore more difficult to compare and evaluate.

The differences between the plane the Wright brothers flew at Kitty Hawk in 1903 and the 747s of today are obvious and demonstrable when put alongside the differences between the leading political figures of the same two eras. People and their behavior don't seem to be marching forward and "improving" in quite the same way as machines are. The one exception to this is in the world of athletics, and this may account for the strong appeal of sports in urban America. Furthermore, this makes it hard to resist the idea that every problem is ultimately a technical one, the kind of dilemma that will eventually be solved when the right machine or pill or system is invented. Even machine metaphors are popular as tools for describing everything from language to cities (Move #3). The belief that problems in areas such as housing, the environment, psychological health, and the like will all be solved through technology is a popular one in contemporary urban America and blinds us to some of the legitimate criticisms of the machine.

Ned Lud's realization in England, at the beginning of the Industrial Revolution, that the introduction of the mechanical loom would end the way of life that he and his fellow weavers depended on to survive, was one of the earliest examples of negative attitudes toward technology. And broader attacks have been made by contemporary by social critics such as Jacques Ellul on a set of values where *what* one does is somehow less important than *how* one does it, an ethos that he called "technique." This is evident everywhere from television quiz shows to prestigious academic programs, and his views have been echoed by many others and seem to have a good deal of relevance in today's world. For all the idealization of the machine (Move #3), there seems to be a growing awareness that a more critical attitude is necessary if ecological and social tragedy are to be avoided.

In *Communitas: Means of Livelihood and Ways of Life* (New York: Vintage Books, 1960), writer and critic Paul Goodman, along with his brother, city planner Percival Goodman, offered up some elementary principles for what they called the moral selection of machines. Along with the obvious criterion of "utility"—does the thing work?—the Goodmans believed that the "good" machine should be "transparent," that is, simple enough to be understood through visual inspection. This is reminiscent of Lynch's "imageability" (Move #17), where similar criteria are used to judge the "good" city. This transparency should result in a machine that the average well-educated person would be able to repair, and it should also diminish the amount of "environmental mystery" present in the city (see Part IV), a mystery that can result in general feelings of unease. This is the dread we all feel when we realize that if we don't know how it works, then we'll be helpless if it breaks down.

Lenny Bruce had a comedy bit where he suggested people learn at least a few phrases of different kinds of technical language so that when they inevitably had to call in that specialist to fix the machine, they could feign competence and perhaps avoid being taken advantage of—little did he realize that some twenty years later people would already be listing computer language proficiencies on job applications.

The "good" machine should also be free from nonubiquitous power, and even more important, there should be a sensible proportion between the total effort needed to acquire and maintain the machine and its utility. According to this way of thinking, when you calculate the speed of an automobile and its cost per unit of distance traveled, you really should add in all those extra hours and dollars invested in acquiring and maintaining the vehicle. And there should be some thought given to whether the trip itself is worth making. For Goodman and Goodman, speed devoid of purpose was not quite the cause for celebration some would have it be (Move #21).

The advice on "freedom from nonubiquitous power" seems a sound anticipation of those ecologically minded critics who strongly argued for the development of ubiquitous power sources such as sun, wind, and sea. And this final cautionary note introduced an element of sanity in a world where the technological solution often becomes more of a difficulty than the original problem it was designed to deal with. It's not so much that the baby is thrown out with the bath water, but rather that the tub itself attacks the child it was supposed to clean.

A report done by Bryn Mawr College just after World War II stated that women still devoted more than eighty hours a week to cleaning the house, cooking meals, and taking care of the children even with the introduction of all those "labor saving" appliances. And in an extensive study in *Scientific American* in 1974, titled "Time Spent in Housework," Jo Ann Vanek reported that the full-time housewife spent more hours doing laundry in the 1970s than she did in the 1920s, despite all the new washing machines, dryers, detergents, and bleaches. The main change was that the family had acquired more clothing and now had even higher expectations about cleanliness and grooming. "Ring around the collar" had been transformed into a character flaw.

Nevertheless, the city is still the bastion of technology, and life in urban America would *not* be possible in anything like its present form without this technology. Imagine the situation without it. Think back to floods and weather-induced power failures and technological breakdowns. What's life like in the city during the summer heat waves when extremely high user demand can sometimes result in entire metropolitan regions blowing a fuse? And without cars, planes, trains, telephones, televisions, and computers, everything suddenly becomes very different. Work, play, transportation, and communication aren't the same as they were before. And even the essential elements of light, air, and water can become problematical and almost impossible to obtain.

Imagine spending a day without any of these machines. What

would it be like to eliminate just two of the more powerful, the telephone and television, from your life for a week? Aside from the obvious—no Monday night football without television—what would be some of the other consequences? If the city is the place of the "distant friend" (see Part IV), and important relationships with other people are often maintained over great distances through technology, how can these relationships continue without machines such as telephones and cars? What is the impact of technology on our sense of "place," and how does it influence the criteria that are used to decide whether or not something is important? Can any news stations give us the world if we give them twenty-two minutes, as WINS in New York says it can? And what exactly is this "world" that we are being given?

NOTES

Friendship

First, without technology we might well say goodbye to the distant friend. Without being able to "reach out and touch someone" via the telephone, we lose one of the primary ways of connecting with the distant friend. Technology has made possible wider networks of people, where geography itself is irrelevant as in a telephone conversation where any reference to what the landscape is like will be viewed as quite odd and out of place. Ironically, there seems to be evidence that it's harder to establish friendships on the telephone than it is when meeting face to face. Studies using the prisoners' dilemma game, where people can maximize their benefits by cooperating rather than competing, show that people meeting for the first time will like each other and tend to be more cooperative when they meet face to face rather than over the telephone.

Common wisdom has it that city people just don't have that many friends. Or as Charles C. Colton, an English clergyman, put it in *Lacoon; or Many Things in Few Words Addressed to Those Who Think* (1820), "If you would be known and not know, vegetate in a village; if you would know and not be known, live in a city." How true is this bit of folk psychology? Do people in the city really have fewer friends, and is the quality of those relationships inferior to the friendships that exist in other places?

Systematic investigations don't seem to support these assumptions. One of the best of these investigations was carried out by the sociologist Claude Fischer. Fischer surveyed 1,050 people living in fifty northern California neighborhoods and communities, varying from cities such as San Francisco and Oakland to rural areas.

People taking part in Fischer's study listed as many key associates as they could think of and also provided information about the nature of their relationships—for example, what they and their friends did together, what kinds of help and support they could count on from one another, whether or not they were related, and how physically close their places of residence were. Fischer did not find that people living in larger communities had fewer numbers of friends, nor did he find that those urban relationships were lacking in quality. Although friendships in the cities were scattered over a greater area, quality, as measured in terms of available social support, did *not* decline.

But what *was* different was the process of making friends. In a study of newcomers to New York City and to a small town, it was found that the process of making friends in the city took longer and was more difficult than the same process in the small town. The environmental psychologist Karen Franck found that within two months of their arrival people in the urban settings had an average of 3.5 friends, while people in the small town reported 6.32 friends. But seven and eight months later, the numbers were almost identical, with people in both groups reporting slightly more than five friends. So, while the manner of making friends was somewhat different in the two situations, the ultimate results appeared to be similar.

Technology may well be changing the very nature of friendship itself. In an article written in the 1950s ("Mass Communication and Para-Social Interaction: Observations on Intimacy at a Distance," *Psychiatry*, 1956), Donald Horton and R. Richard Wohl, both social scientists, argued that the new electronic media offered the illusion of face-to-face interaction, and as a result, people were responding to figures on the television screen as if they were close friends. During his five-year stint on network television, Robert Young, who played Marcus Welby, M.D., received over a quarter of a million letters, many requesting medical advice. And actors on soap operas regularly receive communications from fans warning them of the schemes and machinations of other characters in the show.

A talk show host such as Johnny Carson is perceived as likable and interesting, and viewers take an interest in the details of his life—his divorces, will he leave the *Tonight* show, and so on— the same way they would with a close friend. Carson's real skill as a performer is convincing millions of people that they "know" him by establishing a "false" sense of intimacy—a "false" sense, because while "Heeeeere's Johnny," wheeeeere's you? Usually at home in bed, flat on your back, which seemingly makes the encounter with Johnny even more intimate. Horton and Wohl call these relationships "para-social interactions," and they help explain why Walter Cronkite is perceived as one of the most trusted men in America or the deep sense of grief experienced by many people upon the death of someone such as John F. Kennedy or John Lennon. Even though they leave behind visual and audio recordings, which is the most people ever saw and heard of them in the first place, there's a feeling that the people behind the pictures and sounds were known, and there can be a profound sense of loss when they're gone.

The Medium, the Message, and the Metaphor

Marshall McLuhan argued in his classic work *Understanding Media* (Toronto: New American Library of Canada, 1964) that the way television has impact on peoples' lives has less to do with the content of the medium and more to do with certain formal properties of television. "A TV show is a TV show is a TV show," and what's important is not what the program is about, but rather that the experience of watching television consists of looking at a rapid succession of continuously changing visual images on a small electronic screen.

As far back as the Second Commandment in the Decalogue of the Old Testament, where the Israelites were prohibited from making images and were commanded to record and represent their experiences, particularly those of God, with the Word, there has been a recognition that the form of a medium was related to the type of message it might best convey. The author of the Decalogue clearly thought that an abstract, universal deity could best be approached with words rather than with pictures or three-dimensional representations such as idols. Words are inherently abstract and capable of dealing with the general rather than the particular in a way that pictures and statues often are not. These last two have a certain materiality that words lack, and it may well be that this characteristic conveys some messages of its own.

While a number of thinkers have put forth this idea, among them Lewis Mumford in *Technics and Civilization* (New York: Harcourt Brace Jovanovich, 1934) and Harold Innis in *The Bias of Communication* (Toronto: University of Toronto Press, 1951), Marshall McLuhan was its great prophet and popularizer in modern times. "The medium is the message" was the way he put it, and he spent a good part of his career documenting the transition from a culture dominated by the printed word to a world where the electronic media, and particularly television, reign supreme.

With the average American family having television on nearly fifty hours a week, according to a recent Nielsen poll, by the time most people graduate from high school, they've spent considerably more time in front of the screen then they did in the womb.

For the educator and scholar Neil Postman, media are more like metaphors than messages. They don't convey particular bits of information the way a message does (Los Angeles had a population of 3, 567, 879 in 1975) but operate "by unobtrusive but powerful implication to enforce their special definition of reality. Whether we are experiencing the world through the lens of speech or the printed word or the television camera, our media-metaphors classify the world for us, sequence it, frame it, enlarge it, reduce it, color it, argue a case for what the world is like" (*Amusing Ourselves to Death*; New York: Viking, 1985).

And what the world is like, according to television, is Las Vegas. And for Postman, this is a very different city than that portrayed by Robert Venturi and Denise Scott Brown in *Learning from Las Vegas* (Cambridge: MIT Press, 1972) (Move #9). It's a city devoted to show business and entertainment, which has become a symbol for the entire nation just the way Boston was at the time of the American Revolution or New York was in the "melting pot" period of the mid–nineteenth century (Move #25). The values and orientations of show business have totally permeated politics, religion, education, commerce, and every other aspect of contemporary life. According to Postman, this has introduced irrelevance, impotence, and incoherence as significant elements in daily discourse. Much of what is communicated to us by television has these qualities.

In the world of entertainment, questions of coherence, relevance, and potency are entirely beside the point. What exactly does a quiz show or a hockey game "mean"? And how is the issue of meaning dealt with on those more "serious" programs where presidential candidates are given twenty minutes to summarize their political programs and respond to the other candidates? A single session of the Lincoln–Douglas debates took more than seven hours, and they weren't even candidates for the presidency. As a medium, television seems singularly unequipped for dealing with issues of meaning. And no wonder, for most people there's nothing quite as boring as watching other people think. Thinking is just not a spectator sport and gets short shrift in an age when the first thing a political candidate does is hire a media consultant who is responsible for developing an image. Only later is any concern shown for thinking about issues, and even then it's really only a shadow of the full-blown process because true searches for meaning may be too subtle, complex, and nonvisual to be conveyed by a medium such as television.

When was the last time you watched something on television that was directly related to your life and made you think and behave differently from the way you would have otherwise? Except for the weather report and perhaps some sports and business news, much of what you see probably isn't immediately relevant to your life. Sports have succeeded brilliantly in insinuating themselves into millions of peoples' lives, while the horror of the large majority of the typical daily news broadcast—murder, pillage, and mayhem in the main—makes us want to protect ourselves from the threat it presents by treating the news as if it were irrelevant.

Consider the issue of potency. When you watch something on the television set, are you ever in a position to do anything about it? Or are these experiences the ultimate in a kind of urban voyeurism where we're forced just to watch knowing full well that we'll rarely, if ever, be able to act on anything we're watching.

All the traditional themes and requirements of print media —a need to think conceptually and sequentially, a high value on reason and order, and a great deal of detachment and objectivity—the usual stance of someone reading the written word, as you are now—are drowned in a concern for visual appearance and the simple, amusing pleasures that are the goal of entertainment. It's not that I don't want you to enjoy reading *City Moves*, but rather the very nature of a book will demand this attitude. The words on a page will stay fixed in place for a while if the printers and binders did their job, and this invites a kind of scrutiny that the 3.5-second life of a television image makes impossible.

When everything from education to politics is viewed as entertainment and often *is* entertainment—because whatever else those benefit concerts for disease victims and farmers and starving Africans are they're also rock concerts—then the values and attitudes of entertainment will be used. These values are often totally inappropriate for the activity being judged. It could be argued, for example, that a politician's looks are as irrelevant in the performance of his or her duties as those of a writer and focusing on this aspect of the event may lead to the *Brave New World* (London: Chatto & Windus, 1932) of Aldous Huxley, a world where the entire culture is trivialized by the incredible technologies totally devoted to pleasure and entertainment. Have we already arrived at Huxley's world of "feelies," "orgy porgy," the "centrifugal bumblepuppy," and the universal feel-good drug of "soma"?

Sense of Place

In *No Sense of Place* (New York: Oxford University Press, 1985), the media scholar Joshua Meyrowitz argued that television has had tremendous impact on American conceptions of secrecy, gender, childhood, and authority by breaking down the traditional sense of place. What one does and with whom one does it rarely depend upon where one is these days in quite the same way that it did before the development of electronic communication systems. Aspatial communities (Move #22) are now possible.

In a world dominated by television, it's almost as if

> many of the walls that separate rooms, offices and houses in our society were suddenly moved or removed and that many once distinct situations were suddenly combined. Under such circumstances, the distinction between our private and public selves and between the different selves we project in different situations might not entirely disappear, but our ability to segregate encounters would be greatly diminished. We could not play different roles in different situations because the clear spatial segregation of situations would no longer exist.

The metaphor of drama and performance (Move #14) illustrates this point: It's as if the barrier separating the front stage and back stage, the place where performances are given and the place where performances are prepared, no longer existed. Suddenly everything is visible and on camera. Heroes in sports and politics have a more difficult time maintaining their stature when television invites the public into what in the past had been considered back stage areas of their lives.

From "Entertainment Tonight" to "Lifestyles of the Rich and Famous" many of the old secrets are gone, or perhaps more accurately, the very idea of secrecy itself has been changed. Childhood innocence is lost when the most intimate aspects of adulthood can be examined with the flick of a switch. And the observation of Simone de Beauvoir that women always behave differently in front of men than they do in front of other women seems meaningless in an era when people seem to be pouring their souls out on national TV. Just turn on Phil Donahue or Oprah Winfrey, among others, to witness women, men, gays, straights, victims, criminals, and others regularly discussing the most intimate aspects of their lives in front of audiences of millions. Segments of the population that wouldn't ordinarily have been observable in the past, because their lives were led in special places hidden behind "gates" (Move #2), are now out in the open, out of the closet, insisting that the rest of the population have a close look.

Some scholars have speculated that we're moving into an age similar to the Paleolithic (Move #4), but that now we're hunters and gatherers of information rather than food, the era when people are nomadic and have no loyalty to specific physical settings and everyone is involved in everyone else's business. Careful to point out that this leveling of specialization and hierarchical status doesn't necessarily mean the beginning of a utopia, Meyrowitz is reluctant to classify these changes as either good or bad. In the tradition of Marshall McLuhan, he argues that new media environments are neither better nor worse than old media environments, but that they're simply different.

Not so in the horrific world of the future that J. G. Ballard paints in his short story "Intensive Care Unit." Here, in a time when all relationships take place via television, the father of a family gets the bright idea of actually meeting face to face, for the first time, his wife of many years and their two children. The meeting is a disaster, with family members trying to kill one another, and thinking back on an earlier encounter, the narrator reflects:

> True closeness, I now knew, was television closeness—the intimacy of the zoom lens, the throat microphone, the close-up itself. On the television screen there were no body odors or strained breathing, no pupil contractions and facial reflexes, no mutual sizing up of emotion and advantage, no distrust and insecurity. Affection and compassion demanded distance. Only at a distance could one find that true closeness to another human being which, with grace, might transform itself into love.

Undoubtedly, just as friendship has been transformed in this age of electronic technology, so will other kinds of feelings surrounding interpersonal relationships. "I found love on a two-way street and lost it on a super highway" was the way a once-popular song had it. Just where exactly is this particular road leading in the city of the future?

ADDITIONAL READING

Ballard, J. G. *Myths of the Future*. Triad/Panther Books, 1984.

Gitlin, Todd ed. *Watching Television*. New York: Pantheon Books, 1987.

Gumpert, Gary. *Talking Tombstones & Other Tales of the Media Age*. New York: Oxford University Press, 1987.

McLuhan, Marshall. *Understanding Media*. Toronto: New American Library of Canada, 1964.

Meyrowitz, Joshua. *No Sense of Place*. New York: Oxford University Press, 1985.

Mumford, Lewis. *Technics and Civilization*. New York: Harcourt Brace Jovanovich, 1934.

Postman, Neil. *Amusing Ourselves to Death*. New York: Viking Press, 1985.

MOVE #20

Marathon Drive

IN 490 B.C., ON THE TWENTY-EIGHTH DAY OF THE ANCIENT GREEK month of Metaeitnon, legend has it that the runner Pheidippides was dispatched from Marathon to Athens to get help in fighting the invading Persian army of Darius. He was unsuccessful in his bid and ran the twenty-six miles back to Marathon two days later. Without Spartan aid, the Athenians under the leadership of Miltiades, defeated the Persians, and again Pheidippides made the run back to Sparta to give news of the victory. He died as he spoke the words, "Rejoice, we are victorious."

Historians like to point out that Herodotus, a contemporary of the battle, gave no account of the feat, and it was only Plutarch, some 560 years later, who made reference to it. It's also been mentioned that the actual distance from the tiny village of Marathon to the center of Athens is about 38 kilometers and not the 42.195 kilometers or 26 miles and 385 yards of a certified marathon course. But the legend aside, the modern marathon originated at the 1896 Olympic Games in Athens, and just a year later, Boston began the first annual running event in the United States that has continued to this day. The time has dropped from 2 hours, 55 minutes, and 10 seconds in the first race by John McDermott to 2 hours, 7 minutes, and 51 seconds by Rob de Castella in 1986. Is it possible to drive a marathon course through a modern American city in a comparable time?

In 1987, close to 400 marathon races took place in the United States. Among those cities which have sponsored such events in the last ten years have been New York, Fairbanks, Chicago, Tucson, Boston, Little Rock, San Francisco, Fort Worth, Los Angeles, Philadelphia, Seattle, San Diego, Washington, D.C., Miami, Atlanta, Honolulu, Boise, Fort Wayne, Iowa City, Topeka, Lexington, New Orleans, Baltimore, Detroit, Minneapolis, St. Louis, Helena, Omaha, Las Vegas, Albuquerque, Charlotte, Grand Forks, Toledo, Tulsa, Eugene, Newport, Columbus, Chattanooga, Salt Lake City, Richmond, Madison, and Cheyenne.

How long would a drive along one of these routes take during an average nine-to-five working day with all the lights, traffic, and construction delays? Try it. Lay out one of these urban courses on a map and then set out to drive the route. Do it at first during the working day so that you can see the city in its everyday glory and then try it at less busy hours when the journey can offer other pleasures.

There is a certain irony about a machine with incredible horsepower that has totally transformed city life (Move #9) with its speed (Move #21), bringing itself and often everything else around it to an almost complete halt. But apparently this was also true of its predecessor, the horse and carriage, which was the major urban transportation system before the development of the "horseless carriage."

According to urban historians, the faithful horse created problems similar to those that the automobile causes today: air contaminants dangerous to health, noxious odors, and noise. And here's an image worth thinking about in a pollution-conscious era when things are often so bad that, according to the Environmental Protection Agency, in 1981 five major metropolitan areas—the Los Angeles, Long Beach area; New York City; the Riverside, San Bernadino, Ontario area; Phoenix; and the Anaheim, Santa Ana, Garden Grove area—had air quality judged to have adverse short-term effects on health more than 20 percent of the time. In a city the size of Rochester, with a horse population of 15,000 producing an average of twenty-two pounds of dung a day, a manure pile an acre in size and 175 feet high would be generated in a single year. That's a lot of dung to drop on the city.

While the first marathon was run to solicit help from the distant Spartans, today the automobile can be the perfect machine for getting in touch with the "distant friend" (Move #2). It allows people who are separated geographically to have enough contact with one another so that relationships and communities (Move #22) can be sustained. And a good deal of the popularity of the automobile also rests on the fact that it's such an effective filter in dealing with the incredible abundance of the city (Move #16). A car can be a private box on a public stage (Move #14) and combine the advantages of privacy and access to a broader public world. Just out the windshield there's everything in the city, and if you don't like what it is you see, you can drive on to a scene that's more congenial and to your liking.

Take that marathon ride. How long does it take, and what are the things that speed up and slow down the trip? Do you feel ready to write the definitive history of the grid and gridlock yet (Move #6)? Maybe the chapter after the one on Theseus being chased by the Minotaur in the labyrinth of Knossos should deal with the Exodus of the Jews from Egypt. What's it like sitting there behind the wheel, and how is the landscape experienced from this vantage point? What's seen and noticed, and what isn't? Can the automobile be considered just a transportation system to move from point A to point B, or does the trip itself have any unique features or intrinsic value? Is it still possible "just to go for a ride" in a country that is estimated to have close to 4 million miles of streets and highways, in a country where "wilderness" is legally defined as any contiguous area "at least five miles from the nearest road."

NOTES

Joys of Driving

The national passion for the automobile and the experience of driving date back to the turn of the century (Move #9). Even before the automobile, Walt Whitman wrote, "Oh public road, you express me better than I can express myself." Cars are and have been everywhere in American life and thought, from the utopian proposals of American architect Frank Lloyd Wright (Move #10) to the literature of that quintessential American movement, the "beat generation." In On the Road (New York: Viking Press, 1957), Jack Kerouac wrote, "We were leaving confusion and nonsense behind and performing our one and only noble function of the time, to move." In his book Los Angeles: The Architecture of

Four Ecologies (Harmondsworth, Middlesex, England: Penguin Press, 1971), Reyner Banham described some of the demands and attractions of the freeways of Los Angeles, "It demands, first of all, an open but decisive attitude toward the placing of the car on the road-surface, a constant stream of decisions that it would be fashionable to describe as 'existential' or even 'situational,' but would be better to regard simply as a higher form of pragmatism."

While Los Angeles is a city that may have a somewhat unusual, and perhaps excessive, involvement with the automobile—Joan Didion had her protagonist in *Play It as It Lays* (New York: Farrar, Straus & Giroux, 1970) regularly take to the freeways for reasons of mental health, and Tom Wolfe documented the Baroque glories of the automobile customizer's art in *The Kandy Kolored Tangerine Flake Streamline Baby* (New York: Farrar, Straus & Giroux, 1965) —much of this excitement seems inherent in the driving experience itself. It *can* be had even on the older streets of downtown areas in cities such as New York, Boston, Philadelphia, and Chicago.

But here precision rather than speed becomes the primary element of the experience: the slalom instead of the downhill, white-water canoeing rather than racing in a sleek shell. Every city driver knows the thrill of racing against a light at a familiar intersection. And then there are the joys of covering large urban distances without stopping, thanks to luck, timing, and intimate knowledge of traffic patterns and the progressively timed lights on a particular route. How many mini–grand prix take place during the morning commute, and does the marathon drive have any of this quality?

Driving and Viewing

Looking out the window when riding in an automobile is unavoidable, and many of America's earliest roads were designed with this in mind. Calvert Vaux, a collaborator of Frederick Law Olmsted (Move #8), first coined the word *parkway* and participated in the design of two early examples of this type of path (Move #1), Ocean Parkway and Eastern Parkway, in Brooklyn. They were inspired in part by some of the grand boulevards in Europe, particularly those of Georges-Eugène Haussmann in Paris. The nation's first public motor parkway, the Bronx River Parkway, had some 30,000 trees planted along its margins and was designed for speeds no higher than thirty-five miles per hour; commercial vehicles were banned, and the entire driving experience was clearly meant to be a recreational one. This was also true for a whole series of parkways built throughout the area and reached a culmination with the construction of the Taconic Parkway between 1940 and 1950. Even Lewis Mumford, a strong critic of most highways, who often viewed them as enemies of the city, praised the parkway as a "consummate work of art" that was responsible for "opening up great views across country, enhanced by a lavish planting of flowering bushes along borders."

The marathon drive resembles another central experience of modern American urban culture; television watching (Move #19). Both require participants to sit and look out on the world through a rectangular screen from what is, usually, a private place. Of course, the automobile typically allows more choice on what can be seen, but in the age of home video systems, even this difference is rapidly disappearing. Is travel itself, and particularly automobile travel, coming to resemble its portrayal on television more and more? Certainly the speed of the changing images and much of the content of both experiences seem similar. Ronald McDonald and his golden arches, Joe Isuzu, and a musical track in the background seem to be everywhere.

Automobile journeys through the city can be wonderful ways to explore certain aspects of the place, and if your timing's right, you can even move with relative ease. That downtown street filled solid with cars during the workday—the "largest parking lot in the world" is the way it's often described by radio traffic reporters—is completely empty several hours later. And then there are the weekends and special holidays such as the Fourth of July and Labor Day when many people try to escape the summer city heat. Those are the times that movement becomes easier, and with any luck, it's even possible to stop without paying exorbitantly for the privilege. The fact that meters and parking lots generally make it more expensive to come to a halt in urban America than to keep moving is strong testimony for both a cultural commitment to movement and speed (Move #21) and the virtual omnipresence of the automobile on the American urban scene (Move #9).

Automobile journeys through the city complement exercises such as those of Move #1 where the goal is to get an impression of the city in its entirety. Now you're at ground level and can see everything up close, but during the marathon ride, you're undoubtedly busy just keeping an eye out for the surrounding traffic. Nowhere is the coordination, which is so much a part of the crowded urban room (Move #2), as much in evidence as in the intricate patterns that automobiles weave through the city.

In *Everyday Life in the Modern World* (New York: Harper & Row, 1971), the French writer H. Lefebvre commented, "motorized traffic enables people and objects to congregate and mix without meeting . . . each element remaining enclosed in its own compartment, tucked away in its own shell." The city becomes converted to a visual experience, with all other elements removed or at least set at a distance.

The visual seems to dominate much in American life. In *Amusing Ourselves to Death* (New York: Viking Press, 1985), mentioned in Move #19, the media observer Neil Postman pointed out that today it would be virtually impossible for anyone physically unattractive to be elected to a high political office such as the presidency. To be a president is to look like a president, in an era when most of our encounters with this official are mediated by the electronic screen. And it's certainly the case that architectural students spend much more time becoming acquainted with the vagaries of visual composition than they do thinking about the social compositions that will be generated as a result of their designs. In a similar vein, researchers report that children who are perceived as physically attractive are punished less often in classroom situations and in general receive better treatment as they move through life.

In their book *The View from the Road* (Cambridge: MIT Press, 1964), researchers Donald Appleyard, Kevin Lynch, and John Meyer portrayed the driver's view of the city as "a sequence played to the eyes of a captive, somewhat fearful, but particularly inattentive audience whose vision is filtered [Move #16] and directed forward." This is the image of the harried commuter desperately trying to get to work on time while dealing with seemingly unending obstacles. It can be a very different experience cruising around in a car in light traffic, just looking at the city—sort of the urban equivalent of the traditional Sunday drive in the country.

Researchers Stephen Carr and Dale Schissler studied the way people form cognitive maps (Move #17) of the city while driving in "The City as a Trip" (*Environment and Behavior*, Volume 1, 1969). Subjects were first asked about their prior conceptions of the city and the roads they were about to travel on and then were either passengers or drivers in cars on the Northeast Expressway in Boston. Their eye movements were recorded with special cameras, and their memories of the trip were tested just after the trip, one day later, and then again a week after that. Memory for different elements of the trip—a particular building, or intersection, or stretch of road—was found to be influenced by a number of factors, including the amount of time the object was in view, the ease with which it could be assigned a verbal label ("What the hell was that thing anyway?"), how much it dominated and stood out from the surrounding cityscape, and the degree of general familiarity that the viewer had with the thing being observed.

What recollections of the marathon drive do you have a week later? And what do you remember about those special rides you take visitors on when they come in from out of town and you want to show them the place? And what kinds of automobile journeys do you sometimes take alone when you just want to look around? What might be on a list of the great urban automobile rides of the United States, and what Moves could cities make, of either a design or policy nature, to improve these experiences?

ADDITIONAL READING

Appleyard, Donald, Kevin Lynch, and John Meyer. *The View from the Road.* Cambridge: MIT Press, 1964.

Banham, Reyner. *Los Angeles: The Architecture of Four Ecologies.* Harmondsworth, Middlesex, England: Penguin Press, 1971.

Kerouac, Jack. *On the Road.* New York: Viking Press, 1957.

MOVE #21

Fast City

In his classic book *Mechanization Takes Command: A Contribution to Anonymous History* (New York: Oxford University Press, 1948), Siegfried Giedion wrote, "Our thinking and feeling in all their ramifications are fraught with the concept of movement." Movement is everywhere in urban America, and any impediments to it are looked at with extreme disfavor. In 1984 near the town of Caldwell, Idaho, "red-eyed Pete," the last traffic light on the extensive system of interstate highways built throughout the United States, was removed, placed in a coffin, and ceremonially buried. The anthropologist Robert Redfield may have used the traffic light's regulating function as an example of the impersonalized social relations of "civilization" (Move #3), but in general we don't seem to like to stop.

This change in sensibility has been accompanied by an incredible increase in the actual amounts of physical movement that the average person engages in compared with earlier times in history. Modern transportation and communication systems make possible speeds undreamed of less than a century ago. What would those two bicycle mechanics, Orville and Wilbur Wright, have to say about a transcontinental 747 flight? Can you even imagine what it's like to attain speeds reached by those unmanned spacecraft reaching out to the edges of the solar system?

The first part of this Move can be thought of as something like a journal. At the end of every day throughout the course of a week, keep a record of your movement patterns, concentrating particularly on the amount of time spent at different speeds. Should you choose not to take these instructions literally, believing that you're past the point in life where you really want additional writing assignments, then use whatever techniques you like to focus on those aspects of your experience that are concerned with speed and movement. Like many other parts of daily life, these themes become habitual to the point where we don't even notice them. The purpose of this Move is to help bring them back into a more conscious awareness. The suggestions and questions below should be helpful whether or not you choose to write.

Include in your notes some mention of the method of transportation, your attitude toward the movement itself *and* toward the geography being passed through. Was it a leisurely ride in the country where all your attention was focused out at the world, or was it a commute on the train where your head was buried in a newspaper? Was the event designed to be a sensory experience itself, such as a ride on a roller coaster or in a fast sports car on a winding country road, or was every effort made to lessen the awareness of the actual physical circumstances?

Airlines are quite good at convincing passengers that although they're six miles high in the sky speeding along at hundreds of miles an hour in a pressurized metal tube made of hundreds of parts all manufactured by the lowest bidder, they're really as safe as they are at home in front of the television set having an evening meal. The only thing that's missing is Rover wagging his tail and fetching the evening paper.

The second part of this Move is more in the form of a list. What would be on a compilation of all those products you regularly encounter—tools, foods, books, and so forth—that sell themselves through declarations of speed: computers that do thousands of operations per second, microwaved cheeseburgers or escargot, puddings that can be made faster than the old-fashioned kind, and that self-help book that shows you how to get your life in order very quickly—say, in about the next minute.

NOTES

Attitudes Toward Speed

The city is the place of speed. In *The Man Without Qualities* (London: Secker and Warburg, 1953), Thomas Musil wrote about "a kind of super-American city where everyone rushes about, or stands still with a stop watch in his hand. . . ." The social psychologist Ed Krupat found that more than 75 percent of his respondents characterized the atmosphere of big cities as being "fast paced," while other researchers have found that people actually do things, such as walking and making change, faster in big cities than they do in rural areas. Le Corbusier captured the generally positive attitude toward this speed when he wrote in 1925, "The city of speed is the city of success."

"Speed" in this Move refers both to ways of thinking *and* to ways of behaving—the thoughts that flash through your mind while you're deciding when and how to cross that city street (Move #16) and the actual physical movement made possible by modern transportation systems such as cars, trains, and planes. Then there's the metaphoric speed of the "fast" city mouse, who's always out looking for thrills while country cousin is home leading the virtuous life. A good deal of the anti-urban bias that has existed almost from the beginnings of th city (see "American Attitudes Toward Urbanization" in the Introduction) stems from this condemnation of supposed urban decadence. The Old Testament reported that the first city was built by Cain seeking protection from God's wrath after killing his brother, Abel, protection he wouldn't have needed if he hadn't been "fast." Is it any wonder that amphetamines and cocaine, which accelerate certain physiological processes and often give the user a feeling of speeding, seem to be such popular drugs in today's urban America?

Le Corbusier's sentiment was merely the affirmation of more than one hundred years of social and technological change that began with the Industrial Revolution. Observers of the modern scene have pointed out that up until the nineteenth century there was no real production of speed, but then with the Industrial Revolution suddenly it was everywhere. One of the major newspapers of nineteenth-century New York, the *Clipper*, ran a line from Shakespeare under its masthead, "The spirit of the time shall teach me speed." And it's even been speculated by historians such as Gunther Barth that baseball achieved its popularity in urban America at the end of the nineteenth century because of its association with speed. The game can be viewed as a series of quiet lulls punctuated by quick bursts of intense activity. The great pitcher Christy Mathewson said, "The American public wants its excitement rolled up in a package and handed out quickly."

Speed is also the essence of violence and war. The difference between a caress and a fatal blow can be thought of in terms of speed of delivery. War itself has been totally transformed by a technological revolution that has generated an enthusiasm for speed so great that the Italian Futurist art movement in the early twentieth century urged compatriots to dress in a style that would be appropriate for the new age of speed.

In the first Futurist Manifesto of 1909, the sculptor Marinetti wrote, "We declare that the splendor of the world has been enriched by a new beauty—the beauty of speed. A racing car with its bonnet draped with exhaust pipes like fire breathing serpents—a roaring racing car rattling along like a machine gun is more beautiful than the Winged Victory of Samothrace."

While speed still tends to be perceived as a virtue in modern urban society, it *has* had its detractors. Some have objected that speed can be viewed as evidence of laziness and lack of concern. If you do it fast, then you can't have much respect for either "it" or the people for whom you're doing it.

When Maxwell House first came out with instant coffee, they were quite disappointed with sales and hired the industrial psychologist Mason Haire to find out exactly what was going wrong. Why weren't people buying the new product when it was so much easier to prepare and earlier tests had demonstrated that people couldn't tell the difference in taste between the two types of coffee?

Haire developed an ingenious strategy for answering the question. He made up two shopping lists that were identical except for the presence of instant coffee on one list and regular coffee on the other. He then asked a sample of people to describe the type of person who would make the purchases on the two lists.

To the surprise of all, he found that potential customers tended to associate the instant-coffee purchaser with several negative traits. *Lazy, spendthrift*, and *poor planner* were the words that came up again and again. For these people, speed wasn't being equated with efficiency and success, as it was for Le Corbusier and the Italian Futurists, but rather with sloth and a lack of concern for family well-being. The denial of an investment in time was interpreted as not caring. Sales increased dramatically when Maxwell House changed their marketing strategy and began selling customers on the idea that their time could be put to better use if they just used the instant product.

Even today, many items are marketed using the same strategy. "Would you rather spend Saturday morning mowing the lawn with that old hand-powered machine you have or buy our power mower and finish the job in less than half the time? Then you can take the kids to the zoo." And save them from drugs, crime, and all the other perils of fast modern life is always the unstated, but strongly implied, final message in these ads.

An eloquent protest against this obsession with speed came from the noted writer William Gass. In an article in the *New York Times Book Review* (April 1, 1984) attacking the idiocy of "speed reading" and celebrating the pleasures of leisurely reading and drinking, he had the following to say,

> Well, there's another way of drinking that I'd like to recommend. We've already dealt with the first way. Gulp. Get the gist. And the gist is the level of alcohol in your blood, the pilixated breath you blow into the test balloon. It makes appropriate the expression: have a belt. We can toss down a text, a time of life, a love affair, that walk in the park that goes from here to there. You have no doubt encountered people who impatiently wait for the payoff; they urge you to come to the point; at dinner the early courses merely delay the dessert; they look only at the bottom line (that obscene phrase); they are persons consumed by consequences; they want to climax without crescendo.

How many sex therapists have built careers around that last dilemma and have made fortunes in teaching people how to go slow? Perhaps to make up for lost time a chain of speed-eating schools with the motto "where the fleet meet to eat" should be established.

Separation of Space and Time

If you've been keeping a journal of your movements as suggested, you'll find that because we live in an age where such great speed is possible, space and time have become almost entirely separated. A thousand miles can be a walk of two months, a ten-day bike trip, an overnight train ride, a two-hour plane flight, or a seven-second phone call. And even the same amount of space can require extremely different amounts of time to cross at different times of the day. Every commuter knows this. While this is not exactly a profound observation, the extent to which this is true is always startling. It has been argued that a large part of contemporary city life revolves around the availability of parking space. This conjures up an image of Romeo in today's Verona, unable to play his balcony scene because all the lots are full, cruising endlessly looking for that empty space and musing over the travails of modern love.

Much of the recent popularity of jogging is probably because in this activity space and time *do* maintain their traditional historical relationship. Other things being equal, a two-mile run *does* take about twice the amount of time as a one-mile run. This is an unusual occurrence in the modern world where a twelve-mile trip into the city can take anywhere from fifteen minutes to two hours, depending on the time of day and the conditions under which it is made.

All sporting events tend to treat space and time as they were in the traditional pre-electronic world. This, along with their explicitness, everything is the way it seems to be and there's little room for debate or interpretation the way there is in judging the winner of a family argument or a presidential campaign debate, undoubtedly accounts for much of their immense popularity. The yardage between the thirty-five and forty yard line is the same as that between the fifteen and the twenty yard line, and it's always the same ninety feet between the bases of baseball. This can be comforting in a world where space seems to expand and contract regularly, continuously changing its relationship to time. The sharp edge of the playing field, which defines exactly what is "in" and what is "out of bounds," creates an all too rare strong sense of place (Move #19) in a world where speed has all but eliminated most "edges" (Move #1), including the ancient city wall. What would city life be like if Le Corbusier's maxim were turned on its head and suddenly everything slowed down?

ADDITIONAL READING

De Pomaine, Edouard. *French Cooking in Ten Minutes*. New York: Farrar, Straus & Giroux, 1977. Originally published by Editions Paul Martial, Paris, 1930, this is one of the earliest and most delightful "how to do it fast" books, and the author suggests, in a vein similar to childbirth scenes in American movies, westerns and otherwise, that you immediately boil a pot of water upon arriving home from work. It's bound to be good for something. A recent edition of *Books in Print* reveals approximately thirty book titles beginning with the words "one minute," and these address topics including Bible stories, business letters, motherhood, and wisdom. Things are getting faster and faster.

V

THE COMMUNITY

THE FIVE MOVES IN THIS SECTION ALL DEAL WITH people in groups. More than anything else, the city is made up of collections of people who come together in different ways to form communities. If an important dimension of human behavior is establishing the appropriate distance between oneself and other people (Move #15)—moving toward them when company is needed or desired and in the opposite direction when solitude is the goal—then the establishment of groups and communities is clearly an essential part of this. As a species, we seem to be decidedly social, and the city is both a product of this social behavior and the place where a great deal of group activity takes place.

Community has been defined by the sociologist Gideon Sjoberg as "a collectivity of actors sharing a limited territorial area as the base for carrying out the greatest share of their activities"—collections of people who hang out and do things together. This implies more than just using screens and filters (Move #16) and choreography (Move #18) to distance the close stranger. The term social scientists use is *interaction*, and this activity turns mere collections of people into communities. Three central components appear again and again in almost every definition of community. The first is a certain commonality or shared set of characteristics among people. This is often the very reason people associate with one another—social scientists have confirmed that birds of a feather do indeed flock together—and it also allows for the possibility of communication between them. Traditional definitions of *community* also include mention of the mechanisms of social interaction—the rules, rituals, and technologies that people use to get together—*and* references to the particular place where the community is located.

Among those definitions of *community* provided by the *Oxford English Dictionary* are the following: "1. The quality of appertaining to all in common; common ownership, liability, etc. 1561, 2. Common character, agreement, identity, 1587, 3. Social intercourse, communion, 1570, 4. A body of people organized into a political, municipal or social identity, ME, 5. A body of persons living together and practicing a community of goods, 1727."

Many contemporary thinkers view the establishment of community in modern society as quite problematical. How can people figure out ways of being with one another when so many of the traditional activities and institutions that, in the past sustained group behavior no longer seem to be able to do this? Family, religion, and leisure are all changing in ways that seem to be making the formation of groups and collections of people more difficult. The great American social ritual of going to the movies, for example, is being challenged by video viewing in the privacy of the home (Move #11); at the same time, the American family seems to be in serious difficulty—and not just the families of the poor or particular social and ethnic groups.

Changes in the institution of the family are so

widespread and have occurred so quickly that we seem to have run out of appropriate language to describe what is going on. Our kinship terminology seems highly outmoded. Terms such as *stepmother* and *half brother* conjure up images of witches, poison apples, and late-night TV with Vincent Price where something has gone terribly wrong in that laboratory in the basement.

All the Moves in Part V deal with aspects of urban group behavior. Move #22 explores two different images of community. With the development of modern technology, it's become possible for people to interact with others who aren't in the same physical location. "Aspatial" communities are collections of people who form communities even though they're scattered over wide expanses of the landscape. Lewis Mumford said it when he wrote that the appropriate image for the city had moved from the Neolithic container—a walled, clay object designed to keep some things in and most things out—to that of the electronic net. Social scientists use the term *network analysis*, while the planner Melvin Webber wrote about "community without propinquity." The two popular children's television shows, "Sesame Street" and "Mr. Rogers' Neighborhood," can be helpful when thinking about the distinctions between spatial and aspatial communities.

Move #23 deals with urban preferences and the way people go about ranking cities, while Move #24 explores a frequently encountered type of urban spatial community, the neighborhood. It's in this part of the city that the paradox of the close stranger and distant friend (Move #2) doesn't seem to hold. And it's here, according to advocates such as Clarence Perry, Clarence Stein (Move #9), and Jane Jacobs, that the salvation of the American city lies. Move #25 deals with where we've come from, the origins of the many racial and ethnic groups that make up urban America. Move #26 is your Move, an invitation to you, the reader, to share the

Moves you make in American cities with a wider audience and perhaps begin to form something of an aspatial community whose focus is an interest in sharing and exploring city Moves.

MOVE #22

Images of Community

"Sesame Street" and "Mr. Rogers' Neighborhood"

THE TWO POPULAR CHILDREN'S TELEVISION SHOWS "SESAME STREET" and "Mr. Rogers' Neighborhood" can serve as useful examples of two very different types of community. They convey different messages to their audiences about the nature of collections of people and how they go about hanging out together. It would probably make some sense to have a look at these two shows while making this Move, particularly if you've never seen them. (I suspect that large numbers of adults are already in the audience of "Sesame Street," and this would appear to be confirmed by the presence of many of the show's characters, such as Big Bird and the Muppets, in a wide variety of other settings, ranging from galas downtown to shopping mall openings. Are we coming to an era where Mr. Rogers will anchor the evening news after even Dan Rather is found by the audience and network officials to be too jaded?) There's almost no television market in the United States where the two shows are unavailable, and their enormous popularity clearly indicates that they appeal to children on levels other than merely communicating specific educational skills such as recognizing specific numbers and letters.

In "Mr. Rogers' Neighborhood," all the characters reside in a particular geographic place, and the community itself is based on this fact. Whenever Mr. Rogers goes to visit anyone, the viewer is informed of how he makes the journey, and this even holds for those trolley rides through the tunnel under the mountain to the "neighborhood of make-believe." Geography is real and is treated as such, and the whole place has a feel of what one scholar of actual urban neighborhoods, Herbert Gans, has called an "urban village." This kind of community can be thought of as a "spatial community." Before the advent of sophisticated transportation and communication systems (Moves #9, #19, #20), all communities had to be spatial. There was no other way for people to stay in touch in an era when staying in touch often meant just that, staying in *touch*. And touch absolutely requires minimal distance between people (Move #15), sharing a location. Villages, residential colleges, urban neighborhoods (Move #24), and that extended family of mother, father, children, aunts, uncles, and grandparents all living in the same house or on the same block are examples of spatial communities.

But "Sesame Street" reveals the possibility of a different kind of community. Here, many different kinds of characters seem to transcend space and are always dropping in. First there's a quiet scene with a child and an adult sitting and talking on a stoop and then, all of a sudden, the numbers 3, 5, and 7 show up to do a dance whose purpose it is to inform the viewer about what it's like to be a number hanging out in a community of numbers. Then a noted sports figure such as Marvin Hagler and perhaps comedian Lily Tomlin show up and have a chat with Big Bird and number 5. To ask where everybody first met or where the numbers come from or where they're going for that matter makes as little sense as it does to talk about the path the electronic television signal makes as it moves through the space between its transmission point and your individual receiver. It really has very little to do with the experience of viewing the show. Continuity in time and space seems a less essential part of the aspatial community than it is of the spatial community.

Commuter colleges, professional societies, and the modern family, which is often scattered halfway across the country and keeps in contact with technology and ritual gatherings on special occasions, are all examples of "aspatial communities." These collections of people aren't located in a specific, special place and, as a community, seem to exist independent of space. A good deal of modern city life seems to have this quality. Many urbanites live in one place, work in another, play in yet others, and have friends and acquaintances scattered all over the landscape. As a consequence, a good deal of time and energy is spent moving among these different locations (Move #20).

Think for a moment about all those different communities of which you are a member—collections of family, friends, professional and vocational colleagues, religious and political associates, and all those other groups whose membership is of some significance to you. How many of those collections are "spatial" and how many are "aspatial"? What are some of the basic differences among these different types of communities in terms of the way people in them think and interact with one another?

NOTES

First, it's important to realize that aspatial communities have become possible only relatively recently, while spatial communities have probably been around as long as there have been people. Even in nomadic hunter-gatherer cultures (Move #4), communities regularly gathered in particular settings for certain kinds of rituals, often having to do with prayer and burying the dead. Lewis Mumford saw this Necropolis as one of the ancestors of the city, but today even the spatial nature of the kingdom of the dead is being transformed. In *Talking Tombstones and Other Tales of the Media Age* (New York: Oxford University Press, 1987), Gary Gumpert reported the plans of one company to market recording devices built into tombstones that would carry prerecorded messages from the deceased, voices from beyond, and at least the suggestion of the ultimate aspatial community.

Some essential differences between spatial and aspatial communities can be thought of in terms of three dichotomies— geography versus technology, spontaneity versus planning, and support in times of crisis as opposed to toleration of diversity.

Geography and Technology

The love of the spatial community for its geographic base is well known and has been amply documented on every scale from the individual family and home (Move #11) to the neighborhood (Move #24), to the patriotism of the modern nation-state. Members of the community are often willing to die in defense of the sacred soil of the homeland, and even when they're not so willing, this is an obligation the national community feels quite comfortable imposing on them. To defend the "special place," whether nation, city, or neighborhood, seems to be an essential part of the role of citizen. The intensity of these feelings is often so strong that they've been compared to the attachments certain species of animals make to their "territories." In his classic study of urban renewal in the West End neighborhood of Boston (Move #11), Marc Fried reported that many people when forced to leave said such things as, "I felt that my heart had been torn out of me." Lamenting the loss of the group's place runs throughout human history and goes back at least as far as the Old Testament and Adam and Eve and the Garden of Eden.

Members of aspatial communities often experience geography merely as something to be moved through (Move #20) rather than anything of significance in its own right. That the relationship with it is tenuous should not be surprising since it's often encountered in a most indirect fashion. Activities such as flying, driving, and talking on the telephone result in a certain distancing from the environment when compared with the activity of actually walking through a particular place (Move #16), where it's possible to see, hear, smell, and touch the landscape. With the advent of such sophisticated communication systems as the automobile telephone, the typical opening line, "How are you?" pales in complexity next to the question, "Where are you?" And this is even more true for those telephones that are being installed on commercial airliners. Does it make any sense at all to imagine the landscape that lies between the two voices on a telephone? It's even less material for us than the scenery we pass on the way home from work (Move #20).

For members of aspatial communities, a good deal of involvement and emotion becomes attached to the technology that sustains the interaction necessary to maintain the community. Certainly, the American love affair with the automobile (Move #9) has become a dominant part of contemporary reality, and television appears to be insinuating itself even further into our communal life (Move #19). Not only does the tube supply mechanisms for staying in touch with other people, but we're even provided with a cast of characters to love, hate, respect, disdain, and ask advice from on everything from financial to sexual strategies. Sex therapists such as Doctor Ruth are regularly asked questions on national television which, before the advent of this medium, would have been asked only in the most private of circumstances. And many people firmly believe that if the world ever does end, it somehow won't be real until its implications have been explored on late-night television by Ted Koppel or some other "serious" newscaster. The aspatial community's love of technology can result in its being viewed as the most "real" aspect of the environment.

Planning Versus Spontaneity

Aspatial communities place a premium on planning and co-ordination (Move #2). This must be the case if any interaction between community members is to take place at all. A day of shopping together for a mother and daughter who live hundreds of miles away from each other certainly requires different attitudes in this regard than the same set of activities would if they lived just a block apart. The likelihood of spontaneous, unplanned encounters between the two disappears with the vast increase of space between them. If they can maintain access to a working technology, they can still interact as much as they want to, but now those encounters have to be planned. This is something everyone deals with when trying to coordinate get-togethers between members of aspatial communities—perhaps a business or professional gathering. After seemingly endless hours of planning and scheduling, suddenly there's a lament for the good old days when everyone was down the hall from everyone else, and all it took was a quick walk, or even shout, to gather the community.

Support and Tolerance

There is also the trade-off between support in times of crisis and a tolerance of diversity. Because members of spatial communities often lead their lives surrounded by friends and acquaintances in typical village fashion, they can count on a good deal of support in times of crisis. It's hard to imagine the Kitty Genovese incident (Move #16) happening in a village atmosphere where everyone knew everyone else. If you're getting hit over the head in the streets, people will quickly come to your aid. But at the same time, there isn't much tolerance of diversity in these settings. People who feel obligated to help others in times of crises also feel little hesitation in telling those same people how to go about leading their lives, how to think, what to wear, who to associate with, and so on. Members of aspatial communities on the other hand are often surrounded by strangers (Move #2) and because of this can't count on as much support (Move #16), but they can rely on the tolerance that groups of strangers must develop toward others' different ways.

The traditional portrait of the city as the place of tolerance, where all preferences in matters political, sexual, and aesthetic can be indulged, is based in large part on the fact that most urbanites are members of aspatial communities and lead a good part of their lives surrounded by strangers. In a book entitled *Cosmopolitan Culture* (New York: Atheneum, 1987), the sociologist Bonnie Kahn developed the theme that many of the best qualities of city life are the result of these strangers; "All cities have strangers, but only some cities prize and encourage them, valuing variety and taking pride in their achievements." These are cosmopolitan centers—back to "Sesame Street" and the incredible diversity of the characters who can show up in the community. Anyone or thing can drop in at any time, and this has always been one of the great appeals of the city.

ADDITIONAL READING

Kahn, Bonnie. *Cosmopolitan Culture*. New York: Atheneum, 1987.

Stoneall, Linda. *Country Life, City Life: Five Theories of Community*. New York: Praeger, 1983.

Webber, Melvin. "Order in Diversity: Community Without Propinquity." In *Cities and Space: The Future Uses of Urban Land: Essays from the Fourth RFF Forum*, edited by L. Wingo et al. Baltimore: Johns Hopkins University Press, 1963.

MOVE #23

Do We Like It Here?
A Survey of Urban Preferences

WHICH CITIES DO WE LIKE AND WHICH CITIES AREN'T WE TOO ENthusiastic about? People have been making judgments about cities from their very beginnings, but only relatively recently have there been attempts to do this in a more systematic fashion. Rationalize the activity so that it might be done more accurately. The interesting thing about these attempts to rank cities in terms of preference is that, similar to the activity of assigning nicknames (Move #3), they often reveal more about the people making the judgments than they do about the places being judged. They clearly tell a story about what people consider to be important when thinking about cities.

Ranking cities is a good example of the strategy of dealing with the abundance and diversity of the urban scene by imposing some sort of order on it, that is "hierarchical thinking and the disregarding of low-priority inputs" in the language of Move #16. This is another example of ranking as a "filter" so that only the good stuff can get through. Figure out which cities are "good" places and which aren't, and then any decisions that have to be made about these places—from where to live to where to visit—will be easier to make.

Which city is your favorite and why? How significant are things such as educational and employment opportunities, the architecture and look of the place, recreational features and issues such as safety from crime and environmental hazards? What is it that makes a city preferable to other cities?

NOTES

Some Early Efforts

"Quality of life" indicators were pioneered by C. Angoff and the noted American journalist H. L. Mencken in an article in the September 1931 *American Mercury* entitled "Worst American State." Angoff and Mencken used the state, rather than the city, as a unit of analysis, and one criterion they adopted was compliance with the laws of Prohibition. They no doubt felt that while it probably wasn't really important whether drinking was going on or not, it *was* important whether particular urban populations were obeying the laws of the land.

In other early efforts, *Your City* (New York: Harcourt Brace Jovanovich, 1939) and *144 Smaller Cities* (New York: Harcourt Brace Jovanovich, 1940), the noted psychologist Edward Lee Thorndike compiled a list of thirty-seven items that he claimed represented "those which all reasonable persons would regard as significant for the goodness of life for good people in a city." Using these measures, Thorndike ranked 310 large American cities. Thorndike's numbers dealt with educational opportunities for the public, health, recreational opportunities, something he called "creature comforts," the degree of literacy, and a number of miscellaneous issues. He found that the three factors that accounted for most of the differences among city rankings were wealth, income, and something labeled the "quality of people." This last factor was measured by, among other things, the extent of public library usage and the percentage of high school graduates in the urban population.

In a 1951 article in *The American Journal of Sociology* entitled "The Moral Integration of American Cities," the sociologist Robert Angell objected to the idea that the quality of urban life could somehow be judged by a mere summation of different factors in the manner of Thorndike. He suggested that a better measure would be what he called "moral integration"—the "degree to which there is a common set of ends and values toward which all are oriented and in terms of which the life of the group is oriented." Angell developed two ways of measuring this "moral integration." The first dealt with the amount of welfare money raised by city residents to be used by their less fortunate neighbors, and the other considered the amount of crime that was present. Statistics on murder, robbery, burglary, and other felonies were used. Interestingly enough, these measures didn't correlate very highly with one another. That is, if a city had a high score on one of the measures, crime for instance, this didn't necessarily mean that it would have a similar score on the other measure, the Welfare Effort Index. According to Angell, the four best cities in the United States were Rochester and Syracuse, New York; Erie, Pennsylvania; and Worcester, Massachusetts. The four worst were Atlanta, Miami, Tulsa, and Memphis.

Three More Recent Attempts

In 1976, Ben-Chieh Liu of the Midwest Research Institute published one of the most highly regarded studies of comparative urban quality. He gathered data in five broadly defined areas he considered important in the ranking of cities. The first was an "economic component." This included measures of personal income, wealth, and indicators of broader community-wide economic health. Then there was the "political component," with data having to do with local government performance, the amount of citizen participation in municipal affairs, and the degree of public welfare assistance. The "environmental component" was made up of measures of air quality, noise, water, pollution, and availability of outdoor recreational facilities. The "health and education component" included the infant mortality rate, the death rate, the availability of medical care, and educational opportunities. The "social component" was the broadest of all the categories. It included measures of discrimination based on the differences in income and employment among various racial groups and between men and women, the general cost of living, the crime rate, housing quality, and the availability of sports and cultural opportunities.

Liu compared sixty-five cities of 500,000 or more in population, eighty-three cities of between 200,000 and 500,000, and ninety-five cities of between 50,000 and 200,000 people. For every city the quantitative measures used for each component were combined into a single score. These were then assigned grades ranging from A for "outstanding," to E for "substandard." A total score was then computed by summing up the five scores for each city.

Only Portland, Oregon, received straight As, with Sacramento, California, in second place with four As and a C in economic quality.

Liu's rankings of the sixty-five largest cities of the United States were as follows:

OUTSTANDING

1. Portland
2. Sacramento
3. Seattle
4. San Jose
5. Minneapolis–St. Paul
6. Rochester
7. Hartford
8. Denver
9. San Francisco–Oakland
10. San Diego
11. Grand Rapids
12. Milwaukee
13. Salt Lake City

EXCELLENT

14. Anaheim–Santa Ana– Garden Grove
15. Buffalo
16. Oklahoma City
17. Omaha
18. Albany–Schenectady– Troy
19. Syracuse
20. Washington, D.C.
21. Los Angeles–Long Beach
22. Columbus
23. Boston
24. Cleveland
25. Toledo

GOOD

26. San Bernadino– Riverside–Ontario
27. Houston
28. Phoenix
29. Akron
30. Cincinnati
31. Honolulu
32. Dayton
33. New York
34. Dallas
35. Kansas City
36. Indianapolis
37. Chicago

ADEQUATE

38. Newark
39. Patterson–Clifton–Passaic
40. Springfield–Chicopee–Holyoke
41. Youngstown–Warren
42. Detroit
43. Richmond
44. Fort Worth
45. Atlanta
46. Fort Lauderdale–Hollywood
47. Miami
48. Nashville–Davidson
49. Pittsburgh
50. Allentown–Bethlehem–Easton
51. St. Louis
52. Gary–Hammond–East Chicago
53. Louisville
54. Providence–Pawtucket–Warwick
55. Baltimore

SUBSTANDARD

56. Tampa–St. Petersburg
57. Philadelphia
58. Memphis
59. Norfolk–Portsmouth
60. Greensboro–Winston-Salem–High Point
61. Jacksonville
62. San Antonio
63. New Orleans
64. Birmingham
65. Jersey City

It's important to keep in mind when looking at this data that the five components were simply added up to reach a total score, and no attention was paid to how much of each component actually contributed to quality of urban life. There's also the difficulty of giving an area as large as an entire city a single rating and thereby implicitly assuming that every part of the city is the equivalent of every other part. Anyone who has searched for a place to live or a site on which to locate a business within a specific city knows that this is nonsense. As a matter of fact, one of the essential qualities of the American city and in a way all cities is that widely different events and experiences are all located within a relatively small area. Then there are those subjective aspects of deciding what is really worth measuring and how to go about measuring it. And consider all the individual little quirks and preferences in matters ranging from weather to the availability of specific groups and activities? Someone interested in jazz, American history, good food, tropical flora, and fishing would have to rank New Orleans much higher than sixty-third.

In an attempt to take into account the more subjective aspects of urban description, the geographers D. Lowenthal and M. Riel used a somewhat different method. They had observers from a wide range of backgrounds, including nurses, architects, senior citizens, and boy scouts, walk along a number of different routes in one of four cities. New York, Boston, Cambridge, Massachusetts, and Columbus, Ohio, were explored. The subjects were then asked to give impressions of their walks in interviews and by responding to questionnaires. Words typically used to describe New York were "busy, wealthy, fashionable, alive, crowds, depressing, varied, colorful, touristy, happy, cheap and vulgar, and rundown." Boston was viewed as "crowded, old and quaint, busy, rundown, different, having shops and stores, peaceful, green, messy, colorful, filthy, and high-class." Cambridge was seen as "green, rundown, varied, busy, having a lot of traffic, peaceful, depressing, a mess, academic, residential, old and quaint, and dull." Columbus was, in many ways, described as the opposite of New York. It was portrayed as "green, rundown, messy, varied, peaceful, neat, depressing, hilly, and having lots of children, apartments, churches and schools"—in many ways, the perfect suburb (Move #9).

In a somewhat similar approach, the psychologists W. Guild and E. Krupat built on the extensive work of Rudolph Moos in assessing environmental quality. Moos has written, "environments have unique personalities just the way people do," an interesting use of the organic metaphor (Move #3). They asked one hundred undergraduates to describe a big city to a person who had just arrived from Mars. Their instructions read, "Suppose a Martian landed and asked you where you lived and you said, 'A big city.' But he said, 'We have no such words in our language. Tell me the 10 most important things you can so I can know what one is.' "

This procedure generated 300 different words and phrases which were then edited down to a list of 75 terms. This list was then presented to college students who came from a wide range of settings, and they rated each of the seventy-five terms for its applicability to a large metropolis, a mid-sized city, and a small town. For thirty-three of the terms, there was agreement among

75 percent or more of the students that a trait was either characteristic or uncharacteristic of a large metropolis.

People in cities were seen as "untrusting, interesting, often lonely, liberal, and not intrusive in other people's affairs." The general atmosphere was viewed as "competitive, very active, entertaining, cultured, fast paced, anonymous, isolating, allowing choice in friendship, diverse, modern, impersonal, and confusing." Large metropolises were *not* described as "peaceful, safe, healthful, close-knit, relaxed or intimate." Krupat and Guild reported that much more consensus was reached about the general atmosphere of the city than about the people who inhabited the place. For many, the city is indeed the place where the people who are close are often strangers (Move #2).

ADDITIONAL READING

Krupat, E. *People in Cities: The Urban Environment and Its Effects.* Cambridge: Cambridge University Press, 1985. This is a good introduction to some aspects of the two relatively new subfields of social psychology that have come to be known as "environmental psychology" and "urban psychology."

Liu, Ben-Chien. *Quality of Life Indicators in U.S. Metropolitan Areas: A Statistical Analysis.* New York: Praeger, 1976.

MOVE #24

The Neighborhood

IN HIS CLASSIC STUDY OF BOSTON'S NORTH END, *THE URBAN VIL-LAGERS* (New York: The Free Press, 1962), the sociologist Herbert Gans coined the term "urban village." This is as good a description as any of the typical city neighborhood and a prime example of a spatial community (Move #22) where the paradox of the "close stranger and distant friend" (Move #2) doesn't hold. Neighborhoods are those places in the city where everyone seems to know everyone else, and there's a lot of life right out there on the streets.

The term *neighborhood* as it's being used in this Move implies that the occupants of a particular place have a lot to do with one another, a "high interaction rate" in the language of social science. When this is used as a criterion, it's quickly realized that many urbanites don't live in neighborhoods at all. All those places where anonymity reigns supreme and the only interactions over the years are the ritual "good mornings" and "good evenings" on the way to and from work clearly don't qualify. In this Move, the term *neighborhood* is being used for those places that have the feel of a village.

And village life is characterized by people's always running into one another. In their study of the East London neighborhood of Bethnal Green, for example, the English sociologists Peter Willmott and Michael Young found that married women encountered their parents and siblings and the parents and siblings of their husbands or wives on the average of more than twice a day. After a Move out of the neighborhood, this was reduced to little more than twice a week, and this had a great deal of impact on the kinds of relationships people could have with one another. Suddenly, friends, neighbors, and family who had always been around for support and company were no longer immediately available and life was led amidst strangers.

While neighborhoods, along with many other types of spatial communities, seem to be rapidly disappearing under the onslaught of technology and other conditions of contemporary life, large numbers of people still seem to consider them to be one of the quintessential urban experiences. To know the American city one must visit these places, and within them are housed the full range of racial and ethnic diversity to be found in the United States. Visiting an ethnic neighborhood can be like a trip to another country and another time, and although one would have to be a fool to equate the place with the Old Country—San Francisco's Chinatown is no more China than any of the numerous Little Italies found throughout the country are villages in southern Italy—there can be more than a touch of the foreign about them. And you don't have to worry about passports, changing money, and all those other inconveniences that are unavoidable when going abroad.

And in a sense, a trip to any neighborhood is like moving backwards in time. The scale of the place is more manageable than the immensity of the skyscrapers (Move #12) encountered in other parts of the city, and while the area is often dominated by a specific racial or ethnic group, the more public nature of much of their activity gives a vivid impression of vibrancy and movement. Here's where street life can be observed, and these parts of the city are wonderful places for people-watching (see Part IV).

Of course, a certain amount of discretion is called for since no one appreciates strangers snooping around in his or her home (Move #11). While a good percentage of the population of contemporary America has some of its origins in city neighborhoods, the visitor should be aware of the relationships among different local racial and ethnic groups. No one has ever made friends by asking for Turkish coffee in a Greek restaurant, and Columbus

Day isn't quite the same thing in Scandinavian neighborhoods as it is in Italian ones. (The Scandinavians are always talking about Viking visitors to the New World centuries before Columbus.)

And then of course there's racism, which seems almost endemic throughout this country and the world. Here the term is most often used to describe negative attitudes toward blacks and hispanics, but since this is a multi-racial, multi-ethnic society, examples of every possible kind of group antagonism—from "dot bashing" (racial violence against persons of Indian descent) to anti-Catholicism—can be found.

Although there are considerable amounts of violence in some urban neighborhoods, a not altogether surprising fact given the incredible range of wealth in urban America, from a statistical point of view, it's still a relatively rare phenomenon. Think back to your own experience and then compare it to the number of bodies you regularly see piled up on television. This is said less in the spirit of trying to convince you that it's safe to visit neighborhoods, which is something many people already know, and more as a piece of information that anyone trying to understand urban behavior should have. Most of the time most of the people don't run around shooting one another in the fashion of those gory television shows, some of which are unfortunately the news, and with a little common sense, you should be fine. Nevertheless, a certain amount of "street smarts" are called for. You wouldn't want to be burned by some of the heat given off by the "melting pot" (Move #25).

Neighborhood settings are usually identified along ethnic, racial, social class, and stylistic lines and can be discovered in many of the traditional sources that claim to "know" the city—guidebooks, chamber of commerce publications, ethnic associations, and so on. Trips to these settings can be rewarding city Moves.

NOTES

The Street

If the typical spatial community has strong feelings for its geography (Move #22), then the geography of the neighborhood is mainly composed of its streets. In *Manchild in the Promised Land* (New York: Macmillan, 1965), Claude Brown told of this love of the streets: "I always thought of Harlem as home, but I never thought of Harlem as being in the house. To me, home was the streets."

Contrast this with the traditional negative attitudes expressed toward this part of the geography in many other places in urban America—programs to "keep the kids off the streets" and the general association of the word *street* with everything wicked, dangerous, and evil in modern life. What are some of the images that first come to mind when you hear the word *street*?

A partial list of those things illegal on the streets of one typical mid-sized city, Ann Arbor, Michigan, clearly reflect this attitude. Among those things not permitted are "begging; uttering vile, profane or obscene language; to wrongfully accost, ogle, insult, annoy, follow; stand in crowds, or loiter." The whole idea of forbidding loitering actively discourages the very kinds of public face-to-face encounters that lie at the heart of a spatial community such as a neighborhood. And the assumption that the street would be the natural setting for some of these less civilized types of behavior is hardly conducive to encouraging an active street life.

Not so in the neighborhood—here there's a lot going on out on the street. It's where everyone runs into everyone else and isn't just considered a path (Move #1) to get from one location to another. It's a place that has significance in its own right, and the many religious festivals that regularly transport holy objects through some of these neighborhoods even lend a sacred air to the setting. This is true whether the objects of veneration are saints from Sicily or Thanksgiving Day parade floats. The geography of the village, whether urban or rural, is often considered sacred.

In her classic study *The Death and Life of Great American Cities* (New York: Vintage Books, 1961), Jane Jacobs argued strongly for a resurgence of neighborhoods. Along with this was her recognition of the street and sidewalk as an essential part of the city. According to Jacobs, streets are the generators of safety and one of the most important means of contact for members of the community. They are also important vehicles for the assimilation of children. Planners and designers are often quite upset when children of all ages seem to prefer the excitement of the street to those places that have been designed specifically for their exclusive use, playgrounds, parks, plazas, and so on. This preference shows an awareness people seem to have of the central roles of spontaneity and serendipity in play and communal life.

Jacobs has taken strong issue with many important figures in architecture and city planning, including Ebenezer Howard and Le Corbusier (Move #10), those of the City Beautiful Movement (Move #7), and many modern architects (Move #12) for their disregard of the street. She claims that their attempts to sanitize it by limiting its use to particular kinds of traffic or geographically isolating it from other parts of the city are essentially anti-urban in sentiment. For her, the streets are the skeleton that supports and holds together the body of the city.

Interestingly enough, with all this reverence for the street, in studies conducted by Donald Appleyard and his colleagues it was found that one factor that significantly influenced the amount of satisfaction people expressed with particular streets in a neighborhood was the amount of traffic on them.

Researchers examined three streets in an Italian neighborhood in San Francisco. One was identified as having heavy traffic (15,750 vehicles per day); one, moderate traffic (8,700); and one, light traffic (2,000). Residents in the three different settings were asked questions about traffic hazards, stress, noise, pollution, social interaction, privacy, and home territoriality. People who lived on the heavy traffic street perceived higher levels of hazard, more environmental degradation, and tended to confine their friendships to the side of the street where their residences were located. On the light and moderate traffic streets, friendships extended across the street. In these situations, spatial propinquity, or nearness, became an important factor in establishing friendships. And perhaps even more significantly, when asked to draw their home territories, light-traffic street residents typically included the whole street, while those on heavy-traffic streets tended to include only their apartments or on occasion their apartment houses—a pulling back similar to the use of the filter (Move #16) as a way of dealing with the numbers, variety, and density of the city.

Building Neighborhoods

Within the last several decades there's been a resurgence of neighborhood activity in many American cities. This has been happening in blue-collar communities, lower-middle-class white ethnic neighborhoods, and inner-city neighborhoods to which many middle-class residents have been returning. The joys of the spatial community (Move #22) are being discovered by large numbers of people who seem to be tired of all the movement required of those who lead more aspatial lives.

Neighborhood organizations have played a vital role in neighborhood renewal and revitalization, and the National Commission on Neighborhoods has listed more than 8,000 neighborhood organizations nationwide. In communities with more than 50,000 residents, according to a Gallup poll conducted in 1977, 12 percent of the adult population belonged to a neighborhood group.

The Neighborhood Participation project was conducted by the community psychologist Abe Wandersman and his colleagues J. F. Jakubs and G. Giamartino in Nashville, Tennessee. They were trying to answer the question of why some people participated in these groups while others didn't, and what it was that made some of these groups so much more successful than others. The hope was that once these questions were answered the information could be of use for those who were trying to build neighborhoods.

Much of their data was collected on thirty-nine blocks, from more than 1,200 people in the Waverly-Belmont neighborhood of Nashville. The neighborhood was typical of many American transitional urban neighborhoods that experienced an exodus of much of the middle class to the suburbs (Move #9) after World War II. This usually resulted in a general deterioration of the physical and social environment, but recently there has been something of a movement back to these areas by middle-class residents who have rediscovered reasonably priced and placed real estate. The Waverly-Belmont neighborhood was racially integrated, although individual blocks tended to be primarily white or black, and was composed for the most part of one- and two-family dwellings, with a few three- and four-family units mixed in.

Wandersman and his colleagues found that those who were somehow more "rooted" (Move #11) to the place tended to participate in block organizations. These people had usually lived on the block for a longer period of time and were often older, married, homeowners, and female. When asked to name the most important reason for joining the group, they talked most often about improving the residential environment. Less frequently mentioned were the influence of other people and a sense of duty. Those who didn't join these organizations talked about lack of time, scheduling difficulties, and, on occasion, their poor physical condition.

In related work, it was found that in those locations where a lot of residents tended to join volunteer organizations and had feelings of civic duty, block organizations were usually formed. What was interesting about these findings was the discovery that while these characteristics didn't distinguish between members and nonmembers on an individual level, they were important when averaged across the entire block. The authors postulated that they created a "block climate" that influenced organizational development.

The neighborhood, like the city itself, is more than just the sum of its parts (Move #1), and it's clear that neighborhoods, like the blocks of which they're composed, develop distinctive climates. It's this particular climate, or atmosphere, which results in its being experienced as a specific place, a "district" in the language of Kevin Lynch (Move #1), and one of the four quarters made up by the crossroads in the ancient Egyptian hieroglyph ⊗. The word *quarter* has even been retained to label these places in many older cities.

In a work dealing with how to maintain these small-scale grassroots organizations, Wandersman and Giamartino reported that it was important for members to feel satisfied with the progress of the organization and enjoy their membership. Organizations that survived generally had a social climate that was more cohesive and had greater clarity of group rules, norms, and sanctions. They were also generally led by people who helped direct the group, made decisions, and enforced the rules of the group. Members of these groups tended to see the organization as strong and felt that the leaders displayed concern and friendship. They also felt that the group was practical and "down to earth" in its orientation. According to the authors of *Psychology and Community Change* (Homewood, IL: Dorsey Press, 1984), in which this research was reported, "these results suggest that structure and strong, supportive leadership are important to the functioning of block organizations." These are points worth remembering for all those who want help stimulate neighborhood growth.

ADDITIONAL READING

Gans, Herbert. *The Urban Villagers*. New York: The Free Press, 1962.

Heller, K., R. Price, S. Reinharz, S. Riger, and A. Wandersman. *Psychology and Community Change*. Homewood, IL: Dorsey Press, 1984.

Jacobs, Jane. *The Death and Life of Great American Cities.* New York: Vintage Books, 1961.

Willmott, Peter, and Michael Young. *Family and Kinship in East London.* New York: Humanities Press, 1957.

MOVE #25

Who Came from Where?

Ethnic Groups and Their Origins

WHO CAME

The whole history of the United States during the past three and a half centuries has been molded by successive waves of immigrants who responded to the lure of the New World and whose labors, together with those of their descendants, have transformed an almost empty continent into the world's most powerful nation. The population of the United States today, except for the Indians, consists entirely of immigrants and the descendants of immigrants. American society, economic life, politics, religion and thought all bear witness to the fact that the United States has been the principal beneficiary of the greatest folk-migration in human history.

So wrote the historian Maldwyn Allan Jones in his book *American Immigration* (Chicago: University of Chicago Press, 1960), and it has certainly been true that from their very beginnings (Move #5), the cities of the United States have been characterized by a great deal of racial and ethnic diversity. The story of America *has* been the story of immigration and unfortunately also the story of slavery and the extermination of much of the Native American population. Estimates of the total number of blacks taken from Africa into the Atlantic slave trade over its 350-year history from

1500 to 1850 range from 10 to 20 million, with about 400,000 bound for the territories that were first the colonies and later the United States.

But right from the beginning, movement of people from other places was on the minds of the settlers. Even the Declaration of Independence attacked the ruling English government for trying "to prevent the population of these states" by not giving in to colonial demands for a more open immigration policy. William Kielft, the Dutch governor of New Netherlands, commented in 1660 that there were eighteen languages spoken at the tip of Manhattan in Fort Amsterdam, and little more than a hundred years later, in 1776, Thomas Paine wrote, "Europe, and not England, is the parent country of America."

Since the founding of Jamestown, Virginia, in 1607, an estimated 45 million people have immigrated to the present area of the United States. During the colonial period, from 1630 to 1790, immigration was well under 1 million people, but it rapidly increased after that. Based on a classification of surnames in the 1790 census, the white population of the United States was 60.9 percent English, 8.3 percent Scottish, 9.7 percent Irish, 8.7 percent German, 3.4 percent Dutch, 1.7 percent French, .7 percent Swedish, and 6.6 percent unknown. Most were native-born Americans whose names were part of the heritage their families had brought from Europe. Estimates of the black population of the time were approximately three-quarters of a million people, or just over 19 percent. From 1810 onward, when the accuracy of record-keeping greatly improved, a rough estimate of the excess of arriving immigrants over departing emigrants is about 38 million.

While the motivation of people who move from one country to another is always complex, many of those who followed the founders were trying to improve their economic situation. And while it's true that many of the earliest colonists were here for religious reasons, even these were often combined with economic motives. One of the Jesuit leaders who was involved with Lord Baltimore's founding of Maryland as a refuge for English Catholics wrote, "while we sow spiritual seed, we shall reap carnal things in abundance." Certainly all those who came as indentured servants—between 50 and 67 percent of all white people who emigrated to colonial America—were engaged in the economic venture of trading years of their service for passage to the New World. And the African slave trade, beginning in 1619 with a

Dutch man-of-war bringing twenty blacks to Jamestown, was about nothing if not property and profit.

In the mid–eighteenth century, out of the Boston area alone, almost a thousand vessels were engaged in the three-cornered trade of rum, slaves, and molasses. Rum was brought from New England to the Guinea coast of Africa to be traded for slaves who were then transported to the West Indies in exchange for molasses that was used to feed the rum distilleries of New England. The colonial import in slaves was to reach its climax in the ten years from 1764 to 1773. The booming crops of the time, rice and indigo, required more and more labor and from November 1, 1772, to September 27, 1773, in Charleston, South Carolina, more than 8,000 blacks were sold.

For those who arrived not as the property of other people, the immigration figures generally reveal that the trip was often a response to the availability of work. For a long time, single males of prime working age dominated these statistics. In the nineteenth century, males comprised about 60 percent of the total immigration, and people between the ages of fifteen and thirty-nine, about 67 percent. Just before World War I, the period of the "New Immigration" when large numbers of Slavs, Jews, and Italians were added to the population, the dominance of prime working-age males grew. The male proportion rose to about 67 percent and the proportion aged fifteen to thirty-nine climbed to about 75 percent. Females became the dominant group each year after 1930, and married people were also in the majority after that date.

As can be seen from Table 6, relatively few immigrants came to the United States in the first third of the nineteenth century, but then a notable increase began in 1830. This continued into the first ten years of the twentieth century, but even at the peak of immigration, between 1900 and 1910, it accounted for less than 40 percent of the total national population increase. Between World Wars I and II, restrictive legislation and the Depression served to limit greatly the number of people coming to the United States, and in the 1930s, the country actually lost more people by migration than it gained, some 85,000.

As shown in Table 7, throughout most of the nineteenth century, northwestern Europe accounted for more than two-thirds of U.S. immigration. Germany and Scandinavia became increasingly important, together equaling or exceeding the British Isles in their contributions from the 1870s until World War I. In the

Table 6 Increase in U.S. Population by Component of Change, 1810–1970 (Thousands per Decade)

Period	Total Increase	Natural Increase[a]	Net Arrivals[b]
1810–1820	2,399	2,328	71
1821–1830	3,228	3,105	123
1831–1840	4,203	3,710	493
1841–1850	6,122	4,702	1,420
1851–1860	8,251	5,614	2,593
1861–1870	8,375	6,291	2,102
1871–1880	10,337	7,675	2,622
1881–1890	12,792	7,527	4,966
1891–1900	13,047	9,345	3,711
1901–1910	15,978	9,656	6,294
1911–1920	13,738	11,489	2,484
1921–1930	17,604	14,500	3,187
1931–1940	8,894	9,962	−85
1941–1950	19,028	17,666	1,362
1951–1960	28,626	25,446	3,180
1961–1970	23,912	19,894	4,018

a. Excess of births over deaths.
b. Excess of immigrants arrivals over departures. Estimated natural increase and estimated net arrivals do not coincide precisely with total increase figures because of imperfect data for births, deaths, and immigration.

SOURCE: Conrad Taeuber and Irene Taeuber, *The Changing Population of the United States* (New York, 1958), p. 294, table 91; U.S. Bureau of the Census, *Historical Statistics of the United States: Colonial Times to 1970* (Washington, D.C., 1975), pp. 8, 49.

1890s, southern and eastern Europe together became the major source of newcomers.

While it was customary to distinguish "colonial stock" from those who arrived after the American Revolution and then to further distinguish between "old" and "new" immigrants, this distinction was more often made for purposes of justifying exclusionary practices than for any other reason. In 1910 a congres-

Table 7 Distribution of Total Reported Immigration, by Continent, 1821–1970 (in percentages)[a]

Period	Distribution by Area of Origin				Western Hemisphere	Asia	All other
	Europe						
	Total Europe	North and West[b]	East and Central[c]	South and Other[d]			
1821–1830	69.2	67.1	—	2.1	8.4	—	22.4
1831–1840	82.8	81.8	—	1.0	5.5	—	11.7
1841–1850	93.3	92.9	0.1	0.3	3.6	—	3.1
1851–1860	94.4	93.6	0.1	0.8	2.9	1.6	1.1
1861–1870	89.2	87.8	0.5	0.9	7.2	2.8	0.8
1871–1880	80.8	73.6	4.5	2.7	14.4	4.4	0.4
1881–1890	90.3	72.0	11.9	6.3	8.1	1.3	0.3
1891–1900	96.5	44.5	32.8	19.1	1.1	1.9	0.5

1901–1910	92.5	21.7	44.5	26.3	4.1	2.8	0.6
1911–1920	76.3	17.4	33.4	25.5	19.9	3.4	0.4
1921–1930	60.3	31.7	14.4	14.3	36.9	2.4	0.4
1931–1940	65.9	38.8	11.0	16.1	30.3	2.8	0.9
1941–1950	60.1	47.5	4.6	7.9	34.3	3.1	2.5
1951–1960	52.8	17.7	24.3	10.8	39.6	6.0	1.6
1961–1970	34.0	11.7	9.4	12.9	51.7	12.7	1.7

a. Figures for 1821–1867 represent alien passengers arriving in steerage; 1868–1891 and 1895–1897, immigrant aliens arriving; 1892–1894 and 1898–1970, immigrant aliens admitted; 1819–1868, by nationality; 1869–1898, by country of origin or nationality; 1899–1970, by country of last permanent residence.

b. Great Britain, Ireland, Norway, Sweden, Denmark, Iceland, Netherlands, Belgium, Luxembourg, Switzerland, France.

c. Germany (Austria included, 1938–1945), Poland, Czechoslovakia (since 1920), Yugoslavia (since 1920), Hungary (since 1861), Austria (since 1861, except 1938–1945), U.S.S.R. (excludes Asian U.S.S.R. between 1931 and 1963), Latvia, Estonia, Lithuania, Finland, Romania, Bulgaria, Turkey (in Europe).

d. Italy, Spain, Portugal, Greece, and other European countries not classified elsewhere.

Source: Conrad Taeuber and Irene Taeuber, *The Changing Population of the United States* (New York, 1958), p. 53, table 11; U.S. Bureau of the Census, *Historical Statistics of the United States: Colonial Times to 1970* (Washington, D.C., 1975), pp. 105–109.

sional committee headed by Vermont Senator William P. Dillingham issued a forty-two-volume report that supposedly substantiated the racial inferiority of immigrants from southern and eastern Europe compared with those from northern and western Europe. In spite of the fact that the evidence in the famous report directly contradicted the conclusions, these "data" were to serve as the basis for much of the restrictive legislation that soon followed. The portrait of the "new" immigrant was the traditional one of the "other" (Move #2), with the full array of negative traits including lack of ambition, an inability to take time seriously, and loose moral character.

In 1902 the Chinese Exclusion Act was renewed indefinitely, and in 1903 anarchists, saboteurs, epileptics, and professional beggars were barred from entry. The Immigration Act of 1917 established an Asiatic Barred Zone and imposed literacy tests. It was hoped that these would keep the wrong kind of people out, but when it soon became apparent that the literacy tests weren't achieving their desired goal of reducing immigration from southern and eastern Europe, the Quota Act of 1921, also known as the Johnson Act, was passed. This limited the annual number of entrants of each admissable nationality to 3 percent of the foreign-born of that nationality as recorded in the U.S. census of 1910. And then the Immigration Act of 1924 further reduced the admissable annual total to 165,000, less than 20 percent of the prewar level.

These were attempts to make sure that no one else came into the crowded room (Move #2), except the same kinds of people who were already there—a strategy of dealing with the "close stranger" by making sure that people who *were* allowed to get close weren't members of groups that were thought of as "strange." The image of the closed gate can also be useful in describing these restrictive immigration laws, and even the popular name of the period of liberal immigration policy from 1776 to 1881, which directly preceded this era of restriction, drew on a similar image. It was known as the "open door" era. With the partial closing of this open door, there was a conscious attempt to strengthen the original racial stock of the United States by keeping out the same kinds of people who had also prompted the enactment of zoning legislation (Move #7).

In a study of the impact of immigration on urban America,

Send These to Me: Jews and Other Immigrants in Urban America (New York: Atheneum, 1975), John Higham observed:

> Probably one of the crucial determinants of ethnic status has simply been the order of arrival. In the founding of communities, in the settlement of new areas, and in the development of new industries, the first comers secured a preferential position. Groups arriving later have usually had to enter on terms acceptable to their predecessors, who owned the land, offered the jobs, provided the credit, and controlled the sources of power and prestige.

With the beginning of another era of liberalization and the passage of the Hart-Celler Act in 1965, the door was again opened a bit. This act abolished both the national origins quota system and the designation of certain Asian populations as ineligible for entry into the United States. Even with this liberalization, estimates place between 1 and 8 million illegal aliens presently within the United States, and debate on how to deal with this issue has evoked the entire spectrum of responses to immigration from "open the door" to "keep them out." One of the traditional paradoxes of American life has been that while we seem to have been a multi-racial and multi-ethnic society from the very beginning (Move #5), attempts to achieve a national identity have often excluded large numbers of the population.

THE IMAGE OF THE MELTING POT

Even with restrictive legislation, compared with many other nations in the world, the United States has indeed been something of a "melting pot," although clearly not all groups have been considered worthy of inclusion in the pot. The image of the "melting pot" goes back quite far in the country's history. In 1782, a naturalized New Yorker, M-G Jean de Crevecoure, wrote of a family "whose grandfather was an Englishman, whose son married a French woman, and whose present four sons have now four wives of different nations. *He* is an American, who leaving behind him all his ancient prejudices and manners, receive new ones from the new mode of life he has embraced. . . . Here individuals of all nations are melted into a new race of men."

While the image of the melting pot *does* have a number of problems, not the least of which is, just how do you "melt" together all those different kinds of people to get an "American," and then what exactly is an "American," it does suggest a possible strategy for thinking about issues of immigration and ethnicity. For instance, explore the world of food. It's not that the different groups can be reduced to their national cuisines, but rather that many of the significant issues having to do with the ethnic and racial variety of American society and American cities can be approached in terms of food.

First, cities often reveal what groups of people are located in the area by the types of foods that are available. Just open the telephone directory Yellow Pages to those sections dealing with restaurants, food distributors, and retail markets, and there are often clues about what cultures and countries of origin are represented in the local population. There are few urban ethnic neighborhoods (Move #24) without their complement of local restaurants, bakeries, and markets, and even when groups have dispersed and assimilated into the larger culture, that is, no longer think of themselves as "Irish" or "German" or "Italian," but rather as "American," a good deal of their heritage can often be revealed in the kinds of specialty items that the local supermarkets carry.

Issues such as assimilation, status, and the variety of relationships among different groups can all be encountered in the world of food. The difference between a moussaka in a diner in New Jersey and a moussaka in Athens not only is the difference between the two places but also has something to do with what it means to be "Greek" and how this differs from being "Greek American." In *Miami: City of the Future* (Boston: Atlantic Monthly Press, 1987), T. D. Allman compares the experience of walking through Little Havana on Southwest 8th Street with that of making *café con leche*: "It starts out black, quickly turns brown, and, as you add more and more milk, winds up white as any 'real' American with a Florida suntan."

He also argues that the new technology, particularly that of automobiles and television, has sped up everything (Move #21) including assimilation so that while earlier it might have taken four generations for an immigrant group to assimilate and become fully American, experts call it the "three generation concept," later groups such as the Cubans of Miami are accomplishing it much faster. It took the Irish more than forty years after they arrived in Boston to elect their first mayor, while the Cubans of Miami have accomplished it in twenty-five years. This probably says less about the differences between the Irish and the Cubans and more about the different conditions under which the two assimilation experiences are occurring.

How often do immigration statistics mislead by assuming that the specific country of origin means the same thing for all those who emigrated from it—or what exactly is Italian food anyway? For example, were there even such things as "Italians" when their immigration to this country began; at that time people from the region tended to identify on the level of the province and not the recently established nation-state. Those first arrivals must have found it strange to learn that they were "Italians" and not "Calabrians" or "Sicilians" or "Neapolitans." Then there are those situations where there are more immigrants and their descendants than inhabitants of the country of origin as is the case with the Irish. And finally, the theme of adaptation to the surrounding setting introduces diversity and regionalism in everything from food to values and rituals of particular national groups located in different places. To experience the vagaries of the hot dog in different parts of the country—from the Coney Island red hot to the foot-long chili dog to the corn dog on a stick to the miniature canape of formal receptions—is to directly encounter this theme on a gut level.

What determines the status of a particular food or style of preparation? And aren't all those strange and wonderful creations, such as Cuban-Chinese food and garlic bagels, a constant reminder of the gratuitous and unforseen encounters among groups in urban settings that could never happen in the places of origin of these same groups? It is these serendipitous encounters that proponents of the city as far back as Aristotle have always celebrated.

WHO WENT WHERE?

Two great geographic movements have dominated the general distribution of the American population. One was the westward expansion, which came to an end by the close of the nineteenth century, and the other was urbanization. Westward expansion was accomplished primarily by native-born whites, except in areas of the south, where many blacks were also involved, but in urban growth, immigrants have played a very large part. This was particularly true after 1840 and in the growth of large cities.

In 1890, 55 percent of the U.S. population was native-born white stock, 33 percent foreign-born white stock with at least one foreign-born parent, and 12 percent were nonwhite. In north-central and western regions, 62 percent of the rural population was native-born white stock, 37 percent foreign-born white stock, and 1 percent nonwhite. The south-central region of the United States was composed of 67 percent native-born white stock, 2 percent foreign-born white stock, and 31 percent nonwhite. In all three of these areas the native-born white stock was disproportionately represented. At the same time, foreign-born white stock made up 53 percent of the urban population, indicating a disproportionately large number of immigrants heading to America's cities, where the jobs and opportunities generally were.

Tables 8, 9, and 10 show which cities blacks and Hispanics were located in for the 1980 U.S. census, and what regions of the country specific European ethnic groups were located in according to the 1970 census.

Table 8 Black Population of U.S. Cities, 1980

Rank	City	Black Population	Percentage Black
1	Washington, D.C.	448,229	70.29
2	Atlanta	282,912	66.56
3	Detroit	758,939	63.07
4	Newark	191,743	58.24
5	Birmingham	158,223	55.63
6	New Orleans	308,136	55.27
7	Baltimore	431,151	54.80
8	Richmond	112,357	51.25
9	Memphis	307,702	47.61
10	Jackson	95,357	47.00
11	Oakland	159,234	46.93
12	St. Louis	206,386	45.55

Table 8 **Black Population of U.S. Cities, 1980 (continued)**

Rank	City	Black Population	Percentage Black
13	Cleveland	251,347	43.80
14	Flint	66,124	41.43
15	Shreveport	84,627	41.12
16	Chicago	1,197,000	39.83
17	Montgomery	69,765	39.16
18	Philadelphia	638,878	37.84
19	Dayton	75,031	36.85
20	Baton Rouge	80,119	36.50
21	Mobile	72,568	36.20
22	Norfolk	93,987	35.20
23	Columbus, Ga.	57,884	34.16
24	Cincinnati	130,467	33.89
25	Greensboro	51,373	33.01
26	Little Rock	51,091	32.24
27	Chattanooga	53,716	31.68
28	Charlotte	97,627	31.05
29	Dallas	265,594	29.38
30	Louisville	84,080	28.17
31	Jersey City	61,954	27.72
32	Houston	440,257	27.62
33	Kansas City, Mo.	122,699	27.38
34	Buffalo	95,116	26.58
35	Rochester	62,332	25.78
36	Jacksonville	137,324	25.39
37	Tampa	68,835	25.35
38	Kansas City, Kan.	40,826	25.34
39	New York	1,784,124	25.23
40	Miami	87,110	25.11
41	Pittsburgh	101,813	24.02
42	Nashville-Davidson	105,942	23.25

Table 8 **Black Population of U.S. Cities, 1980** *(continued)*

Rank	City	Black Population	Percentage Black
43	Milwaukee	146,940	23.10
44	Fort Worth	87,723	22.78
45	Akron	52,719	22.23
46	Columbus, Ohio	124,880	22.11
47	Indianapolis	152,626	21.78
48	Boston	126,229	19.69
49	Toledo	61,750	17.41
50	St. Petersburg	41,000	17.31
51	Los Angeles	505,208	17.03
52	Syracuse	26,767	15.74
53	Grand Rapids	28,602	15.73
54	Oklahoma City	58,702	14.56
55	Fort Wayne	25,063	14.55
56	Knoxville	25,881	14.13
57	Sacramento	36,866	13.37
58	Lexington-Fayette	27,121	13.28
59	Las Vegas	21,054	12.79
60	San Francisco	86,414	12.73
61	Austin	42,118	12.19
62	Omaha	37,852	12.14
63	Denver	59,252	12.06
64	Providence	18,546	11.83
65	Tulsa	42,594	11.80
66	Long Beach	40,732	11.27
67	Wichita	30,200	10.81
68	Yonkers	20,583	10.54
69	Virginia Beach	26,291	10.03
70	Fresno	20,665	9.47
70	Seattle	46,755	9.47
72	Tacoma	14,507	9.15

Table 8   Black Population of U.S. Cities, 1980 (continued)

Rank	City	Black Population	Percentage Black
73	San Diego	77,700	8.87
74	Lubbock	14,204	8.16
75	Minneapolis	28,433	7.66
76	Portland, Ore.	27,734	7.57
77	Riverside	11,776	6.89
78	Aurora	10,889	6.87
79	Des Moines	13,054	6.83
80	Colorado Springs	11,961	5.56
81	Anchorage	9,242	5.34
82	Corpus Christi	11,889	5.12
83	Phoenix	37,682	4.93
84	St. Paul	13,305	4.92
85	San Jose	29,157	4.58
86	Santa Ana	8,232	4.04
87	Tucson	12,301	3.72
88	El Paso	13,466	3.17
89	Arlington, Texas	4,660	2.91
90	Worcester	4,625	2.86
91	Madison	4,603	2.70
92	Albuquerque	8,361	2.52
93	Lincoln	3,444	2.00
94	Spokane	2,767	1.62
95	Salt Lake City	2,523	1.55
96	Honolulu	4,247	1.16
97	Anaheim	2,557	1.15
98	Huntington Beach	1,218	.71
99	Warren	297	.18

SOURCE: U.S. Department of Commerce, Bureau of the Census, *1980 Census of Population: Standard Metropolitan Statistical Areas and Standard Consolidated Statistical Areas: 1980* (October 1981).

Table 9 **Hispanic Population of U.S. Cities, 1980**

Rank	City	Total Hispanic Population	Percentage Hispanic
1	El Paso	265,819	62.51
2	Miami	194,987	56.20
3	San Antonio	421,774	53.70
4	Corpus Christi	108,175	46.63
5	Santa Ana	90,646	44.50
6	Albuquerque	112,084	33.78
7	Los Angeles	815,989	27.50
8	Tucson	82,189	24.87
9	Fresno	51,489	23.60
10	San Jose	140,574	22.08
11	New York	1,405,957	19.88
12	Lubbock	32,791	18.85
13	Austin	64,766	18.75
14	Denver	91,937	18.71
15	Jersey City	41,672	18.64
16	Newark	61,254	18.60
17	Houston	281,224	17.64
18	Anaheim	38,015	17.14
19	Riverside	27,604	16.15
20	Phoenix	115,572	15.11
21	San Diego	130,610	14.92
22	Sacramento	39,160	14.20
23	Chicago	422,061	14.04
24	Long Beach	50,700	14.03
25	Tampa	35,982	13.25
26	Fort Worth	48,696	12.64
27	Dallas	111,082	12.29
28	San Francisco	83,373	12.28
29	Oakland	32,491	9.58

Table 9 Hispanic Population of U.S. Cities, 1980 *(continued)*

Rank	City	Total Hispanic Population	Percentage Hispanic
30	Colorado Springs	18,268	8.49
31	Las Vegas	12,787	7.77
32	Salt Lake City	12,311	7.55
33	Boston	36,068	6.41
34	Providence	9,071	5.78
35	Rochester	13,153	5.44
36	Honolulu	19,127	5.24
37	Worcester	6,877	4.25
38	Milwaukee	26,111	4.10
39	Philadelphia	65,570	3.88
40	Wichita	9,902	3.55
41	New Orleans	19,219	3.45
42	Kansas City, Mo.	14,703	3.28
43	Grand Rapids	5,752	3.16
44	Cleveland	17,772	3.10
45	Anchorage	5,209	3.01
45	Toledo	10,667	3.01
47	St. Paul	7,864	2.91
48	Oklahoma City	11,295	2.80
49	Washington, D.C.	17,652	2.77
50	Buffalo	9,499	2.65
51	Seattle	12,646	2.56
52	Flint	3,974	2.49
53	Tacoma	3,869	2.44
54	Detroit	28,970	2.41
55	Omaha	7,304	2.34
56	Norfolk	6,074	2.28
57	Fort Wayne	3,786	2.20
58	Portland, Ore.	7,807	2.13

Table 9 Hispanic Population of U.S. Cities, 1980 *(continued)*

Rank	City	Total Hispanic Population	Percentage Hispanic
59	Columbus, Ga.	3,521	2.08
60	Virginia Beach	5,160	1.97
61	Des Moines	3,523	1.84
62	Baton Rouge	3,985	1.82
63	Jacksonville	9,775	1.81
64	St. Petersburg	4,210	1.78
65	Tulsa	6,189	1.71
66	Syracuse	2,819	1.66
67	Lincoln	2,745	1.60
68	Spokane	2,554	1.49
69	Atlanta	5,842	1.37
70	Shreveport	2,769	1.35
71	Madison	2,242	1.31
72	Minneapolis	4,684	1.26
73	St. Louis	5,531	1.22
74	Mobile	2,265	1.13
75	Charlotte	3,418	1.09
76	Louisville	2,005	1.01
76	Richmond	2,210	1.01
78	Baltimore	7,641	.97
79	Montgomery	1,641	.92
80	Indianapolis	6,145	.88
81	Dayton	1,748	.86
82	Little Rock	1,315	.83
83	Columbus, Ohio	4,651	.82
84	Memphis	5,225	.81
85	Nashville-Davidson	3,627	.80
86	Birmingham	2,227	.78
86	Cincinnati	2,988	.78

Table 9 Hispanic Population of U.S. Cities, 1980 *(continued)*

Rank	City	Total Hispanic Population	Percentage Hispanic
88	Greensboro	1,201	.77
88	Chattanooga	1,295	.76
90	Pittsburgh	3,196	.75
91	Jackson	1,508	.74
92	Lexington-Fayette	1,488	.73
93	Knoxville	1,260	.69
94	Akron	1,534	.65

SOURCE: U.S. Department of Commerce, Bureau of the Census, *1980 Census of Population: Standard Metropolitan Statistical Areas and Standard Consolidated Statistical Areas: 1980* (October 1981).

The census data of 1970 revealed quite strongly that some ethnic groups were confined to extremely small areas of the country. More than 75 percent of the population of Puerto Rican origin were to be found in the Mid-Atlantic states, mainly in the New York City area, and almost half the Cuban population were centered in the Southeast, especially in and around Miami. Most of the other half were to be found in the New York area. California and the Southwest contained about half the population of Mexican origin, and most of the remaining half lived in the west-south-central region. About half the Native American population also lived in these two adjacent regions (Southwest and west-south-central) with the remaining half widely dispersed throughout all the western states. About a third of all people of Japanese and Chinese descent were to be found in California, with an equally large group of Chinese clustered in the Mid-Atlantic region and a large group of Japanese in Hawaii.

Groups of European origin also showed patterns of concentration. New England and the Mid-Atlantic states contained two-thirds of first- and second-generation Irish and Italians. Russians, mainly but not entirely Jewish, were also concentrated in the Northeast. Almost 70 percent lived in the Mid-Atlantic States with most in New York and Philadelphia. More than 50 percent of the Greeks and two-thirds of the first- and second-generation Poles,

Table 10 Relative Regional Representation of European Ethnic Groups By Country of Origin, 1970[a]

Country of origin	New England	Mid-Atlantic	Eastern Midwest	Northern Midwest	Southern Midwest	Upper South Atlantic	Southeast	Eastern South Central	Western South Central	California-Southwest	Mountain	Pacific Northwest
United Kingdom	2.0	1.6	0.9	0.6	0.5	0.7	0.6	0.2	0.3	1.5	1.3	1.3
Ireland	3.8	2.4	0.7	0.4	0.4	0.5	0.3	0.1	0.1	0.7	0.5	0.5
Germany	0.7	1.4	1.2	2.5	1.4	0.5	0.5	0.2	0.4	1.0	1.0	1.1
Norway	0.5	0.6	0.5	7.7	0.8	0.2	0.3	0.1	0.1	1.1	1.8	4.7
Sweden	1.6	0.6	1.1	4.2	1.2	0.2	0.4	0.1	0.2	1.3	1.7	2.9
Denmark	0.7	0.6	0.7	3.4	2.2	0.3	0.4	0.1	0.2	1.8	3.0	2.6
Netherlands	0.5	0.9	1.7	1.9	1.2	0.3	0.4	0.1	0.2	1.7	1.6	1.7
France	0.4	1.6	0.8	0.6	0.7	0.8	0.6	0.3	0.5	1.8	1.0	1.0
Switzerland	0.8	1.1	0.9	1.9	1.2	0.5	0.4	0.2	0.3	2.0	1.8	2.4

Austria	0.8	2.6	1.0	1.0	0.5	0.5	0.4	0.1	0.2	0.8	0.7	0.6
Hungary	0.8	2.2	1.6	0.6	0.3	0.5	0.5	0.1	0.1	0.9	0.3	0.4
Poland	1.8	2.3	1.6	0.9	0.2	0.5	0.3	0.1	0.1	0.5	0.2	0.2
U.S.S.R.	1.5	2.4	0.7	1.0	0.5	0.6	0.5	0.1	0.1	1.1	0.7	0.7
Czechoslovakia	0.6	1.9	1.7	1.4	1.0	0.5	0.3	0.1	0.5	0.6	0.5	0.5
Yugoslavia	0.2	1.4	2.3	1.6	0.6	0.3	0.2	0.1	0.1	1.2	1.1	0.9
Italy	2.5	3.0	0.7	0.2	0.2	0.4	0.2	0.1	0.2	0.8	0.4	0.3
Greece	2.4	1.8	1.3	0.4	0.3	0.9	0.5	0.2	0.2	1.0	0.8	0.6
Canada	5.3	0.7	1.0	0.8	0.3	0.4	0.5	0.3	0.2	1.4	0.9	2.3
French mother tongue[b]	6.0	0.6	0.4	0.5	0.2	0.4	0.3	0.2	2.7	0.8	0.4	0.5

a. The value of 1.0 indicates that the proportion of an ethnic group living in a given region equaled the proportion of the total national population living in that region. Values below 1.0 indicate underrepresentation, and values above 1.0 indicate overrepresentation.
b. Primarily people of Quebec origin living in New England and those of Acadian origin living in Louisiana.

SOURCE: U.S. Bureau of the Census, *Census of the Population, 1970*, vol. 1, *Characteristics of the Population*, pt. 1, *U.S. Summary* (Washington, D.C., 1973), I, pp. 473–480, tables 144–147.

Czechs, Hungarians, and Yugoslavs lived in the Mid-Atlantic and Eastern Midwest regions. While people of Scandinavian origin were more dispersed, significant proportions were to be found in the Midwest and the Pacific Northwest.

American cities undoubtedly benefit from the multi-ethnic and multi-racial composition. This is one of the major contributors to that traditional urban characteristic of "variety" (Move #16), but on the collective level, one question worth thinking about is, what next? In the twenty-first century where will the newcomers from abroad originate from, and what will their vehicles of acceptance and rejection be?

ADDITIONAL READING

Conover, Ted. *Coyotes*. New York: Vintage Books, 1987. Conover tells the fascinating story of how many of the country's illegal aliens cross from Mexico to be met by arrest and opportunities for employment.

Easterlin, R. A., D. Ward, W. Bernard, and R. Ueda. *Immigration*. Cambridge: Belknap Press of Harvard University Press, 1982. This is a series of selections from the *Harvard Encyclopedia of American Ethnic Groups*, published in 1980 and considered a classic work by scholars on the origins, history, and present situation of the more than one hundred ethnic groups that make up the U.S. population.

Glazer, N., and D. Moynihan. *Beyond the Melting Pot*. Cambridge: MIT Press, 1963. This interesting study covers blacks, Puerto Ricans, Jews, Italians, and Irish of New York City.

Jones, Maldwyn Allen. *American Immigration*. Chicago: University of Chicago Press, 1960. This is a classic treatment of American immigration from colonial times to the middle of the twentieth century.

Sollors, Werner. *Beyond Ethnicity: Consent and Descent in American Culture*. New York: Oxford University Press, 1986. Sollor's book is an important look at ethnicity in the United States, including an investigation of the image of the "melting pot."

MOVE #26

Post Script

Your Move

IN THE FINAL ANALYSIS, WE ALL HAVE OUR OWN MOVES FOR DEALING with the city, those strategies that we use every day in the landscape of urban America. If the *Oxford English Dictionary* includes in its definition of *move* "a proposal or motion, a change of house or place of sojourn, the changing of the position of a piece in the regular course of a game, a device or trick or action calculated to secure some end, to shake or disturb," then what are the Moves that you make? All those things—books, observations, trips, information, images, and metaphors—that help you think about cities in new ways that bring both understanding and delight.

The author of *City Moves* would be grateful for your sharing some favorite strategies. In a postcard or short letter, send them in to *City Moves*, c/o McGraw-Hill Publishing Company, 1221 Avenue of the Americas, New York, NY 10020. And remember, just like the Moves presented in this book, your suggestions can be highly specific and make reference to a particular city, or they can be those more general strategies that are helpful in a wide variety of urban settings. It may be helpful to think about the situation where you're suddenly faced with the task of acquainting a visitor with urban America. Not all of it, but just that part of the scene that you find most interesting and intriguing. How would you go about doing it? How *do* you go about doing it, since everyone has undoubtedly found him- or herself in this position at one time or another.

There's the possibility of a sequel—something like *Son of City Moves Returns* or maybe a series of radio and television spots, a key club, a breakfast cereal, perhaps a T-shirt, or maybe even a Broadway show with a big orchestra in the pit? And then there's all that computer software. Like almost everything else in urban life, city Moves are nothing if not ambitious in their aspirations. We see this as soon as we go to the top of a tall building and look down (Move #1).

NOTES

This is the part that you write. It's your Move. . . .

Index

Moses, Robert, 116
Mossdorf, Heinrich, 169
Motels, 121
Movement:
  concept of, 242–248
  space and time, separation of, 246–247
  speed, attitude toward, 243–246
Moves, definition and general
  considerations, 1–5, 295–296
"Mr. Rogers' Neighborhood" (TV), 251,
  253–254
Muck and sublimity, 11
Multiple nuclei, city structure, 64–65
Mumford, Lewis, 33, 34, 54, 60, 71, 74,
  90–91, 116, 133, 141, 230, 239, 251,
  255
Muncie, Ind., 112
Musil, Thomas, 244
Mussolini, Benito, 35
Mythologies (Barthes), 29, 38, 114

Name of the place, 49–61
  definitions, 49–53
  metaphors, 54–57
  nicknames, 57–60
  paradox, 53–54
Nashville, Neighborhood Participation
  project, 271–272
National Commission on Neighborhoods,
  271
National Survey, 83, 90
Native American population, 274, 291
Natural History of the West Indies
  (Fernandez), 75–76
"Nature of Cities, The" (Harris &
  Ullman), 63–64, 65
Nature and the city, 108–111, 141
  (*See also* Utopias)
Necropolis, 255
Neighborhood Participation project, 271–
  272
Neighborhoods, 34–35, 251, 266–273
  block organizations, 272
  building, renewal, 270–272
  streets, 268–270
  urban villages, 254, 266–268
  and violence, 268
  (*See also* Ethnic groups)
Neolithic revolution and cities, 69–74,
  223, 251
Network analysis, 251
Neve, Philippe de, 82
New Amsterdam, 77, 275
  zoning legislation in, 93
"New Citroen, The" (Barthes), 114
New Orleans, La.:
  founding and early history of, 80
  nicknames for, 60
  population density of, 31

New Orleans, La.: (*cont.*)
  proportion of blacks and hispanics in,
    284, 289
  ranking, by quality, 263, 264
  tall buildings in, 26
New York City, N.Y.:
  beginnings, 77–78, 90
  garment district in, 96–97
  malls in, 125
  "melting pot," 230
  nicknames for, 57
  parks and plazas in, 197
    (*See also* Central Park; Prospect Park)
  population statistics of, 9
    density, 28–29, 30, 32
    proportion of blacks and hispanics in,
      285, 288
  ranking, by quality, 262, 264
  tall buildings in, 16, 36, 98–99
  zoning regulations, 93–94, 96, 98–99,
    102, 169
New York magazine, 28–29
New York Times, The, 240
  Book Review, 246
Newark, N.J.:
  beginning and early growth of, 78–79
  population density of, 30
  proportion of blacks and hispanics in,
    284, 288
  ranking, by quality, 263
  suburbanization of, 117
Newman, Oscar, 157–158
News reports and the atypical, 8
Nicknames of cities, 57–60, 259
No Sense of Place (Meyrowitz), 232
Nodes, city, 33, 35
Nomadic cultures, 147–148, 233
Norris, Frank, 96
North, Oliver, 189
Nostalgia, 145, 150
Nothing Gained by Overcrowding (Unwin),
  118
Novelty and complexity, 56
Numbers, quantities, 28–30, 270

Oakie, Jack, 35
Oakland, Calif.:
  population density of, 20
  proportion of blacks and hispanics in,
    284, 288
  tall buildings in, 20
Observation, interest, 183–184
"Of Exactitude in Science" (Borges), 216
Oglethorpe, James Edward, 81
Olmsted, Frederick Law, 67, 95, 105–111,
  238
  campus designs, 107, 108
  community designs, 106–107